FootprintFrance

Normandy

S0-ARO-365

Andrew Sanger

Introducing the region

About the region

Rouen

Upper Normandy

Calvados

Cotentin

Southern Normandy

Practicalities

Contents

About the author

Andrew Sanger is a well-established travel writer who has lived and worked in a number of countries including several years in France. Since returning to the UK, he has contributed hundreds of travel articles to a wide spectrum of British national newspapers, popular news-stand magazines, customer magazines and travel websites, winning awards for his travel journalism. For 10 years Andrew was the editor of French Railways' travel magazine, *Top Rail* (later *Rail Europe Magazine*). Andrew Sanger is also the author of more than 30 guidebooks to a wide range of destinations including Ireland, Israel, the Canaries and especially France and its regions. In addition, his first novel, The J-Word, published by Snowbooks in 2009, has been widely acclaimed. He now lives in northwest London. A devoted francophile, Andrew has a special love for Normandy, which he visits frequently. Read more about Andrew's work at www.andrewsanger.com.

Acknowledgements

Andrew would like to thank the travel writer and playwright Laurence Phillips, whose generosity made it possible to write this book, and Geraldine Dunham, whose companionship has made exploring Normandy a delight.

About the book

The guide is divided into four sections: **Introducing the region**; **About the region**; **Around the region**; and **Practicalities**.

Introducing the region comprises: **At a glance**, which explains how the region fits together by giving the reader a snapshot of what to look out for; **Best of Normandy** (top 20 highlights); **A year in Normandy**, which is a month-by-month guide to pros and cons of visiting at certain times of year; and **Screen & page**, which is a list of suggested books and films.

About the region comprises: **History**; **Art & architecture**; **Normandy today**, which presents different aspects of life in the region today; **Nature & environment** (an overview of the landscape and wildlife); **Festivals & events**; **Sleeping** (an overview of accommodation options); **Eating & drinking** (an overview of the region's cuisine, as well as advice on eating out); **Entertainment** (an overview of the region's cultural credentials, explaining what entertainment is on offer); **Shopping** (the region's specialities and recommendations for the best buys); and **Activities & tours**.

Around the region is then broken down into five areas, each with its own chapter. Here you'll find all the main sights and at the end of each chapter is a listings section with all the best **sleeping**, **eating & drinking**, **entertainment**, **shopping** and **activities & tours** options

Sleeping price codes

€€€€ more than €200 per night for a double room in high season

€€€ €100-200

€€ €60-100

€ under €60

Eating & drinking price codes

€€€€ more than €40 per person for a 2-course meal with a drink, including service and cover charge

€€€ €30-40

€€ €20-30

€ under €20

Map symbols

 l'Information
Information

 Endroit d'intérêt
Place of interest

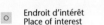 Musée/galerie
Museum/gallery

 Théâtre
Theatre

 Poste
Post office

 Eglise/cathédrale
Church/cathedral

 Mur de ville
City wall

 Parking

 Gare
Train station

 Gare routière
Bus station

 Station de métro
Metro station

 Ligne de tram
Tram route

 Marché
Market

 Hôpital
Hospital

Pharmacie
Pharmacy

Lycée
College

Picture credits

Andrew Sanger
pg 10, 114, 143, 153, 183, 190, 202, 218, 223, 230

Hemis.Fr
Gil Giuglio: pg 108, 267; **Hervé Hughes:** pg 29, 40, 56, 113, 117, 145, 149, 151, 165, 169, 171, 211, 217, 219, 237, 238, 239, 243; **Jean-Daniel Sudres:** pg 48, 59, 60, 148, 154, 163, 195, 232, 256, 268; **John Frumm:** pg 11, 15, 50; **Philippe Renaul:** pg 38; **Sylvain Sonnet:** pg 2, 9, 66, 73; **Annette Soumillard:** pg 43, 240, 248; **Bertrand Rieger:** pg 16, 22, 53, 98, 121, 123, 146, 157, 168, 177, 203, 207, 208, 220, 250, 279; **Camille Moirenc:** pg 62, 65, 231; **Frances Cormon:** pg 84, 126, 176; **Gilles Rigoulet:** pg 13, 18, 20, 30, 51, 61, 68, 77, 78, 79, 81, 91, 95, 96, 101, 129, 162, 167, 200, 212, 253, 262, 271, 272, 273; **Hervé Hughes:** pg 111; **Hervé Lenain:** pg 24, 46, 107, 166, 180, 235; **Jacques Boulay:** pg 159; **Jean-Pierre Degas:** pg 127; **Michel Gotin:** pg 32; **Patrick Escudero:** pg 6, 52; **Pawel Wysocki:** pg 34; **Philippe Body:** pg 58, 247; **Stéphane Frances:** pg 161, 270; **Wysocki Frances:** pg 205

iStock
ACMPhoto: pg 259; bparren: pg 215; brytta: pg 21; dubassy: pg 213; Duncan 1890: pg 26, 173; Elenathewise: pg 274; Melbye: pg 244; Squiddly: pg 17

Shutterstock
Carsten Medom Madsen: pg 278; Christopher Walker: pg 179; Claudio Giovanni Colombo: pg 69, 75, 131, 264; dubassy: pg 214; Elena Elisseeva: pg 234; Pete Hoffman: pg 213; PHB.cz (Richard Semik): pg 181; Philip Lange: pg 49; Rebeka Skalja: pg 277; Robert Young: pg 14; Sternstunden: pg 10

Tips Images
Imagestate: pg 37, 160; Mond'Image: pg 175; Photononstop: pg 100, 119

Photononstop/Tips Images Front cover
Paul Atkinson/Shutterstock Inside back cover
Michel Gotin/Hemis.fr Back cover
Mont Saint Michel_Jean-Daniel Sudres/Hemis.fr Back cover

Contents

Côte d'Albâtre, Etretat.

Introducing the region

Introduction

Tranquil, picturesque and profoundly rural, the Duchy of Normandy today conveys a deep peace and contentment. At its heart there is picture-book charm, with half-timbered cottages, quiet lanes and mature hedges, pretty copses, orchards and small farms in rolling green countryside. Such a richly productive land gave rise to Normandy's long tradition of hearty, flavoursome cooking served in generous quantities.

Yet Normandy has seen more than its share of strife over the centuries, and never more so than during the 1944 Liberation of France, when Allied troops landed on its beaches and swept through the region battling the German occupiers. The coastal areas, especially, preserve the memory of those days. In the struggle, some fine historic towns were almost completely destroyed but fortunately others escaped, and much has been restored, including some of France's loveliest Gothic masterpieces.

Normandy has long been a place of high art and culture, too, especially beside the River Seine. Its winding valley was the focal point of the Vikings' original Duchy of Normandy, and here they began to develop a distinctive Norman style of design and architecture. Some of Normandy's greatest Romanesque and Gothic buildings stand on its banks. The Seine also gave birth to modern art, as the Impressionists gathered here to capture on canvas the pearly skies over the river and its estuary.

Monet's inspiration, Giverny.

At a glance
A whistle-stop tour of Normandy

Normandy is large, and varies hugely across its range. Indeed, the old Duchy is big enough that administratively it is not one region, but two: Haute Normandie (Upper Normandy) and Basse Normandie (Lower Normandy).

Upper Normandy reaches the Channel in spectacular white cliffs, sedate beach resorts and busy harbours, such as Dieppe, Etretat and Fécamp. The meandering River Seine twists through Upper Normandy between forests and cliffs, abbeys and hilltop castles. Astride the river sits the city of Rouen, once capital of the whole

Duchy, now the chef-lieu of Haute Normandie. Lower Normandy reaches from its capital, the Conqueror's city of Caen, down the maritime Cotentin Peninsula, to dramatic Mont-St-Michel abbey rising pyramid-like from sea-washed sands. The heart of Lower Normandy is the Pays d'Auge, a world of half-timbered cottages and *manoirs*, apple orchards and grazing cows. This is the classic Normandy of crème fraîche, apple tart, dry cider, Camembert cheese and Calvados apple brandy.

Whether you arrive in Normandy from the sea at Dieppe, Le Havre or Cherbourg-Octeville, or by road from Paris or the Channel Tunnel, you will experience contrasting faces of the region. Upper

The lowdown

Money matters
In addition to accommodation costs you'll need about €40-€50 per person each day for breakfast, simple lunch and dinner with wine. Sights and attractions usually cost around €5-€7 per person, and don't forget to allow some €20 a day for coffees and other drinks. If you're driving, petrol costs around €1.25 per litre.

Opening hours
Most museums and attractions are closed at least one day a week, generally Monday or Tuesday, and often on Sundays too. Standard opening hours for offices and shops are 0900-1200 and 1400-1700, but you'll find countless variations. Shops are usually closed Sunday and Monday (except for butchers and bakers, which open on Sunday morning). In towns or resorts popular with tourists, shops tend to keep longer hours.

Normandy Pass
For just €1 you can buy the Normandy Pass, which gives discounts at 40 museums, sights and attractions. The emphasis is on the D-Day Landing Beaches, and the pass can be purchased at any of the 26 sites connected with the 1944 Normandy Campaign. In addition, more than a dozen other sites around Normandy participate in the scheme. Discounts vary from 30c to as much as €4.50. normandiepass.com.

Rouen.

Tourist information
There are tourist offices in all main towns and many smaller communities too. The main tourist office for the whole of Normandy is CRT de Normandie, 14 rue Charles Corbeau, 27000 Evreux, France. T02 32 33 79 00, normandie-tourisme.fr. The Normandy region has its own website, normandie-tourisme.fr. Websites for its five *départements* are: Orne, ornetourisme.com; Calvados, calvados-tourisme.com; Eure, cdt-eure.fr; Seine-Maritime, seine-maritime-tourisme.com; and Manche, manchetourisme.com.

Normandy is high plateau country with a patchwork of fields under wide skies. The Cotentin Peninsula in Lower Normandy presents a wilder and more rustic face, with wooded hills, tiny villages and fishing harbours, and cliffs rising from Normandy's rocky western coastline. And on the shores of the Seine Bay, extending west of Le Havre to Caen, are chic beach resorts and bustling ports that have attracted visitors for over a century.

Rouen
Normandy's historic capital Rouen is one of the most attractive places in Northern France. In the old heart of the city, on the river Seine's north bank, cobbled lanes ramble among exquisite houses of timber, stone, and a dozen lace-delicate Gothic churches. From the exuberant Flamboyant cathedral – which was painted again and again by Claude Monet – the old quarter's narrow main street, rue du Gros Horloge, straddled by a gilded medieval clock tower, runs into place du Vieux Marché, where Joan of Arc was burnt alive in 1431. The city makes much of its connection to St Joan and has a remarkable modern church dedicated to her. With an array of good museums, public gardens and remnants of its long history, there's a tremendous amount to do and see in the city, from the Fine Arts Museum where a string of rooms is devoted to the Impressionists who loved this area so much and a world-class collection of Flemish art is sited, to Rouen's other great pleasures – strolling, shopping and sampling local specialities.

Introducing the region

Upper Normandy

Upper Normandy is made up of the *départements* of Seine-Maritime, which climbs from the right bank of the River Seine, and Eure, most of which lies on the left bank. Through the middle of the region flows the wide River Seine, making its way to the sea in great meandering twists and turns, along which the Vikings rowed deep into the

In a southern corner of Normandy is one of the most visited places in France – the abbey of Le Mont-St-Michel, rising spectacularly from the seawaters and tidal marshes where Normandy touches Brittany…

territory of the Franks. On its banks stand the cities of Rouen and Le Havre, and other long-established towns, ancient abbeys, medieval castles, forests and some of the greatest landmarks of Normandy's cultural heritage, like Monet's house and garden at Giverny. Apart from the more populous Seine Valley, though, much of Upper Normandy is high chalk-plateau country, broad and open, clothed in big grain fields and sparsely dotted with villages. There are some surprises, like the fertile Pays de Bray district, or the vast beech woods of the Forêt de Lyons. South of the Seine, the region is quietly rustic and resolutely traditional. North of the Seine, Upper Normandy meets the English Channel in lofty white cliffs and sandy beaches, and bustling towns like the popular port and market-town of Dieppe and the charming pre-war resorts of the Alabaster Coast.

Calvados

At the centre of Normandy's broad spread, the *département* of Calvados seems to conjure all that's most evocative of the Duchy. It extends from a long Channel coastline of wartime Landing Beaches and attractive old harbours like Honfleur or the belle epoque resorts of the Côte Fleurie, to

fine historic towns like Bayeux, the thriving capital Caen, and to exquisite old-fashioned countryside like the apples-and-cream Pays d'Auge with its half-timbered manor houses. Calvados produces some of Normandy's most famous products, and gives its own name to a refined but fiery apple brandy drunk as a digestif. The farms and dairies of southern Calvados put several other familiar names on the gourmet table, such as the strong, creamy cheeses of Pont l'Evêque and Livarot, while the area around Isigny-sur-Mer in western Calvados is famed for its high-quality milk, cream and butter.

Cotentin

Despite the ferry traffic passing through its largest town, the busy port of Cherbourg-Octeville, Normandy's westerly *département* of Manche remains probably the least known region in Normandy. It is dominated by the distinctive character of the Cotentin Peninsula, projecting granite headlands far into the English Channel (*La Manche* in French), but this is no wilderness. The region was densely populated in ancient times, and put up the strongest resistance to Roman rule. It was the first part of Normandy to be settled by the invading Norsemen. In the Middle Ages, too, it prospered. Today it preserves a powerful sense of history, with some of the finest Norman churches, a rustic hinterland of fields, woodland and hedges and many distinctive Viking place names. There are appealing working towns like Villedieu-les-Poêles, and a small cathedral city, Coutances. Heading south, the steep, wild and rocky coast gives way to many little harbours and long sandy beaches, with a string of traditional family resorts like Carteret and Granville. At its foot, the Cotentin Peninsula skirts the edge of evocative Mont-St-Michel Bay.

Southern Normandy

In a southern corner of Normandy is one of the most visited places in France – the abbey of Le Mont-St-Michel, rising spectacularly from the seawaters and tidal marshes where Normandy touches Brittany. Travel in a gentle curve from Le Mont-St-Michel towards Paris and the Seine, and

you will pass through the beautiful natural landscapes of Southern Normandy, encompassing the *département* of Orne and extending a little beyond to include la Suisse Normande. Here is a world of cool rivers and streams and steep green hills, thickly wooded in places. A large part of the region falls within the Parc Naturel Régional Normandie Maine, which includes woods, countless small farms, a mosaic of tiny fields and orchards, delightful villages and quiet country towns among its charms. Of them, St-Céneri-le-

Gérei is one of *Les Plus Beaux Villages de France* (the most beautiful French villages), while Bagnoles-de-l'Orne is an elegant spa resort in the midst of woodland. In Alençon, the region's capital – once synonymous with high-quality needlepoint lace – the impressive historic architecture luckily survived the Second World War almost intact. Further east, the Perche region is a place of quiet, unspoiled villages, rolling hills, forests and farms and paddocks where Percheron horses graze.

Best of Normandy

Top 20 things to see & do ▼

4 Etretat cliffs.

❶ Rouen cathedral

Among Europe's finest Gothic buildings, Rouen's Cathédrale Notre-Dame is a masterpiece of elaborate and intricate stonework, its interior light and spacious, with beautiful stained glass. The awesome west façade inspired Claude Monet to paint it 28 times, each one expressing something different about the interplay between stone and light. See page 73.

❷ Rue du Gros Horloge, Rouen

Busy, atmospheric and breathtakingly photogenic, rue du Gros Horloge is the main street of Rouen's old quarter. It's straddled by an archway topped by the twin faces of a gorgeously gilded medieval clock, the Gros Horloge. With just one hand on each clock face, it's still accurate to this day. See page 78.

❸ Dieppe Market

The crowded, colourful Saturday morning market reaches along Dieppe's Grand'Rue from the busy quayside of the fishing harbour to the heart of the

old town, the stalls loaded with cheeses, charcuterie, cider and all the best local produce from Upper Normandy's dairy farms, orchards and fishing boats. See page 142.

❹ Etretat cliffs

A charming little 100-year-old seafront resort built around a medieval core, the real attraction of Etretat is its remarkable 'doorways' carved into white cliffs projecting into the water. Admire them from a beachfront promenade or get a more stirring vista from the green cliff tops that inspired numerous Impressionist painters. See page 111.

❺ St Joseph Church, Le Havre

The very model of Auguste Perret's belief in concrete as the building material of the future, Le Havre's main church is considered the greatest achievement of his post-war reconstruction of the city. Inside, it's just a vast space lit by 6500 fragments of coloured glass set into a 110-m spire. See page 115.

❻ Giverny: Monet's house and garden

Claude Monet moved to this spacious village house in 1883. At once he began to create the ravishingly beautiful flower gardens behind the building, and later added the famous lily pond and little bridge that feature in so many of his paintings. Everything is preserved as he left it. See page 121.

❼ Château Gaillard

A dramatic, picture-book vision of a medieval castle, the ruins of Richard the Lionheart's mighty white fortress, built to defend Normandy from France, stand high on chalk cliffs rising from the River Seine. Climb up to the château on a steep footpath from the pretty waterside at Petit Andelys. See page 122.

❽ St Etienne Church, Abbaye aux Hommes, Caen

Combining the simple lines of the original Norman Romanesque with a superb and delicate Norman Gothic reconstruction, the majestic and serene

19 Le Mont-St-Michel.

church of the Mens' Abbey – built by William the Conqueror, and where he was buried – puts it among the world's greatest architectural achievements. See page 155.

⑨ Le Mémorial de Caen

An ambitious, dignified museum encompassing the whole subject of the Second World War, how it happened, its horrors and outcome, displaying a vast amount of astonishing original material ranging from a letter from Albert Einstein to President Roosevelt, to uniforms and newsreels, tanks and equipment. See page 157.

⑩ Caen market

The city's main Sunday market is a huge, colourful, vibrant gathering along the marina quayside where you can choose not just the finest products of the Calvados coast and countryside, but also browse fascinating sections devoted to hats and clothes, shoes, carpets, toys and a multitude of arts and crafts. See page 197.

⑪ Honfleur harbour

Brimming with charm, Honfleur's historic fortified Vieux Bassin wowed the Impressionists as it does artists today. Bars and art galleries line the cobbled quays and picturesque lanes lead to enchanting museums, including one devoted to Honfleur-born Impressionist Eugène Boudin and another to local comic artist and composer Erik Satie. See page 159.

⑫ Beuvron-en-Auge

Of all the pretty villages of the Pays d'Auge, few are more delightful than Beuvron, with whole streets of timber-framed cottages and one of the most handsome Normandy manor houses. All around is richly productive Auge countryside of apple orchards and gently rolling pasture where dairy cows graze. See page 170.

⑬ Bayeux Tapestry

Surely the most remarkable cartoon strip in history, this 900-year-old embroidery tells the whole story of 1066. Vivid pictures along its 70-m length, captioned in Latin, show the background, the invasion and the outcome of the battle between Normans and Saxons for the crown of England. See page 173.

⑭ Arromanches
The little resort of Arromanches-les-Bains, fronting right on to the sand of Gold Beach, is the place to discover what D-Day and the Normandy Landings were about, with its excellent beachfront D-Day Museum, imposing remnants of the Mulberry Harbour still in place and a vivid film reconstruction at Arromanches 360. See page 178.

⑮ Normandy American Cemetery, Omaha Beach
The toughest of the Landing Beaches was Omaha, where the Americans lost thousands of men in just hours. They are laid out in this calm, respectful and deeply affecting cemetery beside the beach. The opening and closing scenes of the film *Saving Private Ryan* are set here. See page 181.

⑯ Lessay abbey church
This beautifully proportioned little abbey church on the edge of a small country town in the rural Cotentin is one of the best examples of Norman Romanesque architecture: symmetrical, solid and sturdy. Restored after wartime damage using the same stone as the medieval original, it's a haven of tranquillity. See page 215.

⑰ Coutances cathedral
One of Normandy's most pleasing examples of Norman Gothic architecture, this huge Cotentin landmark was actually built on to the framework of a much older Romanesque church. The result is an exquisite combination of refined elegance and robust simplicity, with lovely 14th-century sculpture and 13th-century stained glass. See page 217.

⑱ Granville
As well as one of western Normandy's best sandy beaches, the Cotentin's main coastal resort has an impressively fortified medieval Upper Town, and fascinating one-off museums ranging from Richard Anacréon's collection of modern art and rare books, to the Christian Dior museum in the designer's childhood home. See page 220.

⑲ Le Mont-St-Michel
An ethereal setting between sky and water gives pure magic to this strange abbey-island, reached by a 2-km causeway into the sea. Its stone ramparts are lit up at night, while by day you can climb hundreds of ancient steps on tours of the abbey's evocative churches. See page 242.

⑳ La Suisse Normande
Wild rocks, green hills, sparkling waters and riverside villages are the main attractions of this corner of Normandy, perfect for a leisurely drive, a challenging bike ride or hike, or a thrilling canoe trip. Despite the name, its highest peak is the craggy 120-m Roche d'Oëtre. See page 250.

15 Normandy American Cemetery, Omaha Beach.

Month by month

A year in Normandy

Normandy has numerous apple orchards.

January & February

Throughout this period the Normandy weather usually remains cool and mild. Even in these coldest months it rarely freezes, though it can be windy and humid and feel chilly, especially inland. New Year's Eve or *Réveillon de St-Sylvestre* is a big celebration in France, accompanied by a lavish meal – something the people of Normandy are especially good at. New Year's Day, *Jour de l'An*, is a national holiday. The New Year festivities end on 6 January. In Normandy's holiday areas, especially by the sea, many hotels, restaurants and other businesses are closed and boarded up, while everyday life in the country towns and cities continues quietly. The first sign of a change in the season is the big, popular Granville Carnival, held over the weekend before Shrove Tuesday; see page 44.

March & April

Spring arrives with abundant flowers in town and country. In Normandy's endless fruit groves and orchards, the earliest blossom starts to open; the first to appear is on the cherry trees. The weather is mild, with occasional tempestuous interludes. Easter festivals, fairs, concerts and exhibitions mark the start of the season at the coastal resorts. At Deauville's *Festival de Pâques* the emphasis is on classical music, while Caen puts on its annual Easter funfair. For something more down-to-earth, visit Mortagne au Perche, in Southern Normandy, for its famous international *Foire au Boudin* (Black Pudding Fair). Mortagne's own top-quality *boudin noir* is a long sausage made of pig's blood, onions and pork fat – locals love it. Vast quantities are sold and eaten during the three-day festival, with solemn competitions to find the very best, judged by Knights of the Black Pudding attired in ceremonial robes of velvet and fur in black, red and white. There are lowlier contests to see who can eat the most! See also Festivals and events, page 44.

May & June

By May it's the height of blossom time all across Normandy's countless apple orchards, gloriously draping miles of countryside in rosy white. The Pays d'Auge is especially lovely now. This is an enjoyable time to visit. The weather is generally warm and pleasant throughout Normandy, often with a scattering of scorching hot days, though there is not, of course, any guarantee of good weather in this maritime region. As this is still out of season, it's uncrowded and accommodation prices are low, except for the weekend of Ascension (a movable feast which usually falls in May) and the national holidays of 1 May and 8 May. There's a joyous mood, with festivals of music and flowers.

Bright geraniums decorate the houses and squares in the postcard-pretty villages, notably in Beuvron-en-Auge, while the festival *Jazz Sous Les Pommiers* (jazz under the apple trees) draws big audiences to charming, medieval Coutances; see page 44. At the end of May, the mouth-watering Cherry Fair (*Foire aux Cerises*) is held at Vernon, in the Eure *département* in Upper Normandy. On a very different note, at the same time Rouen stages its important annual *Fête de Ste-Jeanne d'Arc* (Joan of Arc Festival) with both solemn official events and more festive activities, including a medieval street fair, see page 44.

June brings long, hot, sunny days and the calm, fine, rather humid weather typical of a Normandy summer. It's a good time to visit, before the high-summer crowds arrive, especially inland. On the coast, at the start of the month there's an influx of visitors revisiting or commemorating the events of the Second World War. On the coast of Calvados and the eastern Cotentin – forever remembered as the Landing Beaches – D-Day is recalled every 6 June, solemnly and respectfully, yet also in celebration of the victory. The seaside resorts also start to come into their own, with numerous events and attractions. The religious holiday of Pentecost (or Whitsun), which falls in either May or June, is often celebrated in Normandy with a maritime theme. Cherbourg-Octeville and the tip of the Cotentin Peninsula attract thousands of sailing enthusiasts for the annual yacht rally over the Pentecost weekend. At pretty Honfleur, on a more traditional note, Pentecost brings the colourful *Fête des Marins et Pêcheurs* (Festival of Sailors and Fishermen), including a benediction of the sea and a pilgrimage to the cliff-top church of Notre Dame de Grâce. Later comes a more pagan feast as the Summer Solstice is marked with bonfires at Dieppe, and inland at Lyons-la-Forêt and other communities, on the age-old *Fête de la St-Jean*. See also Festivals and events, page 44.

Beachside restaurant on the Côte d'Albâtre in Upper Normandy.

July & August

It's hot through these high summer months, with a holiday air. Maximum temperatures skirt the mid-20s°C. Many of the main resorts, sights and attractions may be crowded – not only foreign visitors but many French tourists and often the local people themselves are enjoying their summer vacation here. Look out for street festivals and open-air jazz, medieval markets (there's a good one at Bayeux) and evening *son-et-lumière* shows. The city of Caen entertains with street theatre and free concerts on Thursday and Friday evenings in July and August. On the coast, while holidaymakers sunbathe and swim, older customs show a traditional respect for the sea. On Upper Normandy's coast of sand and high white cliffs, St Jouin Bruneval makes its Blessing of the Sea at the beginning of July, while at the end of the month, on the rugged Cotentin coast on the other side of the Duchy, Granville puts on its Grand Pardon with processions and blessings of the sea and of the boats. See also Festivals and events, page 45.

September & October

Warm, dry summer lingers into early September, an ideal time for Hollywood stars to fly over for Deauville's Festival du Cinéma Américain, see page 45. There can be heavy rain around the Equinox and by October the mellow early autumn brings cooler days and with it a celebratory harvest atmosphere in the countryside as the year's fruit is gathered and new cider pressed. You'll come across colourful apple and cider fairs, such as the *Fête du Cidre* (cider festival) at Caudebec-en-Caux, in Upper Normandy, at the end of September, while in

Beuvron-en-Auge.

Calvados, the end of October brings the *Foire de la Pomme* (apple fair) at Vimoutiers and the convivial *Grand Marché et Fête du Cidre* at Beuvron-en-Auge. There are other, less fruity, feasts and fairs throughout the Duchy during autumn, such as the *Fête de la Mer* (Sea Festival) at Le Havre (early in September). See also Festivals and events, page 45.

November & December

Tourist attractions and resorts are liable to close up now, and remain closed until next spring. The late autumn weather becomes chilly, but not freezing. There are also local events and festivities, such as Dieppe's *Foire aux Harengs*, the Herring Fair held on the quayside in mid-November; see page 45. Several other autumn herring fairs take place further down the Alabaster Coast, such as at Fécamp and Etretat. There's even an inland herring fair, at Lieurey, in the Eure *département*, celebrated on 11 November, dating back to the Hundred Years War. December brings Christmas markets and fairs to many towns and villages. Events take place all month, and around St Nicholas' Day on 6 December. In Caen, place du Théâtre is the focus of a Christmas market, outdoor activities and parades. In Rouen, the market and Christmas attractions are held in and around place de la Cathédrale.

Screen & page
Normandy in film & literature

The Umbrellas of Cherbourg
(Les Parapluies de Cherbourg)
Jacques Demy, 1963
In this classic film musical starring Catherine Deneuve, umbrella-seller Geneviève gets into a complicated romantic triangle with car mechanic Guy, who is also loved by his aunt's carer Madeleine. Guy vanishes from the scene and a heartbroken Geneviève – pregnant with Guy's child – marries another man. Guy returns, hoping to see Geneviève again, but on learning that she has married, marries Madeleine instead. When a wealthy but unhappy Geneviève bumps into him by chance, Guy simply bids her farewell and realises he is now happy with Madeleine.

The Longest Day
Darryl F Zanuck, 1962
The hugely successful film, based on the book of the same name by Cornelius Ryan, who also wrote the screenplay, details with historical accuracy the emotion, struggle and drama of D-Day and the Allied push to victory.

Madame Bovary
Claude Chabrol, 1991
Chabrol's film follows Gustave Flaubert's classic novel, in which a young wife living in a provincial town in Upper Normandy relieves her boredom with torrid affairs and comes to a sticky end.

Film location

Tess (Roman Polanski, 1979), Polanski's evocative film of Thomas Hardy's tragic novel *Tess of the d'Urbervilles,* describes the rustic world of England's West Country in the 19th century. To find comparable unspoiled landscapes today, Polanski shot most of the film in Normandy's Cotentin Peninsula.

Cotentin Peninsula.

Saving Private Ryan
Steven Spielberg, 1998
This multi-award-winning film starring Tom Hanks and Matt Damon depicts with graphic realism the horrors of the D-Day Landing at Omaha Beach and scenes of warfare as the Battle of Normandy unfolds. It starts and ends at today's Normandy American Cemetery.

Band of Brothers
Steven Spielberg and Tom Hanks, 2001
A 10-part TV series based on a book of the same name by Stephen Ambrose, about the 1944 Normandy invasion experiences of a single company in the US 101st Airborne Division from D-Day to the end of the war, based on real accounts given by veterans.

La Vie en Rose (La Môme)
Olivier Dahan, 2007
Based on the life of Edith Piaf, the scenes of squalor during her childhood are set in Upper Normandy.

Literature

Fiction
Madame Bovary
Gustave Flaubert, 1857
This novel is set in Rouen. One of the most highly regarded of French writers, Flaubert was born in Rouen and much of his fiction, like *Madame Bovary*, is set in and around the city.

Pierre et Jean
Guy de Maupassant, 1887
This giant of French literature wrote popular short stories and novels realistically depicting ordinary daily life in Normandy. He was born in a château near Dieppe and grew up in Upper Normandy. Often considered his finest work, the novel Pierre et Jean is about a lawyer's family in Le Havre. Pierre discovers that his brother Jean is the result of an illicit affair that their mother had years ago. As a result of the anger, bitterness and shame Pierre now exhibits towards their mother, ultimately he is forced out of the family circle, while the illegitimate brother remains at its heart.

Non fiction
Gardens in Normandy
Marie-Françoise Valéry, with photographs by Vincent Motte and Christian Sarramon, 1995
A gorgeous pictorial overview of forty beautiful Normandy gardens, including some created by British landscape designers like Gertrude Jekyll. They range from châteaux gardens to kitchen gardens to Monet's flower gardens at Giverny.

Overlord: D-Day and the Battle for Normandy, 1944
Sir Max Hastings, 1999
Max Hastings's popular study of D-Day and the subsequent battle to free Normandy from German rule makes use of personal testimony from the whole spectrum of viewpoints.

A Journey into Flaubert's Normandy
Susannah Patton, 2007
Flaubert fans will love this absorbing guide to all the places associated with the great author. Packed with old and new photos, maps and biography, it takes in Rouen, Trouville, Ry and more.

D-Day: The Battle for Normandy
Antony Beevor, 2009
Beevor's monumental history of D-Day and the savage conflict in Normandy that followed during summer 1944 has been widely acclaimed as the most authoritative work on the subject.

Contents

A selection of the region's Camembert.

About the region

History

Romans & Franks

The first Roman legionaries marched into Normandy in 58 BC. The might of Rome had advanced northwards through Gaul, crushing any resistance. In many places the local populace put up a strong fight, and even had victories against the Romans – although reinforcements were soon sent and even the fiercest Gallic warriors suffered defeat and savage punishment. Among the toughest of all opponents to Roman rule were the Unelli (or Venelli), a maritime people based in the Cotentin Peninsula. Their capital is thought to have been at or near present-day Carentan. Under their leader Viridovix (which may have been his soubriquet rather than a name, as it seems to have meant Powerful Warrior in the local tongue), the Unelli were strong enough and numerous enough to send many thousands of men to other regions of Gaul to help hold back the Roman advance.

Roman conquest

Through a succession of defeats, gradually these native people of Normandy were weakened. In 56

Vintage engraving of Richard I, Duke of Normandy 942-996.

Richard Cœur de Lion.

BC, Rome eventually confronted the Unelli tribe on their home ground. The battle is believed to have taken place at Mont Castre, near Coutances. (The site was to become the scene of a major battle in 1944 too.) There the local warriors – supported by their allies, among them many Britons – fought their last great battle against Rome. In the five years following this decisive victory, the Romans rapidly colonized the region, building scores of villas and several towns, including Rouen (Rotomagus), Harfleur (Noviomagus) and Evreux (Mediolanum). The Roman forces soon went on to invade and conquer Britain.

The rise of the Franks

For some 500 years Roman rule prevailed in Normandy, at first successfully subduing local rebellions and then resisting incursions by heavily armed Germanic raiders landing on the coast, but their empire was crumbling. When the Romans abandoned the region, the Franks, a Germanic tribe that had already forced the Romans out of much of northeastern France, moved in. Their powerful leader Clovis was a devout Christian, today regarded as the first King of France. Within 100 years of the fall of Rome, throughout Normandy the Franks were building dozens of abbeys, cathedrals and churches on whose foundations stand the great religious buildings of today.

Norsemen

Caudebec, Bricquebec, Houlgate, Caudecotte, Ouistreham, Dieppe… The place names of Normandy, and the name of the region itself, reveal its Viking past. During the ninth century, life became extremely difficult for the Franks of Normandy as attacks by Norse raiders became more and more frequent. The same thing was happening in northern England, Scotland and Ireland. Complex political and economic factors in their native lands caused men of the coastal Scandinavian culture to look beyond the horizon for new sources of income.

Pirate raiders

Ferocious, fearless, pagan seafarers, they arrived in increasing numbers, using shallow-draught boats to travel up the rivers deep into the interior of the country, there to destroy and steal at will, raping and murdering and taking hundreds of men and women as slaves to be worked to death. Religious communities, especially, were their targets for the great booty of gold and slaves to be found there. In AD 820, villages and religious communities along the River Seine were devastated by the Norsemen. In AD 858, the town of Bayeux was all but destroyed. The populous Cotentin Peninsula was continually harassed.

Settlement

However, the rich and mellow land exerted a change on the raiders. Many began to remain, bringing Viking women or taking local female slaves as wives, at first continuing to raid and steal, but eventually beginning to farm and fish. They were even prepared to fight against their brother Vikings to defend the new settlements, which were plentiful by the early 10th century.

In AD 911 the Viking leader Wrolf – later, when he was baptized, he changed his name to Rollo – met the Frankish King Charles the Simple at St Clair on the river Epte, a tributary of the Seine near Giverny. He wanted to make Normandy a Viking territory, living in peace with the Franks. Faced with little choice, Charles agreed to grant everything west of that point to the Norse settlers. It was to be a new Duchy of Normandy, and Rollo its first duke.

The king placed conditions on Rollo: all damaged religious buildings were to be rebuilt, and Normandy was to be loyal to him. To this Rollo agreed. But when the French king demanded that Rollo kiss his foot to seal the agreement and prove his loyalty, so the story goes, the Viking warlord asked one of his men to pick up the French king's foot and present it to him. The king was swiftly up-ended and Rollo kissed the foot without having to bow or kneel. Thus the Norsemen became the Normans.

About the region

An independent Normandy

The Normans restored peace and prosperity to the province, and seem to have rapidly abandoned Viking culture, taking up the language of the Franks. Embracing Christianity with zeal, they built or rebuilt monasteries and abbeys, churches and mansions in a handsome and distinctive Norman style all their own. A great artistic culture began to flourish, and was carried to all the lands being colonized by the Normans, for at this time they were taking control of Sicily, southern Italy and Malta, and invading Byzantium and the Holy Land.

Norman kings of England

In 1066, little more than 150 years after the Treaty of Epte, the French-speaking Normans set sail, under their charismatic leader William the Bastard, to claim the Anglo-Saxon kingdom across the Channel. William became the Conqueror – King of England as well as Duke of Normandy. Rollo's descendants were now the English aristocracy. Within another 50 years, Norman colonies reached from Ireland to Jerusalem.

William died at Rouen in 1087. His successors were the Norman kings of England, Henry I and Henry II, who did not speak English and did not live in England. Calling himself Henry Plantagenet, Henry II was fortunate enough to marry Eleanor of Aquitaine. Her dowry was almost all the lands extending from Anjou to Gascony.

The Norman duke was now ruler not only of England but much of France, too. His son Richard I, the Lionheart (or Cœur de Lion), taking over the throne, consolidated his control over this vast area, as well as spending four years on Crusade in the Holy Land, conquering Cyprus on the way there. In 1195, on his return to Normandy, Richard built the mighty Château Gaillard whose white ruins still overlook the Seine upriver from Rouen.

It was under Richard's successor, his brother John, that Normandy and England became separated and Normandy lost its independence. Coming to the throne in 1202, King John I (nicknamed Lackland) proved a poor strategist.

Almost immediately the soldiers of King Philippe-Auguste of France seized Château Gaillard. Within two years King John had lost the whole of Normandy to the French king. All, that is, except for the Channel Islands – Les Iles Anglo-Normandes, as they are still called in France.

Hundred Years' War

England's Anglo-Norman royalty and aristocracy did not happily accept the loss of their duchy. Attempts were launched to recapture Normandy – by Edward III in 1346 and by Henry V in 1417 – as part of the Hundred Years' War between the French and English royal crowns. Initially Henry V's invasion was a sweeping success. Seizing Caen in 1417 and Rouen two years later, he brought Normandy back under English rule for the first time in two centuries. By 1429 the English and their Burgundian allies were almost ready to divide the French nation between them. But England's grip on all its French territories was dealt a sudden mortal blow by the strange (and miraculous, as the French would have it) appearance on the scene of Joan of Arc. Although she was captured and taken to Rouen to be burnt alive in 1431, her impact on French morale and strategy – which also caused the Burgundians to abandon their alliance with England – was such that by 1449 and 1450, the English were again driven out of Normandy, and out of the whole of France.

French Normandy

Reunited to the French crown, the duchy itself was abolished in 1469 and Normandy was made into a province of France with its own parliament, based at Rouen. The Wars of Religion brought more violence to a mainly Protestant Normandy, causing a great departure of population to foreign lands, but also led eventually to the restoration and enlargement of some of the great cathedrals and churches.

Meanwhile, the people of Normandy, perhaps keeping some of the character of their Viking forebears, had distinguished themselves as

courageous seafarers. Notoriously, they were corsairs (pirates) preying on the trading vessels of other nations. Soon they were sailing to the Americas, even founding Norman colonies in the Caribbean and in what would later become Quebec. In 1682, Robert Cavalier of Lasalle, near Rouen, took possession of Louisiana.

Revolution & Royalism

When Revolution broke out across France (1789), many in Lower Normandy opposed it. In the 1790s they rallied to the Royalist cause under the banners of the Vendéen Army and the Chouans. The Vendéens were a powerful military force that erupted in 1793 in the coastal region south of the Loire, but were soon at large in the whole area of western France from Normandy to the Gironde. Zealously religious and lacking the class tensions of Paris and the revolutionary regions, the Vendéens styled themselves The Catholic Army, their stated objective being only the reopening of the parish churches.

Their struggle widened to oppose the whole Revolution. After impressive initial victories, they suffered a succession of defeats. A decisive setback took place at the end of 1793 at Granville, on Normandy's west-facing coast, where the Vendéen army had expected to find a force of English allies but found instead that the town had already been taken by the Republicans. By 1794 the Vendéen Army was routed and broken up, with thousands of prisoners executed. But in the same year the Chouannerie flared up across the region, including Lower Normandy, and was harder to subdue. The Chouans were royalists, both peasants and nobility, who usually did not confront the Republican army in pitched battles but instead operated successfully in small guerrilla bands. Their operations against the Revolutionary government continued for years, dying away after about 1800, when Les Chouans passed into myth and legend.

Art & leisure

Despite these events, Normandy survived the French Revolution relatively unharmed. Less than 20 years later, the fishing and market town of Dieppe was attracting visitors who came to take the sea air or bathe in its waters. Queen Hortensia of Holland apparently enjoyed her stay in 1813.

About the region

Soon it was a fully functioning holiday resort, where wealthy English families were building villas. Other towns on the coast of Upper Normandy, and then across the Seine on the Calvados coast, began to attract tourists too, especially after the opening of the railway from Paris to Caen in 1843. Deauville, a first example of a purpose-built resort, was constructed in 1859. Throughout the century, the coast of Normandy was frequented by the new aristocracy, and increasingly, by fashionable bourgeois families.

There was a spirit of invention, novelty and modernity in the air. It was in this setting that in the 1860s a group of young Normandy painters emerged who were to transform art beyond all recognition – the Impressionists, none more famous than Claude Monet of Le Havre.

Normandy at war

During the Franco-Prussian War (1870-1871), Upper Normandy was occupied by enemy forces, but this had relatively little effect on the province. Even the First World War, savagely raging across the border in Picardy, did not inflict much damage. However, devastation was to come later in the 20th century.

German occupation

Germany launched its campaign to conquer France and the Low Countries on 10 May 1940. Just two days later, having effectively defeated Belgium and the Netherlands, the Germany army invaded France. The British, French and Canadian forces they engaged in Picardy went into full retreat. From 26 May to 4 June, British forces escaped in disarray from Dunkirk beach. By 5 June, a scorchingly hot day, the Germans crossed the Somme in Picardy and were fast approaching Normandy. Exhausted

British and French regiments tried to prevent the Germans from crossing the River Bresle, the border of Normandy. The French order was to hold the Bresle 'at all costs', but other German regiments were already crossing into Normandy further east – by 8 June, they travelled along the Seine valley as far as Rouen, and the next day took control of Rouen. Just a few days later the Germans occupied all of Normandy, meeting little opposition.

On 17 June, France laid down its arms and unconditionally surrendered. Under the terms of the armistice, northern and western France would be under German occupation, while most of the rest of the country was to be ruled by a French collaborationist government based in Vichy.

Normandy came within the German Occupation Zone. On 30 June, German forces made the short crossing from the Cotentin Peninsula to take control of the Channel Islands. As in most of the Occupation Zone, the Germans and their French officials held a tight grip on the province and there seems to have been little resistance to the occupation. On 19 August 1942, the Dieppe Raid took place – but this attack by 6000 mainly Canadian commandos on the port town was defeated in just four hours, without achieving any of the objectives.

Operation Overlord: the Normandy landings
The key idea for a new Allied attack was the building of artificial ports that could be taken across the Channel and used to land troops at an unexpected location. In 1943 these were constructed, and early in 1944 training exercises were underway. False information was put out to encourage the Germans to focus on defending the Calais coast further north. The complex top-secret plan was coordinated between American and British generals – under the command of General Eisenhower – and code named Operation Overlord.

Preparations on the ground included a campaign of sabotage by the French Resistance but bad weather meant D-Day itself had to be delayed by one day. Then, in the middle of the night, airborne troops were landed and 5000 craft carrying about 170,000 men began their Channel crossing, towing the pieces that would be put together to construct Mulberry Harbours at Arromanches and Omaha. The weather was still bad, with rough seas, and many were seasick. British and Commonwealth troops aimed for the Calvados coast northwest of Caen (known in Operation Overlord as Sword, Juno and Gold beaches), while the Americans made for Omaha and Utah beaches further west.

They arrived at dawn on 6 June 1944. When the order was given, the men literally jumped into the water to wade on to mine-covered beaches while the surprised German troops in coastal bunkers along the shore fired automatic weapons directly at them: large numbers were killed within moments, but gradually they advanced. At the same time, more airborne troops were being landed by parachute.

This assault phase of the landings continued for one ferocious month; the battle for control of Normandy lasted well into August, the Germans slowly retreating towards the Seine. During that time Normandy suffered widespread devastation. Some two million men were engaged in the fighting. Many small towns and villages, inland as well as near the Landing Beaches, were almost entirely destroyed. Thousands of locals were killed. In larger towns, notably Caen, Rouen, Cherbourg and Le Havre, historic areas that had remained unchanged for centuries were obliterated.

Normandy at peace

In the post-war period, an effort of reconstruction in Normandy focused on two tasks: restoring the greatest of the historic structures which had been bombed, and rebuilding commercial and residential streets. Both were carried out with alacrity and efficiency. More than 500 towns and villages were rebuilt. In some places, the urgency of the task led to some charmless construction, while in other places it was achieved with great

D-Day Memorial, Ste-Mère-Eglise, Cotentin.

success and flair. Among good examples are the impeccable repair of the two medieval abbeys of Caen; and in Le Havre, the controversial modernist avenues designed by Auguste Perret using reinforced concrete, which have since caused the port city to be declared a World Heritage Site.

Throughout the region, bombed low-budget urban housing was cleared away from the surroundings of ancient buildings to create finer, more accessible settings for Normandy's architectural heritage. Parks and gardens were opened up too, and higher-standard modern housing built.

In the 1950s, reconstruction expanded to include a widespread upgrading of infrastructure. An outstanding example was the impressive Pont de Tancarville, opened in 1959: the 1400-m suspension bridge linked the two sides of the River Seine where previously a busy car ferry used to ply. In 1995 the elegant, cable-stayed Pont de Normandie opened, its 2140-m length soaring across the Seine estuary from Le Havre to Honfleur.

Monuments of war & peace

Although they have since become holiday resorts, the Landing Beaches have never forgotten the drama, bravery and suffering seen there in June 1944. Numerous museums, memorials large and small, and huge military cemeteries mark the coastal area, and every year D-Day is solemnly commemorated. A memorial and museum at Pegasus Bridge, between Caen and the sea, records that it was the first place to be liberated. At Arromanches-les-Bains, among vivid displays in the Musée du Débarquement (Landings Museum) are models of the artificial port that made the invasion possible.

In June 1988, Caen, which had been the focal point of the fighting (and destruction) in 1944, opened its Memorial Museum of Peace. It follows the story of war and peace in France from 1918 to 1944, and originally was principally dedicated as a memorial to the Battle of Normandy. It deals now with the continuation of war and repression all

around the world, and invites visitors to reflect on the precarious and precious nature of peace. See page 156.

The changing face of tourism

Normandy's economy, still based essentially on farming, shipping and fishing though on an increasingly industrial scale, grew to incorporate large-scale manufacturing and petro-chemicals based on the edges of the main cities, Rouen, Caen and Le Havre.

Normandy's 19th-century chic coastal resorts might have been expected to suffer a steep decline, especially after the 1960s, with the growth of air travel and package tourism favouring Mediterranean sunshine. However, while the resorts did lose much of their aristocratic glamour – though a flavour of it survives – the importance of tourism actually grew considerably, becoming a mainstay of the Normandy economy. The region's rustic, old-fashioned feel and fine traditional cuisine brought many more visitors, especially from outside France. Cross-channel ferries also made Normandy literally the first port of call for thousands of British holidaymakers each year.

Not only beach resorts, but many inland towns developed an extensive tourist infrastructure, ranging from camping or self-catering cottages to high-quality restaurants and luxurious hotels. Specific attractions became a draw for large numbers of visitors, notably Le Mont-St-Michel (see page 242), the Landing Beaches (see page 174) and Monet's home at Giverny (see page 121), which are among the most visited sites in France.

Art & architecture

Abbaye aux Hommes, Caen.

Art of the Norsemen

When the Vikings first settled in Normandy they were feared as brutal destroyers of art and beauty. As raiders they had murdered monks and destroyed monasteries. Yet as settlers they brought a creative and energetic Norse culture to their new Gallic home. Examples of their arts and crafts can be seen at the Musée de Normandie in Caen.

Required to rebuild great buildings they had destroyed, the early Normans became fluent in the architecture of churches and fortresses, making great advances in sturdy, less vulnerable structures and in fortifications.

One of the great Norse art forms was the telling of sagas. Perhaps as part of that legacy, once in possession of their duchy, and with their conversion to Christianity, Normans developed a particular interest in illuminated manuscripts The turn of the 12th century marked a high point in the creation of illustrated manuscripts in Normandy.

Undoubtedly the finest, best-known piece of illustrative art from the early period of the Duchy is not a manuscript but an embroidery: the Bayeux Tapestry. This tells an epic story – in cartoon-like pictures, with captions in Latin – of events before, during and after the Norman invasion of England under William the Conqueror.

Norman Romanesque

In architecture, moving forward from imitation and improvement of Frankish building techniques, a distinctively Norman style of construction developed – sturdy, massive structures of dressed stone, often well fortified; confident simple lines; round pillars; many rounded Roman-style arches to support ceilings and over doors and windows, lightly decorated with simple designs and geometric patterns; and often a substantial square tower (or two), sometimes topped with a stone pyramid, but no spire. This Romanesque style was carried to all the Norman colonies, with local variations. It remains plentiful in England, where it is known simply as 'Norman'. In its later period (12th century), very shallow early Gothic vaulting is introduced and may be found alongside Romanesque in the same buildings.

Norman architecture can be seen especially in the oldest parts of Le Mont-St-Michel and in the ruins of Jumièges abbey on the banks of the Seine – which was destroyed by Viking raiders in the ninth century, then rebuilt by their grandsons in the 10th. One of the best examples still surviving in Normandy are the 11th-century parts of the Abbaye aux Hommes (Mens' Abbey) in Caen, to which some early Gothic vaulting was added in the 12th century.

Five of the best

Norman art & architecture

❶ **Musée de Normandie** Caen, page 153.
❷ **Bayeux Tapestry** page 173.
❸ **Château Gaillard** page 122.
❹ **Abbaye de Jumièges** page 125.
❺ **Abbaye aux Hommes** Caen, page 155.

Gothic masterpieces

Norman architecture was much copied by the French, but from the 12th century onwards, the new Gothic masonry designs and construction skills were being developed in northern France. These were quickly mastered in Normandy, and again, a distinctively Norman Gothic style emerged, combining Gothic arches and skilful stonework with the sturdy proportions and simple lines of traditional Norman architecture. An early example can be seen in the cathedral at Lisieux. Norman Gothic reached perfection after King Philippe-Auguste of France seized the duchy from the Anglo-Norman King John I in 1204. The great surviving examples are the La Merveille buildings at Le Mont-St-Michel, and the cathedral at Coutances.

Late Gothic

The 14th century, after the hundred years of destructive conflict between England and France, saw a change of taste in Normandy, as the skilful Gothic stonework of the repaired and restored churches became extremely elaborate and exuberant, richly carved and decorated, and introduced flame-shaped designs that gave rise to the name Flamboyant. Throughout the region, especially Upper Normandy, remarkably accomplished Flamboyant Gothic structures were added to great religious buildings. In Rouen, the Tour de Beurre at the Cathedral, and Eglise St-Maclou which stands right behind the cathedral, and are two of the good examples of Flamboyant Gothic. Rouen Cathedral is one of several Normandy churches which, built over a period of centuries, is considered a supreme masterpiece of French Gothic art. Normandy's other fine Gothic churches include the Eglise Notre-Dame at Caudebec-en-Caux and Evreux's Cathédrale Notre-Dame.

Manors & mansions

A charming feature of the Normandy scene is the wealth of handsome half-timbered town houses and more substantial mansions with courtyards and, in the countryside, imposing manor houses and picturesque thatched cottages. Many are several centuries old. In a few, authentic Gothic remnants can often be seen. Most, though, date from the 16th century and incorporate mock-Gothic elements like turrets and decorative moats, as well as attractive Renaissance features of that time. Brickwork was often laid at zigzag angles to make patterns between the exposed timbers. Pont-Audemer, in the Eure, is one of many country towns with enchanting streets of half-timbered houses. Close by, the Pays d'Auge is especially lovely with a number of fine, timbered manor houses under steep tile roofs. Many recent country houses have been built to similar designs. It's not unusual to see modern houses painted with 'timbers'.

Impressionism

Sketching and painting out of doors and discovering naturalistic scenes and rural life rather than formal indoor settings, was a growing interest in the art world in the early and middle years of the 19th century. Both Romantic landscape painters and those of the Realist movement would place their easels in the rural countryside south and west of Paris. The interior and coast of Normandy along the River Seine was a popular subject. Three of the most influential names in French outdoor painting were English – Richard Parkes Bonington, John Constable and JMW Turner. Among their admirers were younger artists who were making another leap forward that was a step into the modern age.

Moving on from the growing interest in outdoor scenes, artists had the idea of trying to capture on canvas the very essence of 'outside' –

light itself, whose bright, hazy, pearly effects were such a feature of the Seine river and the resorts around its estuary. Among these painters were two young men who not only pioneered the new style, but remained its greatest exponents. Claude Monet and Eugène Boudin (originally from across the estuary in Honfleur) were both living in Le Havre and painting together in the 1860s. Their principal subjects were open horizons, dawn and dusk, sea mists and hot, hazy days. They worked in villages, in town and at holiday resorts, such as Trouville and Ste-Adresse. They were joined by Pierre-Auguste Renoir and many others.

The artists fled the Franco-Prussian War of 1870-1871 – many going to London – but as soon as it was over, most returned to Normandy, at least temporarily. In the aftermath of the war, the resorts north of Le Havre were thronging in season with artists, writers and musicians. Etretat was a haunt of Boudin, Matisse, Courbet, Monet and Corot, as well as the composer Offenbach and author Guy de Maupassant. The work of the painters continued. Taking the name from one of Monet's own works (*Impression: Soleil Levant*, exhibited in 1872) the art establishment derided them all as 'Impressionists', but the first Impressionist exhibition, held in 1874, established their reputations, and the start of their great popularity. Ten years later, a Monet set up house at Giverny. There he painted the lily pond in his garden again and again, as he did the façade of the cathedral in nearby Rouen, pictures that were to become definitive of the Impressionist movement. Monet died at Giverny in 1926.

Impressionism was just the beginning of modern art. The Seine valley, and Normandy, remained important as these developments advanced. It is remarkable that both Othon Friesz (1879-1949) and Raoul Dufy (1877-1953) were also natives of Le Havre, and that the Cubist pioneer Georges Braque (1882-1963) also grew up there. Other leading modern artists of the early 20th century came to paint in the area. Today, the Musée des Beaux-Arts in Le Havre has the largest collection of Impressionist art in France after the Musée d'Orsay in Paris.

Rouen Cathedral: The Portal (Sunlight) by Claude Monet.

Normandy today

D-Day anniversary celebrations, Ste-Mère-Eglise, Cotentin.

Normandy in France

With the massive project of post-war reconstruction and restoration for Normandy's damaged towns, villages and historic monuments, the region benefited from huge expenditure. Normandy's intense development and modernization has continued ever since, with the construction, for example, of oil refineries at Le Havre, three nuclear power stations and state-of-the-art bridges across the River Seine.

Until recently rustic and remote, Normandy's closer integration into the rest of France arguably began with the 19th-century Seine Valley railway line from Paris to the coastal resorts, but has seen great advances in the latter years of the 20th century and the beginning of the 21st. Autoroutes have been carved across the region to connect Paris with Le Havre and Caen; Calais to Rouen; and eastern Normandy with western Normandy. High-speed (TGV) railway lines have been laid linking Paris to Rouen and Le Havre. Since 2006, a huge programme has been underway to upgrade railway services throughout Normandy, with new lines and new stations constructed. Since 2009, Le Havre is directly connected by TGV not just to the French capital, but also to Strasbourg.

The economic and structural integration of Normandy into the rest of the country has been helped by many other political and social factors. For example, the gathering in Normandy in 2009 of American president Barack Obama, Prince Charles and other international leaders, together with French President Sarkozy, for the 65th anniversary of the Normandy Landings, impacted on public perceptions of the former duchy. Ceremonies on that occasion, and the solemn speeches made, increased awareness of Normandy's historic role in the world.

English-speaking Normandy

Quite apart from 1066, Normandy's historical links to Britain have long continued in another form. Ever since the growth of Dieppe as a resort in the 19th century, with its all-year-round English community, the region has attracted large numbers of British residents – more so now than ever before. An estimated 10,000 British people are living in Normandy.

The area around Dieppe has remained popular with English expats and second-homers. The 'Normandy Riviera', centred on Deauville, has been another area with an established British (and Parisian) presence. While these communities have tended to be well-to-do, Normandy today appeals to British incomers across the social, age and economic spectrums.

Lower Normandy, especially the inexpensive west coast and rural south, is particularly popular with the British today. Many thousands have settled here, both retired and working. In their favour they say of themselves that they save many rural houses from dilapidation. Against them, it is said that they allow first-class orchards to fall into ruin, not tending the trees, not even gathering the fruit. However, a large number are registered to vote and play an active part in French communal life. At least one Normandy village has an English mayor – St-Ceneri-le-Gérei, in the Orne *département*.

The reasons are many. For francophiles, Normandy is the nearest place to England for a taste of the authentic *France profonde*. It's very easy to reach – directly by ferry to Dieppe, Le Havre, Caen and Cherbourg, by car via the Channel Tunnel, or by train using Eurostar and TGV. Coupled with the easy access, property prices are low by English standards. Another important factor is that Normans are still conscious of the great sacrifice made on behalf of France during the Second World War, and in general feel warmly towards the British. And the climate, too – rarely very hot or very cold – suits many British people.

Nature & environment

Field of colza in bloom, Pays de Caux.

Picture the Norman countryside and you'll probably imagine little fields and orchards, densely populated but rustic, with hedgerows and clumps of woodland and narrow lanes. That is an accurate image – of Normandy's most picturesque areas. But Normandy is large and varied. Its diversity is startling, ranging from southern Normandy's rolling green landscapes cloaked with oak, beech and pine forests and cut through by flowing waters, to northeastern Normandy's vast uncluttered uplands under wide skies. The differences come largely from the underlying structure of the land. Upper Normandy is plateau country, more recent geologically than the ancient, rocky Lower Normandy. Between them, and amongst them, are other distinctly different areas carved out by the movement of water across the land.

Thanks to Lower Normandy's less intensive farming, wild flowers bring masses of colour to roadsides and fields, especially in spring and early summer. Normandy lacks extensive wilderness, but it does protect some sand dune areas and woodland and wetland habitats where birdlife thrives. Roe deer, red deer and even wild boar may also be glimpsed in its forests.

Caux & the Alabaster Coast

The high, wide chalk plateau of Upper Normandy extends from Picardy to the Seine. Here is a great sweep of large-scale arable farming untypical of the rest of the province. Extensive fields of sugar beet and golden corn are spread across a sparsely populated landscape. On the eastern side is the curious Bray 'buttonhole' – a slender region of more fertile terrain cut into the landscape. In its southern reaches, a more populous section of the chalk plateau is bordered by the valleys of the rivers Epte, Andelle and Seine. The chalky uplands of the Caux reach the English Channel in majestic white cliffs , home to vast numbers of gulls,

especially around Cap d'Antifer, where you'll see colonies of petrel, great cormorant and shag. Dramatic enough in themselves, in places (most striking around Etretat) these soaring white sea cliffs become even more remarkable where the chalk has been deeply carved into arches by the wind and waves. Upper Normandy has large woodland areas too, the oak and beech forests of Eu, Eawy and Lyons richly coloured by bluebells in spring, gold and copper foliage in autumn, and harbouring wild boar and herds of deer.

River Seine

The wide, flat valley of the Seine meanders through Upper Normandy, edged on its right bank by high white escarpments and on its left bank by lower, wooded farm country. It makes for an inspiring sight. A short distance downriver from Rouen is the Brotonne Forest, an area of beech, oak and pine, home to boar and deer, and smaller mammals including hare. These woods are full of bluebells in spring.

At its mouth the river broadens into an immense estuary of vast mud and sand flats where seabirds gather despite refineries and power stations stretched along the right bank on the approach into Le Havre. A large part of the estuary is a nature reserve, part of the Parc Naturel Régional des Boucles de la Seine Normande (Regional Nature Park of the Normandy Seine Loops). It includes the curious and atmospheric half-wild *Marais Vernier* (Vernier Marshes), lying like a huge bowl among the farmland. Within the once-marshy terrain, the Grand'Mare lake is a protected haven for wildlife, often crowded with vast flocks of ducks and geese and wading birds, teal, mallard, shoveller, as well as cormorant, coot, herons, great egret, crested grebes and even stork among them.

About the region

Calvados coast

Along the prettily named Côte Fleurie (flowery coast) – flowers do indeed flourish beside the Calvados seafront between the mouth of the Seine and the mouth of the Orne – wide sandy beaches and popular little resort towns alternate with harbours. Behind the shore rise hills and cliffs, in places densely tree-covered.

Beyond the Côte Fleurie, the exposed sandy beach continues in a seemingly endless strip beside a windy sea. Called the Côte de Nacre (*nacre* is mother of pearl), this shore – the Landing Beaches of 1944 – is now dotted with small resorts. Yet behind them the land is often a barrier of scrubby, undeveloped terrain of dunes and marshes. Further inland, the grassy open country of the Bessin is known for its stud farms and dairies, but also for extensive marshy areas where tens of thousands of wading birds spend the winter. Among permanent residents are numerous white storks and white wagtail.

Pays d'Auge

Rural yet densely populated, farmed with a mosaic of small fields, pastures and orchards, in places giving way to woodland, this rolling countryside marks the border between Upper and Lower Normandy. The area is well watered by the rivers Touques and Dives, and a multitude of streams, and it consists partly of long-ago reclaimed marshland. Locally the climate tends to be relatively warm and humid, which has encouraged rich pasture for dairy cows, and also for horses, which are bred here. The copses and endless mature hedges are each like a little nature reserve, brimming with nuts and berries and flowers and bursting with insect and bird life.

Cotentin peninsula

Cotentin is geologically part of the same rocky massif as Brittany. It is similar in character too, thrusting into the salty waters of the English Channel. Nowhere on the peninsula is far from the waves. Seabirds fly over the rooftops, rocky ocean-facing spurs are dented with inlets and cottages cluster around harbours. The Cap de la Hague, together with the northern Cotentin coast, is one of the best places in Europe to view them, with an extraordinary number of different species flying close to land. Gulls crowd around the cliffs, mingling with petrels, auks, skuas and terns and shearwaters. Inland you can see marsh harriers and bunting. The Cotentin is good for spotting summer migrant waders and inland species too, including flycatchers, pipits and warblers. There are long sandy beaches too, especially towards the more sheltered St Michael's Bay, in the crook of which the granite wedge of Le Mont-St-Michel rises from sea-washed marshes. In these southern limits of the peninsula, the interior of the country is also gentler and lusher with *bocage* scenery – the word conveys a familiar, traditional Norman countryside of fields, with rough pasture and a few apple trees, enclosed by mature hedges.

Southern hills

Rolling green hills and valleys extend across Southern Normandy from southern Cotentin to the valley of the Eure. Southern Normandy has a character all its own, with extensive forests and rivers and old-fashioned farms, much of which is protected by the Parc Naturel Régional Normandie Maine. Explore in the woods and with luck you'll come across red squirrels, perhaps even red deer, as well as hare. Overhead, raptors swirl, especially kestrel. Although hilly, the area does not achieve great altitudes. The even more unspoiled Perche region, where Normandy plunges further south into Maine, is known for its Percheron horses, while on the eastern fringes are cool landscapes of open pasture.

Horse riding in Calvados.

Festivals & events

Normandy's calendar reflects the two great preoccupations of the duchy and its people – good food and the sea. From spring to autumn, food fairs celebrate local produce, and traditional blessings are made for the sea and those who work on it. There are also prestigious arts and music festivals.

February

Granville Carnival
Four-day carnival celebrations in Granville starting the weekend before Mardi Gras (ville-granville.fr).

March & April

La Foire au Boudin (third weekend)
Much-loved annual festival at Mortagne-au-Perche, a town acclaimed for its black pudding (perche.gastronomie.free.fr/).

Festival de Pâques
Deauville kicks off the Easter holiday season with two weeks of classical music (deauville.org/fr).

La Foire de Pâques
A huge annual Easter funfair at Caen, with more than 130 rides, free to enter and lasting three weeks (caen-expo-congres.com/calend/paques.html).

Journées des Plantes Franco-britanniques
(usually third weekend)
An exquisite weekend festival of garden plants, in the grounds of a handsome country house Château de Crosville-sur-Douve (T02 33 41 67 25).

May & June

Jazz Sous les Pommiers (May)
This important week-long annual 'jazz under the apple trees' festival in Coutances draws big crowds to the medieval country town (jazzsouslespommiers.com).

Les Rencontres de Cambremer
(first weekend in May)
Discover, taste and buy Normandy's 12 traditional quality-assured gourmet products at this festival in Cambremer, Calvados (office-tourisme-cambremer.fr).

Bénédiction de la Mer (May, on Ascension Day)
A devout traditional procession in Etretat to a seashore Mass and a cliff-top blessing.

Fête de Ste-Jeanne d'Arc
(Sunday nearest 30 May)
This Joan of Arc festival in Rouen is both solemn and festive, with religious services but also medieval markets and street theatre (rouentourisme.com).

Pentecôte (May or June)
The religious holiday of Pentecost (or Whitsun) is a holiday weekend in France.

Yacht rally (Pentecost)
Thousands of yachts sail in waters around Cherbourg and the Cotentin.

Fête des Marins et des Pêcheurs (Pentecost)
This festival of sailors and fishermen takes the form of a pilgrimage to cliff-top Eglise Notre Dame de Grâce in Honfleur to bless the sea and the sailors.

D-Day Commemorations (6 June)
Veterans and visitors remember and celebrate the hard-won victories on the Landing Beaches. (normandiememoire.com).

July

Fêtes Médiévales (first weekend)
A jolly celebration of the Middle Ages in the medieval streets of Bayeux with parades in medieval dress, singing, dancing celebrating the end of the Hundred Years' War (bayeux-tourism.com).

Fête de la Mer et du Maquereau
Weekend sea festival in Trouville-sur-Mer with mackerel tasting and a festive procession and blessing of boats (trouvillesurmer.org).

August

Grand Pardon (Sunday nearest end of July; can be in July or August)
Atmospheric traditional events in Granville, with banners, torchlight parade, outdoor Mass and blessings of the sea and of the boats (granville-tourisme.fr).

Fête au Fromage (usually first weekend)
Tasting and competitions at the annual festival of Livarot cheese in Livarot (paysdelivarot.fr).

September

Festival du Cinéma Américain (10 days during first two weeks of September)
Stars, glamour and screenings in Deauville of the year's best releases from Hollywood and American independents (festival-deauville.com).

Fête du Cidre (end of September)
Apple-themed parades, arts and crafts stalls, parades, folk music and cider drinking in celebration of local traditions and of the local brew in Caudebec-en-Caux.

October

Festival des Coquillages et Crustacés (usually first weekend)
The leading shellfish port of Granville celebrates and shares its speciality (granville-tourisme.fr).

Foire de la Pomme (second or third weekend)
Celebrating the new season in Vimoutiers with a fair dedicated to all things apple.

Grand Marché et Fête du Cidre (usually last weekend)
Plenty of local fare on offer in Beuvron-en-Auge and the new season's cider to drink.

November

Foire aux Harengs or Fête du Hareng (mid-November)
Herrings are celebrated at this quayside festival in Dieppe, and at most other towns on the Alabaster Coast (seine-maritime-tourisme.com).

Sleeping

Grand Hotel, on the seafront in Cabourg, Calvados.

Chic pre-war resorts, family beach holidays, lively city breaks and simple country living are all among the favourite holiday options here. Normandy is one of the most popular regions in France and appeals to a wide range of people and interests, with a diverse choice of accommodation to match.

Prices

Most visitors to Normandy are travelling on a package holiday – that is, accommodation and transport (and sometimes meals) combined in an inclusive price, pre-booked with a travel agent or tour operator in their home country. This is normally cheaper and easier than paying for each element of the trip separately. However, package deals usually require a minimum stay of three nights in a hotel, or a week in self-catering or campsite accommodation. You may also be required to arrive at your accommodation on a particular changeover day.

For more freedom and independence, especially on a touring holiday with a flexible itinerary, you may need to find and book accommodation yourself. This is not difficult: the internet has made it easy to make reservations in advance.

Hotel pricing in France is normally for the room, not per person. Breakfast is generally not included, but is available for an extra charge of about €12-€15 in mid-priced establishments – it is usually cheaper to pop out to a café.

Hotels are graded with a star system, but some hotels fall short of a single star (expect to pay under €40), while others exceed the requirements, for France's maximum grade four-star *luxe* (expect to pay more than €300 per night). Most have three stars (around €80-€140 per double room).

Prices vary considerably by season and from place to place. Deauville in high summer makes quite a contrast to similar accommodation at a village on the Cotentin out of season. Prices take a big step up as the summer peak approaches. Expect to see room rates rise sharply at Easter, then in June, and again in July. They step down again at the end of August, making early autumn a good time to visit.

Booking

To visit the most popular parts of Normandy during peak season (July-August), it's wise to plan everything at least two months in advance. To stay near the Landing Beaches for D-Day commemorations at the beginning of June, book well ahead. Out of high season, though, especially away from the main towns, it is not usually necessary to book more than a day in advance.

Hotels and chambres d'hôtes (guest rooms) are easily booked online or by phone. For small, independent, family-run establishments, especially off the beaten track, a smattering of French may be needed. For camping and self-catering, it can be simpler to pre-book a package rather than to arrange independently.

Hotels

In and around Normandy's larger towns, you will find everything from predictable, decent budget hotels to stylish four-star *luxe* hotels. Almost all towns and many villages have at least one modest, comfortable three-star hotel, generally with its own restaurant. They often have a traditional feel and are sometimes in historic mansions and manor houses (do ask in advance if steep stairs or other access issues may be a problem). If prices are very low, ask carefully about facilities – a bargain-priced hotel room may lack modern amenities.

The major international hotel groups are all present. In addition, the big French chains, all with several hotels in the region, include Campanile motels with restaurants, economy motels such as Formule 1, which are modern and simple, Ibis (functional, budget-priced town hotels), and more upmarket chains Meridien and Sofitel.

A high proportion of hotels are independent, most belonging to hotel federations that resemble chains, requiring member establishments to reach a certain standard. Two dependable French hotel and restaurant federations are Relais & Châteaux, which offer classic luxury, and Logis de France, small, traditional family-run hotels, nearly all with a restaurant.

Tip...

Online hotel bookings are often cheaper. Simply turning up at hotels without a booking could result in a higher rate being charged.

About the region

Chambres d'hôtes (B&Bs)

Bed and breakfast accommodation in private homes (usually in a purpose-built extension) is common in rural areas. It provides an inexpensive alternative with the added interest of meeting local people and getting under the surface of Normandy life. These chambres d'hôtes (guest rooms) – often have a simple sign on the front gate. You're welcome to stop and ask for a room. They often provide an evening meal too. All chambres d'hôtes have to be approved by local authorities.

Self-catering gîtes

Gîtes – self-catering country cottages – are found all over Normandy in the most rural areas. They're often a bargain, though facilities can be old-fashioned. It is wise to pre-book, either by phone or online (gites-de-france.fr/, in French and English).

For self-catering with all the comforts of home, choose from thousands of modern holiday houses and villas available from a number of UK tour operators and agencies. You can find self-catering in towns, too: *meublés* (furnished) are vacation apartments. Contact local tourist offices for a list; they can also make bookings.

Campsites

Campsites are the least expensive accommodation and often in the best locations. Most of the larger sites have a number of erected spacious modern tents as well as rows of mobile homes fixed in position. Campsite life gives a freedom and independence ideal for those who don't want to conform with normal mealtimes or dress codes. Children tend to meet and play with others from all over Europe, and parents may find an easy-going atmosphere on a campsite unlike other lodgings.

The region offers perfect camping opportunities.

Campsites are carefully regulated and must meet approved standards. They're graded with stars: anything with two or more stars has hot showers and good facilities. Four-star and the even better four-star 'Grand Confort' sites have excellent amenities, often including a swimming pool. *Camping à la Ferme*, campsites on farms, are a category on their own that tends to be more basic. At the other extreme, Castels et Camping, mainly in superb locations, is a federation of top-quality camps.

Accommodation online

Relais & Châteaux relaischateaux.com
Castels et Camping les-castels.com
Camping and Caravanning Club campingandcaravanningclub.co.uk
Caravan Club (UK) caravanclub.co.uk
Gîtes de France gites-de-france.fr
Logis de France logis-de-france.fr

Eating & drinking

La Mère Poulard restaurant, Le Mont-St-Michel.

Gastronomic region

French tourists happily make their way to Normandy for the pleasures of the table. Normandy's traditional cooking has a highly distinctive regional style, with a strong emphasis on its rich dairy produce, shellfish and good-quality meats, as well as the abundant harvest of its cherry, pear and especially apple orchards.

There are numerous Normandy specialities. The result of all those orchards and dairy farms and picturesque fishing harbours is meals with plenty of local cheeses, butter, and thick, farm-made, semi-sour crème fraîche for savoury cream sauces. Apples may turn up in any course as apple sauces and apple pastry, dry cider and fiery Calvados, and the sherry-like aperitif, *pommeau*. More than that, Normandy is renowned in France for the sheer size of meals. Normans are trenchermen par excellence, spending longer at the table than anyone else in the country. From this arose the tradition of the *trou normand* – literally the 'Norman gap', but the custom itself is more elegant than the phrase: a short break between two main courses, in which a tot of Calvados is sipped, supposedly to aid digestion. Nowadays it is more likely to be a Calvados sorbet.

Dairy produce

Some of the best-known French cheeses come from Normandy. Creamy and pungent 'washed-rind' boxed cheeses, made from the milk of grass-fed cows, carry the names of the towns and villages where they were first produced. Among them are Camembert, Pont l'Evêque, Livarot and Pavé d'Auge, all in the Pays d'Auge, and from the other side of the Seine, Neufchâtel (which is usually made in a cute heart shape). Local farm-made crème fraîche is a staple of Normandy's all-important sauces: a rich, smooth, slightly soured thick cream. Normandy butter, processed and wrapped at Isigny, is also counted among the very best and is exported all over France and abroad.

Seafood

Expect to find lobsters and crayfish, crabs and spider crabs, oysters, scallops and mussels on almost every menu. They are jointly known as *fruits de mer* and often served in large heaps. Such seafood is another essential ingredient of Normandy's sauces and stews. The main area for shellfish is the Cotentin Peninsula, especially around the scenic ports of Granville and St Vaast-la-Hougue. Fresh fish are also abundant.

Apple orchard, Upper Normandy.

Normandy specialities

Almost every good meal in Normandy includes lashings of cream and a good splash of Calvados or cider. Among the most famous of all Normandy's plethora of local specialities is *tripes à la mode de Caen*, a long-cooked stew of tripe, pig's trotters, vegetables, herbs and Calvados. Another is *Marmite Dieppoise*, a creamy fish-and-shellfish stew supposedly invented at the restaurant from which it takes its name. More generally, *dieppoise*, as in the classic *sole à la dieppoise*, means served in a creamy sauce made with white wine, mussels and crayfish. Other local favourites include charcuterie, especially *andouilles* and *andouillettes* (chitterling sausages large and small) from the farms of southwestern Calvados, and *boudin* (black pudding) from Le Perche. *Agneau de pré-salé* is the

About the region

Normandy produces some of France's most famous cheese.

Fresh fish and shellfish are plentiful in Normandy.

distinctive-tasting tender lamb from the flood meadows around Mont-St-Michel Bay. While you're at Le Mont-St-Michel, another local treat is *omelette Mère Poulard*, a thick fluffy soufflé omelette.

For something simple, crêpes have long been Normandy's preferred cheap snack. These paper-thin pancakes can be sprinkled with almost anything, sweet or savoury, and are especially popular on the Cotentin Peninsula. To finish the meal, apples, pears and cherries are served in tasty flans and tarts.

Dining tips

Choose a prix-fixe menu
At most restaurants you'll be offered à la carte (list of dishes, individually priced) and a choice of about three menus, that is, *prix fixe* (fixed price) set meals. Typical menu prices might be €20-€40. The price difference reflects not differences in quality but in number of courses and difficulty of preparation. In general, to get the best out of a restaurant, and the best value for money, order one of the menus, not à la carte.

Formula for a cheap lunch
For a quick light meal, many restaurants and bars offer an inexpensive fixed-price *formule* without specifying the dishes. It's often a starter and simple main course, or main course and dessert, with a quarter-litre of house wine and a coffee.

What's on the bill?
French restaurant prices always include service and all taxes. It's not necessary to give any extra tip. *Vin compris* means wine included (usually a quarter of a litre of house wine per person); *boisson comprise* means you may have a beer or soft drink instead.

Eat at the right time
Away from resorts and big cities, it can be difficult to find something to eat outside normal mealtimes. Lunch is served generally 1200-1400 (Sunday lunch lasts until 1500), and dinner 1900-2200.

Out of hours dining
Brasseries (breweries) are bars that serve food at any time of day. A *salon de thé* is a smarter alternative for between-meals pastries and other light snacks with tea or coffee.

No need to dress for dinner
Smart casual is the norm in even the best places, though you may dress up if you prefer.

The €10 picnic

From the *épicerie*, pick up 100g of Neufchâtel cheese for €1, 500g ripe tomatoes for €1, a bottle of decent Normandy cider or cheap French wine for €2 and a litre of water for €1. From the *traiteur* buy ready-to-eat *coquille St Jacques*, or an *andouille de Vire* sausage for €3. Then from the *boulangerie* or *pâtisserie* get some fresh bread and a pastry for €2.

Menu reader

General

petit déjeuner breakfast
déjeuner lunch
dîner dinner or supper
hors d'œuvre appetisers
entrées starters
plat principal main course
menu/formule set menu
plat du jour dish of the day
carte des vins wine list

Drinks (boissons)

bière German or Belgian-style beer
cidre bouchée sparkling cider
cidre doux, cidre sec dry cider, sweet cider
pommeau strong apple aperitif
Calvados apple brandy
apéritif drink taken before dinner
digestif after-dinner drink, usually a liqueur or spirit
eau gazeuse/pétillante sparkling/slightly sparkling mineral water
eau plat/minérale still/mineral water
bouteille bottle
dégustation tasting
vin rouge/blanc/rosé red/white/rosé wine
pichet jug, used to serve water, wine or cider
une pression a glass of draught beer
une bière a beer
un demi small beer (33cl)
un cidre cider
un panaché beer/lemonade shandy
jus de fruit fruit juice
orange pressée freshly squeezed orange juice
sirop fruit syrup or cordial served with water or soda
un coca Coca-Cola
glaçons ice cubes
un café coffee (black espresso)
un (grand) crème a (large) white coffee
une noisette espresso with a dash of milk
deca decaf
chocolat chaud hot chocolate
lait milk
un thé tea, usually served black with a slice of lemon (*au citron*) – if you want milk ask for *un peu de lait froid*, a little cold milk
une tisane/infusion herbal tea

Fruit (fruits) & vegetables (légumes)

ail garlic
ananas pineapple
artichaut artichoke
asperge asparagus
blettes Swiss chard
cassis blackcurrants
cèpes porcini mushrooms
champignons de Paris button mushrooms
châtaignes chestnuts
chou cabbage
citron lemon
citrouille or *potiron* pumpkin
cocos small, white beans
courge marrow or squash
épinards spinach
fenouil fennel
fèves broad beans
figues figs
fraises strawberries

framboises raspberries
haricots verts green beans
lentilles vertes green lentils
mesclun a mixture of young salad leaves
poires pears
pomme de terre potato, *primeurs* are new potatoes, and *frites* are chips (*chips* being crisps)
pommes apples, the *Reinette d'Orléans* and *Reine des Reinettes* are local varieties
prunes plums
truffe truffle

Sauces & cooking styles

dieppoise with mussels, white wine and cream
jus meat juice with nothing added (may be thickened by reduction)
matelote Normande creamy white sauce with cider and calvados
Normand(e) cooked with cider or calvados, and cream added
à la Normande casseroled with apples, calvados and cream
sauce any kind of sauce or dressing
vallée d'Auge meat flambéed in calvados and served in cream and cider sauce

Fish & seafood (poissons et fruits de mer)

aiglefin haddock
anchoïade anchovy-based spread
anchois anchovies
anguille eel
bar bass
barbue brill
bigorneaux winkles
bulots sea snails, whelks
cabillaud cod
calamar squid
coques cockles
coquillage shellfish
coquilles St Jacques scallops
colin hake
crevettes prawns
dorade sea bream
ecrevisses crayfish
homard lobster
huîtres oysters
langoustines Dublin Bay prawns
lotte monkfish
loup de mer sea bass
maquereau mackerel
morue salt-cod
moules mussels
palourdes a kind of clam
poissons de rivière river fish
poulpe octopus
poutine very tiny, young sardines, most often cooked in an omelette or served raw
praires clams
raie skate
rascasse scorpion fish
rouget red mullet
St-Pierre John Dory
sardines sardines
saumon salmon
soupe de poisson a smooth rockfish-based soup
soupions small squid
thon tuna
truite trout
turbotin small turbot

Meat (viande) & poultry (volaille)

agneau (pré-salé) lamb (from saltwater flood meadows)
andouillette soft sausage made from pig's small intestines, usually grilled
à point medium cooked meat (or tuna steak), usually still pink inside
bien cuit well-cooked
blanquette de veau veal stew in white sauce with cream, vegetables and mushrooms
bleu barely-cooked meat, almost raw
boeuf beef
boucherie butcher's shop or display
boudin black pudding, blood sausage
canard duck
charcuterie encompasses sausages, hams and cured or salted meats
chevreuil venison, roe deer
confit process to preserve meat, usually duck, goose or pork (e.g. confit de canard)
cuisse de grenouille frog's leg
dinde turkey
escalope thin, boneless slice of meat
faux-filet beef sirloin
foie-gras fattened goose or duck liver
fumé(e) smoked
géline de Touraine or la Dame-Noire grain-fed chicken prized by restaurateurs, awarded a Label Rouge
gigot d'agneau leg of lamb
jambon ham; look for jambon d'Amboise, an especially fine ham
lapin rabbit
lardons small pieces of ham
médaillon small, round cut of meat or fish
mouton mutton
pavé thickly cut steak
pintade guinea fowl
porc pork
pot-au-feu slow-cooked beef and vegetable stew
poulet chicken
rillettes coarse pork pâté
rillons big chunks of pork cooked in pork fat
ris de veau sweetbreads
sanglier wild boar
saucisse small sausage
saucisson salami, eaten cold
saucisson sec air-dried salami
taureau bull
veau veal

Desserts (desserts)

chantilly whipped, sweetened cream
compôte stewed fruit, often as a purée
crème anglaise egg custard
crème brûlée chilled custard cream dessert
crème caramel baked custard flavoured with caramel
glace ice cream
boules de glace scoops of ice cream
le parfum flavour, when referring to ice cream or yoghurt
pâtisserie pastries, cakes and tarts – also the place where they are sold
sabayon creamy dessert made with eggs, sugar and wine or cider
tarte au citron lemon tart
tarte Normande apple tart
tarte Tatin upside-down apple tart
teurgoule baked rice pudding sprinkled with cinnamon

Useful phrases

I'd like to reserve a table *Je voudrais réserver une table*
For two people at 8pm *Pour deux personnes, à vingt heures*
What do you recommend? *Qu'est-ce que vous me conseillez?*
I'd like the set menu please *Je vais prendre le menu / la formule s'il vous plait*
Does it come with salad? *Est-ce que c'est servi avec de la salade?*
I'd like something to drink *Je voudrais quelque chose à boire*
I'm a vegetarian *Je suis végétarien / végétarienne*
I don't eat… *Je ne mange pas de…*
Where are the toilets? *Où sont les toilettes?*
The bill, please *L'addition, s'il vous plait*

Other

assiette plate (eg *assiette de charcuterie*)
beurre butter
beurre blanc buttery white wine sauce often served with fish
boulangerie bakery selling bread and *viennoiserie*
brioche a soft, sweet bread made with eggs and butter
casse-croûte literally 'to break a crust' – a snack
une crêpe pancake served with various fillings
croque-monsieur grilled ham and cheese sandwich
croque-madame as above but topped with a fried egg
crudités raw vegetables served sliced or diced with a dressing, as a starter or sandwich filling
en croûte food cooked in a pastry parcel
escargots snails
forestière generally sautéed with mushrooms
fromage cheese
fromage de chèvre goat's milk cheese
galette savoury filled pancake made with buckwheat flour, served as a starter or main course
garniture garnish, side dish
gâteau cake
gaufre waffle, usually served with chocolate sauce
Hollandaise rich oil and egg yolk sauce flavoured with lemon juice
œuf egg
pain bread – choose from a rich variety of flavoured breads as well as the traditional baguette
pain au chocolat similar to a croissant, but pillow-shaped and filled with chocolate
pâte pastry or dough, not to be confused with *pâtes*, which is pasta or *pâté*, the meat terrine
riz rice
rouille saffron, garlic and paprika mayonnaise, served with *soupe de poisson* and *bouillabaisse*
salade verte simple green salad with vinaigrette dressing
soupe/potage soup
viennoiserie baked items such as croissants and brioches

Entertainment

Restaurants and bars line the promenade at Le Havre.

Bars & clubs

Popular town centre bars often stay open until 0200, later at weekends. Some make a late-night transition into dance venues and nightclubs. Bars that focus on coffees and set lunches during the day may turn into nightclubs or cocktail bars after dark. There's often music – sometimes live – in the Irish pub type of bar. You'll find them around place du Vieux Marché in Rouen, the docks area of Le Havre and the Quai Vendeuvre in Caen. Especially at weekends, there are late-night clubs in all the main towns. The Côte Fleurie has late-night clubs along the seafront outside Deauville. Clubs usually open at about 2230 and get going from 0100 onwards. There's often an entrance fee on busy nights at the most popular places, which can be as much as €15, though this usually includes a drink.

If your French is good enough to get the jokes, some city cafés and bars host cabaret, comedians and theatre acts too. For glitzier entertainment and floorshows, dress up for a visit to the casino in the old established resorts such as Deauville on the Channel coast or Bagnoles-de-l'Orne in Southern Normandy, where they have kept some of their pre-war style.

Children

Much of Normandy's sightseeing grabs the imagination of older children. Hilltop castles and forts like Château Gaillard, crossing a causeway to reach Le Mont-St-Michel, seeing the Norman invasion of England in cartoon-strip form on the Bayeux Tapestry, a visit inside the Redoubtable submarine at Cherbourg-Octeville's Cité de la Mer and authentic military equipment used in the Second World War, are all likely to impress. At major attractions, interpretation facilities have been put in place with children in mind. For example, at Bayeux, there's a simplified children's version of the audio-guide, as well as a cinema. Scattered around Normandy, traditional low-tech leisure parks and animal enclosures provide good old-fashioned entertainment for the younger ones. Parc Zoologique Lisieux, for example, in the Pays d'Auge, has over 600 species of wild animal. You travel around by 'Little Train' between the enclosures, meeting some of the friendlier creatures face-to-face.

Music

Classical & opera
The arts are thriving in Normandy's main cities, especially in Rouen and Caen. It's wise to book tickets before your trip. The riverside Opéra de Rouen is a prestigious centre for high-quality dance, ballet, classical music and opera. The Comédie de Caen stages performances at the suburban Théâtre d'Hérouville, while the city's resident Orchestre de Caen plays at the city-centre Grand Auditorium de Caen. Dance and classical music are performed at Le Volcan in the heart of the Quartier Moderne. You can find classical music in smaller towns too. Alençon, in southern Normandy, is the main base of Scène Nationale 61, which puts on a programme of drama, dance and concerts.

Contemporary
Jazz has made its mark on Normandy. One of the best-loved jazz festivals in France is its Jazz Sous les Pommiers at Coutances. Listen out for jazz bars and clubs in the city centres, or ask the tourist office. For rock and pop concerts with top French and international performers, check what's coming up at the Zenith auditorium in Rouen and Caen. Traditional folksy sounds get people on their feet at open-air riverside *guinguettes* on summer weekends; very popular with locals, these come to life especially on national holidays at places like Pont d'Ouilly in the Suisse Normande, or on the Seine near Rouen.

Shopping

Copper workshop in the metalworking town of Villedieu-les-Poêles.

Arts & crafts

Traditional crafts and trades survive in several parts of Normandy. Local hand-made lace can still be bought at the lace museums of Alençon (see page 237) and Argentan, which make it their business to preserve the skills for which they were once famous. Knitted goods (*tricoterie*) are a tradition of the fishing ports, many of which now have fine knitwear boutiques. In the old metalworking town of Villedieu-les-Poêles, gleaming copper pots and pans still hang outside shops in the main street just as they have for centuries. Look out for antiques too, in street markets, *brocantes* (second-hand shops) and *antiquaires* (antiques dealers). You may even discover good pieces of the 18th- and 19th-century local blue and white patterned faïence and porcelain known as Rouen ware.

Food & drink

In any Normandy town you'll find busy specialist stores selling locally produced food and drink. The *traiteur* and *charcuterie* (both delicatessen) have *boudins*, *andouillettes* and other prepared and preserved meats and ready-to-eat cooked dishes and salads. A *boucherie* is a butcher's shop. An *épicerie* stocks everyday foods, including Calvados and cider, while the classier *épicerie fine* caters to gourmet tastes, and generally has a top-quality cheese counter, perhaps crème fraîche ladled from a tub and fresh butter cut from a large slab. A *boulangerie* is a baker's, often selling country-style breads as well as the traditional baguette and flute. They may sell pastries too, but a better place for those is the *pâtisserie*, the pastry-cook's. Chocolatiers and *confiseurs* (or *confiserie*) make and sell confectionery, while a *glacier* (it sounds cold!) specializes in ice cream. A *supermarché* is a small self-service shop, while an edge-of-town *hypermarché* (hypermarket) will stock a full range of goods from around the world.

Seafood stall on the Normandy coast.

Seafood

At fishing ports, the fresh catch is laid out and sold each morning from stalls on the quayside. Sole, brill and mackerel are plentiful. Early in the day, you can see it being carted straight into the kitchens of waterfront restaurants. Queues of discerning locals form to buy the best of fish and shellfish, usually by the half-kilo, the kilo or even larger amounts, such as 5 kg of the popular *coquilles St Jacques* (scallops) for about €20. Remember to keep live shellfish cold, but not on ice, and not in an airtight bag. Eat them within a day or two.

About the region

Producing cider from a press, Le Pays d'Auge.

Markets

Most towns in Normandy have at least one farmers' market (*marché*) per week, either in a centuries-old market square or a covered *halles*. Among the best of Normandy's street markets are Caen, Dieppe, Rouen and in the villages of St-Pierre-sur-Dives and l'Aigle. The bigger markets include dozens of stalls selling inexpensive clothes, kitchenware, household items and other goods. Freshly gathered fruit and vegetables in season are piled high. Look out for stalls with local Normandy cheeses, creamy white heart shapes of Neufchâtel or squares of Livarot and Pont l'Evêque and circles of Camembert, as well as ready-to-eat stews and whole roasted free-range chickens off the spit for as little as €6, a multitude of dried sausages, jars of preserved meats as well as bottles of local cider and other drinks.

Tip...

Markets are usually held in the morning only, from about 0700 to 1300.

Seafood

At fishing ports, the fresh catch is laid out and sold each morning from stalls on the quayside. Sole, brill and mackerel are plentiful. Early in the day, you can see it being carted straight into the kitchens of waterfront restaurants. Queues of discerning locals form to buy the best of fish and shellfish, usually by the half-kilo, the kilo or even larger amounts, such as 5 kg of the popular *coquilles St Jacques* (scallops) for about €20. Remember to keep live shellfish cold, but not on ice, and not in an airtight bag. Eat them within a day or two.

On the farm

All over Normandy, away from the big towns and resorts, quiet country roads pass farm gates with signs inviting you to a *dégustation* (tasting). They are seen especially in the Pays d'Auge and in Southern Normandy. On offer are cider, Calvados and other alcoholic apple drinks, and pear drinks too, as well as fruit juices, cheeses, farmhouse pâtés and preserved meats, and honey. Tastings are usually free, and there may even be a free tour too, showing how the produce is made. Although there is no obligation, etiquette requires that having tasted, you will buy – at least a small amount. Prices are usually less than in a supermarket.

French fashion

Stylish fashion boutiques and small independent stores give character to the shopping streets of all Normandy's main towns. Even smaller towns keep up to date with latest French fashions. Look especially for beautiful shoes, jewellery, handbags and lingerie. Menswear shops no less than womenswear have originality and flair. There are children's clothes too. Most shopping areas have excellent perfumiers. Other shops sell an extensive choice affordable good-quality kitchenware, household goods and wine paraphernalia. Rouen, Le Havre and Caen have pedestrianized shopping areas packed with good shops. Some department store chains are renowned for glamour and style, especially Galeries Lafayette, which has branches in Caen and Rouen.

Fashion shop in rue Beauvoisine, Rouen.

Tip...

Few shops open on Sunday in France and many shops are also closed on Monday. The exception is in popular tourist centres and resorts. Most town centre shops are open Tuesday-Saturday 0900-1200 or 1230 and 1400-1430-1800. Food shops often open earlier in the morning, and a few (especially *boulangeries* and *pâtisseries*) open on Sunday morning. Department stores usually open Monday-Saturday 0900-1830, but often have one or more late evenings in mid-week. Hypermarkets are normally open Monday-Saturday 0900-2200.

Activities & tours

Cliff-top golf course at Etretat.

Cycling

Tourist offices throughout Normandy provide information on cycling routes and trails within their *département*. For many routes, the offices can provide a booklet to enhance the ride. As well as routes marked through the regional nature parks, ranging from easy to challenging, the network of *Voies Vertes* (green ways) enables relatively gradient-free long-distance cycling through the countryside following former railway lines. The Fédération Française de Cyclotourisme.has dedicated websites for Upper Normandy (ffct-haute-normandie.org) and Lower Normandy (ligue.ffct-lbn.org). The Eure *département* has online information about its Voies Vertes (eure-voiesvertes.fr/voies-vertes).

Golf

Golf has become one of Normandy's major attractions. Play on grassy cliff tops with sea views (at Etretat), on plush courses beside a smart resort (Deauville), under big skies beside Omaha Beach, in the grounds of a château (at St-Saens) or at any of the duchy's 37 courses – 23 of them with 18 holes or more. Normandy Tourism's golf brochure can be downloaded from normandie-tourisme.fr.

Guided tours

Landing Beaches
Guided visits to the D-Day Landing Beaches are offered by specialist local firms based in the landings area, especially Bayeux, see page 199. The Mémorial de Caen also runs guided trips to the beaches. Tours generally last either half a day or a full day, and there's a lot of choice between which beaches to see.

Horse riding

Riding along the wide open beaches of Calvados and their flat hinterland is popular with locals and visitors. The Cotentin peninsula too has several riding centres where you can have a horse for a week or a day, as does Southern Normandy, with its prestigious horse breeding tradition (the **Haras National,** or National Stud, is here). Hourly rates are about €12-€15. Information about each centre is available from Comité Régional d'Equitation de Normandie (23 rue Pasteur, 14120 Mondeville, T02-31 84 61 87, chevalnormandie.com).

Nature parks

Much of Normandy's rural interior encompasses unspoiled natural landscapes as well as traditional farm country. Four regional nature parks offer protection to the flora and fauna, landscape and way of life, while also encouraging walking, cycling and other outdoor activities with marked trails and leisure facilities.

Parc Naturel Régional des Marais du Cotentin et du Bessin
(parc-cotentin-bessin.fr)
Covering the area around the Banc du Grand Vey inlet between Cotentin and western Calvados, this wetland habitat is home to huge numbers of wading birds.

Parc Naturel Régional du Perche
(le-perche.org)
A hilly, forested region that also includes many orchards, horse studs and small farms.

Parc Naturel Régional Normandie-Maine
(parc-naturel-normandie-maine.fr)
This follows the border country between Southern Normandy and neighbouring Maine, an area with extensive forests of oak, beech and pine, home to deer, boar and other wildlife.

About the region

Parc Naturel Régional des Boucles de la Seine Normande

(pnr-seine-normande.com)
This clings to the banks of the meandering River Seine below Rouen, partly forested, partly reclaimed marshland.

Walking

Serious hikers can follow all or part of several *Grandes Randonnées* (long-distance trails) that run through Normandy, along the river valleys, beside the channel coast and through woodland areas. In total they add up more than 3000 km of marked paths. In addition, shorter marked walking trails are in place in all the woodland areas of Southern Normandy. See gr-infos.com and normandie-tourisme.fr.

Watersports

Canoeing & kayaking

The River Orne, descending rapidly through the river gorges of the Suisse Normande, is a centre for canoeing and kayaking. Start at Rabodanges, near Putanges-Pont-Ecrepin, and finish at Pont d'Ouilly. Hire is available at both resorts. Another place to paddle your canoe is down the River Vire to Condé-sur-Vire, Normandy's largest canoeing and kayaking resort.

Fishing

In a region with 600 km of coastline and a strong sea fishing tradition, and with so many rivers and lakes too, it's no surprise that local tourist offices produce booklets about angling in their waters. Sea fishing excursions are available from Dieppe and the ports on the Côte d'Albâtre, from Honfleur and the Côte Fleurie, and from Granville and the Cotentin coast. Inland, the rivers Varenne, Risle and Touques are all acclaimed for brown trout fishing, and Lake Rabodanges on the Orne river for pike and carp. Download a pdf about fishing in Normandy from normandie-tourisme.fr.

Sailing

Marinas and harbours around the Cotentin and all along Normandy's Channel coast are a favourite destination for British yachts. There are more than 100 sailing clubs here. Other popular sports along these breezy shores are windsurfing, kite-surfing and paragliding. You can even sail on land – sand-yachting (*char à voile*) on the immense flat beaches of Calvados is a local favourite. Instruction and equipment hire is available on the spot. Sailing information is available at calvados-nautisme.com and manchenautisme.com.

Wellbeing

One of the biggest spa resorts in France is Bagnoles-de-l'Orne in Southern Normandy. Its natural hot spring, together with a big choice of treatments ranging from genuine medical cures to luxurious health and beauty packages, is complemented by a calm woodland setting, see page 241.

Canoe down the river Orne or Vire.

Contents

Rouen

Cathédrale Notre Dame.

Introduction

Today the modern industrial city of Rouen, sprawling on both sides of the River Seine, is the capital of the *département* of Upper Normandy. However, Rouen's standing in Normandy and in France is far greater than that.

At its very heart, on the river's right bank, is the much more ancient city from which it grew. The original capital of the Viking Duchy, previously a Roman town and still earlier a Celtic settlement, Rouen keeps intact that sense of being the first and greatest city in Normandy.

For the French nation, the name of Rouen resonates with that of Ste-Jeanne d'Arc – Joan of Arc – patron saint of France. In 1431 she was burnt alive in the city's market square, where now a church and a towering crucifix stand in memory of her life and death.

Far from being marked with tragedy by those events, Rouen is full of life and joie de vivre, its squares and streets crowded and lined with stylish shops and good restaurants.

There is superb medieval architecture. Despite extensive wartime damage, whole streets of architectural treasures survive, including hundreds of picturesque half-timbered dwellings. Soaring spires and towers rise above the rooftops. Rouen Cathedral – painted nearly 30 times by Monet (at different times of day) – is one of Europe's Gothic masterpieces.

What to see in...

... one day
Start out from Rouen's main square, **place du Vieux Marché**, and stroll along **rue du Gros Horloge**, beneath the clock, to the **Cathedral**. Follow **rue St-Romain**, with its half-timbered houses, to **St-Maclou** church. Narrow, cobbled **rue Damiette** leads straight to **St-Ouen** church, another Gothic jewel. Make your way along pedestrianized **rue de l'Hôpital**, to the **Musée des Beaux Arts**. If time is short, focus on the museum's magnificent 19th-century collections. Make your way back via the **Renaissance Palais de Justice**, to **place du Vieux Marché**.

...a weekend or more
Take in **Aître de St-Maclou**, a beautiful collection of 16th-century buildings around a former plague cemetery. Spend longer in the **Musée des Beaux Arts** – to see the highlights alone could take a couple of hours – and visit some other museums such as the lovely **Musée de la Céramique**.

Rue du Gros Horloge.

Rouen listings

❶ Sleeping

1 Hôtel Andersen *4 rue Pouchet* **B1**
2 Hôtel Arts et Seine *4-6 rue St Etienne des Tonneliers* **B6**
3 Hôtel Astrid *11 place Bernard Tissot/rue Jeanne d'Arc* **C1**
4 Hôtel de Dieppe *place Bernard Tissot* **C1**
5 Hôtel de Paris *12-14 rue de la Champmeslé* **B6**
6 Hôtel des Carmes *33 place des Carmes* **D4**
7 Hôtel du Vieux Marché *33 place du Vieux Palais* **A4**
8 Hôtel Ermitage Bouquet *58 rue Bouquet* **B1**
9 Ibis Rouen Centre Rive Gauche *44 rue Amiral Cécille* **A7**
10 Ibis Rouen Champ de Mars *12 av Aristide Briand* **E7**
11 Le Cardinal *1 place de la Cathédrale* **C5**
12 Le Dandy *93 bis, rue Cauchoise* **A3**
13 Mercure Centre Cathédrale *7 rue Croix de Fer* **C4**
14 Mercure Champ de Mars *12 av Aristide Briand* **E7**
15 Morand Hôtel *1 rue Morand* **C2**
16 Premiere Classe Rouen Petit Quevilly *112 av Jean Jaurès* **A7**
17 Rouen Saint Sever *20 place de l'Eglise St Sever* **C7**
18 Suitehotel Rouen Normandie *Ilot Pasteur, Quai de Boisguilbert* **A5**

❶ Eating & drinking

1 A La Table Gourmande *25 rue des Bonnetiers* **D5**
2 Bar de la Crosse *53 rue de l'Hôpital* **C4**
3 Bistrot des Hallettes *43 place du Vieux Marché* **A4**
4 Brasserie d'Arc *26 place du Vieux Marché* **A3**
5 Brasserie de la Flèche *12 place de la Calende* **C5**
6 Brasserie des Beaux-Arts *35 rue Jean Lecanuet* **C3**
7 Brasserie Paul *1 place de la Cathédrale* **C5**
8 Dufour *67 bis, rue St-Nicolas* **D5**
9 Gill *quai de la Bourse* **B6**
10 Gill Côté Bistro *14 place du Vieux Marché* **A3**
11 La Couronne *31 place du Vieux Marché* **A4**
12 Le 37 *37 rue des Tonneliers* **B6**
13 Le Catelier *134 bis, av des Martyrs de la Résistance* **C7**
14 Le Diplomate *10 place Foch* **B4**
15 L'Euro *41 place du Vieux Marché* **A4**
16 Le Florian *11 rue de Crosne* **A4**
17 Le Maupassant *39 place du Vieux Marché* **A4**
18 Le Métropole *111 rue Jeanne d'Arc* **C1**
19 Le Tyrol *36-38 rue de la Champmeslé* **C5**
20 Le Vicomte *70 rue de la Vicomte* **B5**
21 Les Capucines *16-18 rue Jean Macé* **A7**
22 Les Nymphéas *7/9 rue de la Pie* **A4**
23 Les Petits Parapluies *46 rue Bourg L'Abbé, place de la Rougemare* **D3**
24 Maison Hardy *22 place du Vieux Marché* **A3**
25 Minute et Mijoté *58 rue de Fontenelle* **A3**
26 Tex Mex L'Equateur *5-7 rue du Bac* **C6**

Essentials

❶ Getting around **On foot** Unless you have friends or business within the modern quarters of Rouen, you are unlikely to leave Vieux Rouen, the old heart of the city which contains almost everything of interest. This is a small enough area to be thoroughly explored on foot. Many city centre streets are closed to all vehicles, and several to all except public transport.

By bicycle Another option is the city's Cy'clic bike rental scheme: using your credit card, pick up a bicycle at any of 17 rental points all over town and leave it at any other rental point when you are finished. The first 30 minutes are free.

By public transport If you do decide to go further afield, for example to the Jardin des Plantes in southern Rouen, or if you are staying on the south bank, getting around is simple. The city has an efficient, comprehensive public transportation network. This includes metro, bus and the unusual high-tech Téor system in which wheeled buses, following visual tracks in the road, function as trams on parts of certain city centre routes. Rouen public transport is run by **TCAR** (Transports en Commun de l'Agglomération de Rouen, T02 35 52 52 52 (French only), tcar.fr).

❸ Bus station Gare Routière, 9 rue Jeanne d'Arc.

❸ Train station Gare Rouen Rive Droite, at the north end of rue Jeanne d'Arc. See page 270 for regional travel.

❸ Hospital CHU (Centre Hospitalier Universitaire de Rouen), Hôpital Charles-Nicolle, 1 rue Germont, T02 32 88 89 90, is the city's large modern hospital.

❸ Pharmacy There are 18 pharmacies in the city centre, for example, in rue Jeanne d'Arc and rue du Gros Horloge. One example is **Pharmacie de la République** (21 rue République, T02 35 70 61 11).

❷ Post office Main city office, 45 rue Jeanne d'Arc.

❶ Tourist information 25 place de la Cathédrale (facing the cathedral), T02 32 08 32 40, rouentourisme.com, October-April Monday-Saturday 0930-1230 and 1330-1800, May-September Monday-Saturday 0900-1900, Sunday and holidays 0930-1230 and 1400-1800.

Cathedral Quarter

Not for nothing is Rouen's tourist office located in place de la Cathédrale. Almost every visitor to the city makes their way to this spacious square to see with their own eyes the west front of Cathédrale Notre Dame. Despite over 800 years of eventful history, Rouen's cathedral is probably best known for one 19th-century Impressionist painter. Claude Monet sat in the square with his canvas day after day, painting the glorious Gothic stonework of the building's intricate main west façade 28 times to capture the changing moods and impressions created by changing daylight. One example can be seen in the city's Musée des Beaux Arts, but the others are scattered in the great art museums of the world. If you love Gothic architecture at its finest, linger in this quarter, for close by are two other Gothic masterpieces. The surrounding streets are full of fine domestic architecture too, with half-timbered houses dating back in some cases to the 15th century. From the cathedral, walk beside medieval dwellings along rue St-Romain to St-Maclou church, and from there evocative little rue Damiette heads towards St-Ouen church. For a break or a meal in this quarter, there are tempting outdoor tables of brasseries and restaurants along the edges of place de la Cathédrale.

Cathédrale Notre Dame

Place de la Cathédrale, cathedrale-rouen.net.
Nov-9 Mar: Sun and holidays 0800-1800 (may be closed Sun morning), Tue-Sat 0730-1200 and 1400-1800, closed Mon morning. 10 Mar-Oct: Sun and holidays 0800-1800 (except during services), Tue-Sat 0730-1900, closed Mon morning. Closed to visitors during services, and on 1 Jan, 1 May, 11 Nov. Free.
Map: Rouen, C5, p70.

Its two towers rising high over the Old Quarter, Rouen's cathedral is considered one of the most beautiful examples of Gothic craftsmanship in Europe. Its exuberant architecture is the focal point of the city and provides a living link between today's city and its ancient past.

Immense damage was done to the cathedral during the Second World War and the repair work and restoration continue to this day, but it remains an awesome spectacle. Stand on the edge of place de la Cathédrale, facing the main west front, and you are more or less on the spot where Impressionist artist Claude Monet set up his easel. He painted this ornate façade 28 times. Each of those pictures is today worth tens of millions of dollars, pounds or euros – which is why the city of Rouen itself owns just one of them!

Tip...

A great way to enjoy the main sights of the Old Quarter with an expert guide but at your own pace is simply to hire an audio guide. Available from Rouen tourist office, it costs just €5.

Around the region

The original church on this site was built in AD 393, and marked the beginning of Rouen's rise to prominence as an ecclesiastical centre. In AD 488 the first cathedral was built here, and grew in successive centuries. By the ninth century, the city and its cathedral made a fine target for Viking raiders, who began a 50-year process of destruction and theft. However, when Rollo became the first duke of the new Duchy of Normandy, he converted to Christianity and ordered the rebuilding of all damaged churches. The first Norman cathedral on the site – in the Romanesque style they made their own – dates from about AD 1000 and partly survives as the crypt of the present cathedral.

Following a fire in 1200, the cathedral was entirely rebuilt, with great success, in the new Gothic style. For the next 400 years it was added to and enhanced as the Gothic period evolved. For example, one of the towers, **Tour St Romain**, is partly 12th-century early Gothic and embellished with much later sculpture, while the other tower, oddly called the **Tour de Beurre**, was built 300 years later in a more elaborate style and topped with a Flamboyant crown. It is explained that the Tour de Beurre (literally 'tower of butter') gets its name from having been funded by selling dispensations to those who did not wish to give up butter during Lent. It's easy to see though that this tower's stone is actually a creamier colour than the rest.

Inside, the cathedral has an immense sense of light and space. There are important Gothic and Renaissance tombs, notably that of Rollo, first duke of Normandy, and another containing the heart of Richard the Lionheart. The beautiful stained-glass windows, dating from the 13th to the 16th centuries, survived the war by being removed and put into safe keeping.

It's a fact...

At the west entrance of Rouen's Jardins de l'Hôtel de Ville, near St-Ouen, is the curious Pierre de Jellinge (Jellinge Stone). Made of artificial granite, this was a gift from Denmark to mark the 1000th anniversary of the founding of Normandy.

Eglise St-Maclou

Place Barthélemy.
Apr-Oct Fri-Mon 1000-1200 and 1400-1800;
Nov-Mar Fri-Mon 1000-1200 and 1400-1730;
closed 25 Dec and 1 Jan. Free.
Map: Rouen, D5, p70.

It could do with a clean, and the pigeons are a deterrent, but for all that this magnificent 15th-century church is a beautiful sight with its white, lacy Flamboyant Gothic stonework and fine porch with imposing portals. The central tympanum shows the Last Judgement, while rich carving on the 16th-century wooden doors depicts the Good Shepherd, the Baptism of Christ and the Virgin Mary. The interior is more simple, but elegant, with a Flamboyant Gothic staircase climbing to a Renaissance organ loft.

Aître de St-Maclou

186 rue Martainville.
Daily 0800-2000 (1900 in winter). Free.
Map: Rouen, E5, p70.

This lovely large enclosed courtyard of immaculate timbered buildings, today so enchanting, was originally a communal plague pit dating back to the Black Death. On the same theme, it subsequently served as an ossuary. Skulls and bones and gravediggers' tools carved into the wooden beams hint at its unsettling past. In complete contrast, it now the home of a school of fine arts.

Abbatiale St-Ouen.

Abbatiale St-Ouen

Place du Général de Gaulle.
Daily (except Mon and Fri) 1000-1200 and
1400-1800 (1730 in winter). Free.
Map: Rouen, E4, p70.

Graceful and exuberant, this huge 134-m-long
church is a superb example of Gothic architecture.
It's made of fine white stone, rather blackened
outside but beautiful within, and with lovely
14th-century stained-glass windows. A former
church on the site was originally built to house the
tomb of seventh-century Bishop Ouen, who had
been vitally important in Christianizing the region
and founded a great Benedictine Abbey here. His
abbey was so often harassed and attacked by Norse
raiders that it fell into ruins. The first attempts to
recreate it were made by Duke Rollo, but another
building in Norman style took its place in 1066. In
the 14th century, the abbot had the whole church
almost entirely demolished and elegantly rebuilt in

Tip...

Behind St-Ouen Abbey Church there's
a statue of Rollo, the Viking chieftain
who became first Duke of Normandy.

Gothic style. Much further work was done in the
15th century, and it was not completed for another
100 years. Even after that time, further additions
were made, including the only false note in the
building – the artless alterations to the west front in
the 19th century. The church has a majestic
19th-century organ made by Aristide Cavaillé-Coll,
and one modern stained-glass window by Max
Ingrand, installed in 1960.

Gros Horloge & Vieux Marché

Rouen's main square, place du Vieux Marché, is more than the 'old market square' of its name. It is a focal point for the city's emotions and its history, with a religious, a secular and a patriotic role to play. Here are restaurants, bars and entertainment where the Rouennais come for an evening's pleasant relaxation, yet also in this square are memorials to poignant events that took place on this spot hundreds of years ago. In February 1431, Joan of Arc, having turned the fortunes of France in its 100-year war with England, was tried by a French ecclesiastical court and found guilty of heresy. On 30 May she was tied to a stake in this marketplace, and her judges watched as she was executed by fire. Just 24 years later the verdict was reversed and in 1920 she was beatified and declared a patron saint of France.

Rue du Gros Horloge, the most popular sight in Rouen, links place du Vieux Marché to the town's other great square, place de la Cathédrale. Crowded and commercial, but charming, cobbled, lined with old buildings and utterly picturesque, it's the main shopping street and is spanned by the fascinating Gros Horloge, Rouen's most distinctive landmark.

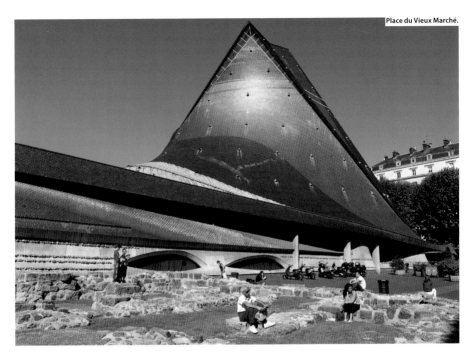

Place du Vieux Marché

Map: Rouen, A4, p70.

Originally the town's medieval marketplace, the square was ingeniously restored in the 1970s and today seems curiously undateable. There is no view across the square as its centre is taken up with the rather unattractive exterior of the modern Joan of Arc church and the small covered market which is part of the same construction. Close to the church a slender modern crucifix, soaring to a height of 20 m, marks the exact place where Joan was tied to the stake and burned while her judges sat and watched. Around the edges are handsome half-timbered buildings with the polish of recent construction. At street level, many of the buildings have been turned into bars and restaurants popular with locals and tourists.

Eglise Ste-Jeanne-d'Arc (Joan of Arc Church)

Place du Vieux Marché.
Daily Apr-Oct 1000-1200 and 1400-1800 (1730 Nov-Mar), closed Fri and Sun morning and during services. Free.
Map: Rouen, A4, p70.

The middle of Rouen's old market square is dominated by the post-war church, designed by Louis Arretche and dedicated to Joan of Arc. It is ultra-modern with concrete construction, with 400-year-old glass along one side. The sanctification of Joan is itself a modern phenomenon (she was canonized in 1920), and the building serves as powerful statement that the Catholic church is still relevant to the present day. The curious twisted architecture, the interior on a different axis than the exterior, is supposed to be drawn from the shapes of shipping and docks. Certainly the bowed wood and metal ceiling

Five of the best

Picturesque streets

❶ **Rue St-Nicolas** Narrow shopping street with half-timbered houses and courtyards.
❷ **Rue du Gros Horloge** The original main street of Old Rouen.
❸ **Rue St-Romain** Charming half-timbered and Renaissance houses.
❹ **Rue Damiette** Narrow lane of half-timbered buildings.
❺ **Rue Martainville** Historic houses near St-Maclou church.

Rue Martainville.

could be reminiscent of the keel of a ship. There is no nave: the church appears to be a meeting hall with rows of pews curved around the altar. The panels of fine 16th-century stained glass, saved from wartime destruction, are the most pleasing aspect of the church.

Gros Horloge

Rue du Gros Horloge, T02 35 71 28 40.
Daily except Mon, Apr-Oct 1000-1300 and 1400-1900, Nov-Mar 1400-1800, last admission 1 hr before closing. €6, €3 child/concession. Map: Rouen, B5, p70.

Rouen's bustling, appealing old thoroughfare, rue du Gros Horloge, gets its name from the mighty clock spanning the street. On this spot in medieval times there was a city gate, Porte Massacre; rising beside it stood a belfry that housed the Gros Horloge. In the 16th century the gate was largely demolished and the clock was moved from the belfry on to the gate's remaining archway, which was reconstructed especially to hold the huge mechanism. Carvings of the Good Shepherd and his flock decorate the archway.

The Gros Horloge itself, gilded and ornate, is a remarkable mechanism, with a clock face on each side so it can be seen whichever way you approach it. One hand revolves around each clock face,

showing the hours of the day, while a central panel shows the phases of the moon and the passing of the weeks. It is accurate to this day.

The old belfry still survives, and still tolls the nightly curfew bell at 2100 as it has for over 700 years. A spiral staircase winds to the top, where a balcony (added in the 18th century) gives a thrilling view of the city's rooftops and spires and landmarks. It was from this vantage point that Corot painted *The Seine near Rouen* in about 1830, showing how surprisingly close the countryside came to the city centre at that time.

Palais de Justice (Law Courts) – Parlement de Normandie

Rue aux Juifs.
The interior is closed to visitors for security reasons, but ask at the tourist office about guided visits, which are sometimes possible. Map: Rouen, C4, p70.

In a narrow street parallel to rue du Gros Horloge, just 100 m away, Rouen's law courts occupy a gorgeous early 16th-century complex in white stone so intricately carved that the upper section of the façade appears to be a screen of delicate lace concealing part of the roof. The whole structure is considered one of northern Europe's finest surviving examples of medieval civic architecture. The west wing is the oldest part, being originally a merchants' trading hall completed in 1509. The central building was then begun, first to house the Exchequer of Rouen, and then the Parlement de Normandie (Normandy Parliament) set up by François I. The east wing was added in the 19th century in the same style.

Parts of the building were bombed to smithereens on the night of 18-19 April 1944, and then bombed again on 26 August. When the war was over a huge project began to repair it; the work still continues. On the side and back of the structure some marks of wartime damage have been left in place.

The best spot to appreciate the beauty of the building is right in front of the main central courtyard set back from rue aux Juifs. A vast amount of exuberant and accomplished Gothic and Renaissance sculpture and stonework decorates its exterior, increasing in complexity and profusion as it rises up the façade. A stone staircase leads up to the only part which may sometimes be open to the public (on guided tours with advance booking at the tourist office), the **Salle des Procureurs** or **Salle des Pas Perdus**, a huge old courtroom with galleries at each end and an impressive modern panelled roof, 16.5 m wide.

The name of the street comes from this having been the heart of medieval Rouen's principal Jewish neighbourhood until Jews were expelled from France in 1306. Their property and possessions were confiscated and sold at auction by the Exchequer of Rouen in the same year. Jews were readmitted nine years later on payment of a fee, then re-expelled (today there is again a Jewish community in Rouen).

Excavation of the Palais de Justice courtyard in 1976, together with a study of contemporary documents, revealed that part of the Palais de Justice stands upon the remains of a medieval *yeshiva* (a Jewish religious academy), sections of which are being exposed to view during work on the east wing. Renamed 'La Maison Sublime' by the municipality, the *yeshiva* ruins are of a substantial three or four-storey Romanesque building dating from about 1100 (lamaisonsublime.fr).

Place du Maréchal Foch and Palais de Justice.

Tip...

Parking is a problem in Rouen. There are plenty of car parks, but they are expensive. Even the cheaper all-day options cost from €6-€14 per day. There is free parking in place Boulingrin. Public transport ticket holders may park free in the car park Parking du Mont-Riboudet.

Museums Quarter

Between the historic heart of the Old Town and the encircling boulevards de la Marne and de l'Yser to its north is a less picturesque district with a more workaday atmosphere. Here wide residential and commercial avenues cut straight lines towards the railway station and the ring road. They are, however, interspersed with many more ancient backstreets and lanes of 18th-century stone mansions and older half-timbered houses. Just two or three streets north of the main sightseeing area, the huge, purpose-built Musée des Beaux Arts is the focal point of this quiet area of museums. Facing the Musée des Beaux Arts, the spacious park of square Verdrel provides a tree-shaded haven of tranquillity and repose. In the 16th century, this neighbourhood was home to a wealthy Irish community of the merchant class, who built the large St-Patrice church, known today for its wealth of good 16th- and 17th-century stained-glass windows. All around the area are intriguing and unusual museums well worth visiting. On the northern edge of the district, Tour Jeanne d'Arc is a last remnant of Rouen's 13th-century fortifications.

Musée des Beaux Arts (Fine Arts Museum)

Esplanade Marcel-Duchamp (Square Verdrel), disabled access 26 bis rue Jean-Lecanuet, T02 35 71 28 40, rouen-musees.com.
Wed-Mon 1000-1800 (South Wing closed 1300-1400), closed during national holidays.
€3, €2 concessions, under-18s free.
Map: Rouen, C3, p70.

This large museum, one of France's premier art collections, contains over 300 works of painting and sculpture from the 15th century up to the modern period, arranged in more than 60 rooms. The galleries devoted to the 15th to 17th centuries are exceptional for Flemish Primitives and Italian Primitives, with superb works by Gérard David and Pietro Perugino, and later, by François Clouet, Paolo Véronèse, Caravaggio, Velasquez, Rubens and many more.

The museum is renowned especially for 19th-century painting. A focal point for visitors is the single example of Monet's paintings of the west façade of Rouen cathedral. There are numerous other outstanding Impressionist works, and views of the Seine appear and reappear in the paintings by Monet, Sisley, Boudin and others. Also on display in this section are works by Ingres, Poussin, Degas, Corot, Millet, and many other great names of early modern art. A good space is devoted to 20th-century art, among which are outstanding pieces by Modigliani, the brothers Duchamp, Dufy and Villon.

Musée de la Céramique (Ceramics Museum)

1 rue Faucon or 94 rue Jeanne d'Arc (square Verdrel), T02 35 07 31 74, rouen-musees.com.
Wed-Mon 1000-1300 and 1400-1800, closed during national holidays. €2.30, €1.55 concessions, under-18s free.
Map: Rouen, C3, p70.

Facing the greenery of Square Verdrel, this neighbour of the Musée des Beaux Arts occupies the imposing neo-Classical 17th-century mansion Hôtel d'Hocqueville. Both the house and the

Musée des Beaux Arts.

museum are interesting. With exceptional rich collections of exquisite porcelain, totalling over 5000 pieces, the museum gives a comprehensive overview of the whole period of Rouen's manufacture of high-quality traditional faience from the mid-16th century up to the 19th century when it went into decline. The work ranges from floor tiles and tableware and ordinary household objects – beautifully coloured and painted – to precious ornaments and creative curiosities like the Celestial and Terrestrial Globes by Pierre Chapelle, dated 1725. As a comparison, there is also some fine faience ware from Nevers, Lille and Delft, and 100 19th- and 20th-century pieces from Sèvres.

Death in Rouen: Joan of Arc

Perhaps the strangest thing of all about the enigmatic St Joan is that she was an ordinary, uneducated country girl. Born in about 1412 in the small farming village of Domrémy (in northeastern France), she lived there with her parents, who owned and worked 50 acres of land. It remains unclear how it came about that at the age of about 17, she was riding with the French army dressed as a knight, carrying a standard into battle against the English at Orléans.

The often-told tale is that from the age of 12 she claimed to be having visions of saints and receiving guidance from them and from God. It is said that by predicting the outcome of a battle she so impressed a local garrison commander, a minor nobleman called Robert de Baudricourt, that he enabled her to travel to Chinon to ask for a private audience with the Dauphin (heir apparent to the throne of France), which was granted. Her motive seems to have been patriotic rather than religious, as her sole ambition was to see the Dauphin crowned king of a France free from foreign control.

On 29 April 1429, she arrived with the rest of the army at Orléans. Excluded from war councils and acting on her own, she led soldiers to seize three nearby English fortresses, and then – again in defiance of the campaign's leaders – took the men into battle against the main English stronghold at Orléans. Their rapid victory had a profound effect on the English, and on the French, who had not had a single important victory against the English for over a generation.

The Dauphin now permitted Joan to lead a campaign to re-take the bridges across the Loire. This was successful, inflicting great losses on the English, and Joan went on to a string of victories. In areas held by the Burgundians – allies of the English – her reputation went before her and many towns submitted to her without a fight. When Joan reached Reims, where traditionally the kings of France were crowned, the city submitted to her. On 17 July 1429, in Notre-Dame Cathedral at Reims, her ambition was achieved, and the Dauphin was crowned King Charles VII of France.

However, the war against the English continued. In a battle in Picardy on 23 May 1430 Joan was captured by the Burgundians. It was the idea of the Duke of Burgundy's former chaplain, Bishop Pierre Cauchon, a strong supporter of the English, that she could be sold to the English and, under their auspices, executed by the church for heresy. This, he believed, would discredit the French king and demoralize the French soldiers.

Following the coronation of Charles VII in Reims, Cauchon had fled to Rouen, the chief city of the English in France. Dismayed by the influence of this strange, inspiring girl, Bishop Cauchon eagerly offered to try her himself, and assembled other leading pro-English churchmen to join him.

Joan was brought from Picardy to Rouen, and the trial began on 21 February 1431. Much depended on her having worn men's clothing – a heretical act. Shown the instruments of torture, she admitted to this former heresy, but said she had repudiated those practices and repented. The judges could not execute a penitent former heretic. In the cells, guarded by soldiers rather than nuns, Joan was tricked into wearing men's clothes once again, when these were all she was given. For this crime she was taken, on 30 May 1431, to be tied to a stake in Rouen's market square and burned alive, watched by the judges.

Bishop Cauchon prospered and continued to live in Rouen, dying there of a heart attack at the age of 71.

Musée le Secq des Tournelles (Le Secq des Tournelles Museum)

2 rue Jacques Villon (disabled access rue Deshays), T02 35 88 42 92, rouen-musees.com. Wed-Mon 1000-1300 and 1400-1800, closed during national holidays. €2.30, €1.55 concessions, under-18s free. Map: Rouen, C3, p70.

Behind the Musée des Beaux Arts rises the elaborate Flamboyant spire of Eglise St-Laurent, deconsecrated since the Revolution. Today this 15th-century Gothic church houses the remarkable collection of wrought-iron work assembled during the late 19th century by father and son Henri Le Secq des Tournelles. It has become Europe's leading collection of such workmanship, covering the whole range imaginable of things that could made of wrought iron. Displays include jewellery,

Smaller museums

❶ **Natural History** (198 rue Beauvoisine) A huge, diverse, rich collection.
❷ **Maritime, River and Port** (13 bd Émile Duchemin) The story of Rouen's docks.
❸ **Education** (185 rue Eau de Robec) Vivid history of schooling.
❹ **Corneille** (4 rue de la Pie) Playwright's preserved 17th-century home.
❺ **Medicine** (54 rue de Lecat – Flaubert's birthplace) An 18th-century surgery.

hairdressers' and surgeons' tools, a 13th-century screen door, fantastically intricate 15th-century locks, a complete 18th-century stair rail from a château, and fascinating centuries-old inn and shop signs.

Musée des Antiquités (Antiquities Museum)

Entrance through Ste-Marie cloister, 198 rue Beauvoisine, T02 35 98 55 10.
Closed Tue and national holidays, open Mon-Sat (except Tue) 1000-1215 and 1330-1730, Sun 1400-1800. €2.30, €1.55 concessions, under-18s free.
Map: Rouen, D2, p70.

Situated inside a former 17th-century monastery, the museum brings together an eclectic assortment of remarkable art, craftsmanship and archaeology. Its great highlight is the Lillebonne Mosaic, uncovered in a town centre garden at Lillebonne (between Rouen and Le Havre). Originally the dining room floor of a Roman villa, the beautifully complete 6-m-square mosaic depicts stag hunting, a sacrifice to Diana and, in the circular central panel, a lustful youth – probably Apollo – seizing a tempting nymph. In another room, the 11th-century Valasse Cross is one of the oldest pieces of Limoges enamel work. Step into the Salle des Tapisseries to see the 15th-century Flemish tapestry *Winged Deer*, displayed among 16th-century furnishings.

The neighbouring Jesuit school, Lycée Corneille, was renamed in honour of its most distinguished old boy, the 17th-century playwright Pierre Corneille, regarded as the father of French drama. Several other former pupils of the school went on to great renown, including the painter Jean-Baptiste Camille Corot and writers Gustave Flaubert and Guy de Maupassant.

Tour Jeanne d'Arc or Le Donjon (Joan of Arc Tower)

Rue du Donjon, but entrance is round the corner in rue Bouvreuil, T02 35 98 16 21.
Closed Tue and national holidays, open Mon-Sat (except Tue) 1000-1230 and 1400-1800, Sun 1400-1830, closes 1 hr earlier Oct-Mar. €1.50, €0.75 child/concessions.
Map: Rouen, C2, p70.

This sturdy round tower under its conical roof is a last remnant of Rouen's medieval fortifications. It looks a little out of place standing alone among modern buildings close to a main road near the station. Originally, it was part of a massive 13th-century castle, long since demolished leaving no other trace. The donjon is a dauntingly solid structure – the walls are 4 m thick. Despite the name, it has little or nothing to do with Joan of Arc. She was imprisoned not here, but in another tower, which no longer exists. However it is possible that this was the place to which she was brought on 9 May 1431, to be threatened with torture and shown the instruments that would be used on her if she did not confess to heresy (she did in fact confess).

Today the tower, with steps spiralling all the way to the top, is used as a small museum, with displays about Joan of Arc's trial, and about the history of the castle that once stood here.

Rouen to Lyons

Around Rouen, in either direction along the chalky cliffs and wooded banks of the Seine, are dozens of interesting and attractive places to visit. Among them are forests, waterfront villages, great ruins dating back to the Duchy of Normandy and majestic vistas.

For a single excursion that takes in all these things, drive out of the city to Lyons-la-Forêt, a short drive northeast of Rouen. From there make your way to Les Andelys on the Seine, and turn along the river's north bank back towards Rouen. Avoiding the major roads beside the river, the easiest exit from Rouen's city centre is rue d'Amiens, a turning off the main road rue de la République between the cathedral and the church of St-Ouen. Rue d'Amiens continues straight out of the city centre, passes beneath N28 and becomes Route de Lyons-la-Forêt. Through the city fringes, follow signs to Lyons-la-Forêt. At St Léger-du-Bourg-Denis, stay on D42 heading towards Lyons. Forest soon appears on the horizon, and the road continues towards woodlands, entering into countryside of dense forest and rustic farmland.

Nestling in a hollow in the middle of the forest, Lyons-la-Forêt is a quiet picture-postcard village of heavily timbered traditional Normandy houses gathered around a splendid old covered market. The Anglo-Norman King Henry I of England died here in 1135 after a notorious 'surfeit of lampreys', which he had eaten the previous night at the Cistercian monastery of Mortemer, 4 km away.

The ruins of Mortemer (see page 117), off the road to Les Andelys, make an enjoyable detour as you head out of Lyons-la-Forêt on D2. The third turning on the left leads to a narrow lane which runs steeply down to the ruins in the valley of the Fouillebroc stream, by a lake.

Back on D2, leave the woodlands for the high open fields of the Caux country towards the double spires of Ecouis. Pause when you reach the village (on the crossroads of the D2 and major road D6014) to have a closer look at this impressive church, the Collégiale Notre Dame de l'Assomption, in place du Cloître.

Inside, there is good 14th-century wood-carving and sculpture. Drive across open, rolling countryside of farmland on narrow D2, changing to D1 after Fresne-de-l'Archevêque and descending into Le Grand Andely.

Le Grand Andely and riverside Le Petit Andely together make up the town of Les Andelys (see page 122) which, straddling a tributary called the Gambon, rises from the River Seine. The most picturesque corners are in Le Petit Andely, close to the Seine, with views of the Seine valley's chalky cliff curving away into the distance. High on a cliff top overlooking the town stands the Château Gaillard (see page 122), Richard the Lionheart's daunting white castle built to defend the Seine valley from the French.

Leave Le Petit Andely on D313, signposted to Pont St-Pierre. After 3 km, turn left to stay on D313. This road, at first mainly running between the broad river and the white cliffs, becomes wooded until the river disappears from view. Still the scene remains typical of the Seine valley: calm, rural, bathed in light. At Muids, follow D313 as it turns away from the river's edge, rejoining it at Andé. Once more follow the river road round to Amfreville and La Côte des Deux Amants, from which there is a good view of the Seine and its Amfreville locks.

Cross the River Andelle through Romilly-sur-Andelle to take D126. This road meets the major road N14 (or D6014) at Boos. Here turn towards Rouen and continue, through some unappealing suburbs, back into the city centre.

Main picture:
Château Gaillard.

Sleeping

Cathedral Quarter

Mercure Centre Cathédrale €€€

7 rue Croix de Fer, T02 35 52 69 52, mercure.com.
Map: Rouen, C4, p70.
Modern and comfortable, with simple, elegant uncluttered decor and rooms with a literary theme including pictures of books and portraits of writers. Some rooms may be on the small side, while others are generously proportioned. The car park is cramped and difficult to use, but is nevertheless a welcome addition here on the edge of the pedestrian zone. Service is professional, willing and helpful. The greatest attraction here is the location, in the heart of Old Rouen almost next door to the cathedral.

Le Cardinal €€

1 place de la Cathédrale, T02 35 70 24 42, cardinal-hotel.fr.
Map: Rouen, C5, p70.
If location is everything, this is hard to beat. With rather cramped but clean and adequately equipped rooms in attractive pastel shades, this small and friendly family-run hotel might be an unremarkable two-star (although it does offer free Wi-Fi) but it stands out for its excellent position facing the cathedral. It's almost impossible to reach by car, though; you'll have to park in a nearby car park and walk to the hotel.

Hôtel des Carmes €€-€

33 place des Carmes, T02 35 71 92 31, hoteldescarmes.com.
Map: Rouen, D4, p70.
An unusual, attractive and utterly charming small hotel in a pleasant post-war square between Rouen's cathedral and St-Ouen church. The Carmes has an arty, eccentric feel with pictures everywhere, and simple decor varying from pleasing warm hues to more striking colour combinations. Adequately comfortable little rooms (with free Wi-Fi) have good bathrooms, and here and there are quirkier touches, like a cloud-painted ceiling. The owners speak English and are helpful and considerate. Guests pay a reduced rate at a nearby car park.

Tip...

Stay outside the city centre if you want to find some of the most inexpensive accommodation. There are budget hotels on the south side of the Seine, see page 88.

Gros Horloge & Vieux Marché

Hôtel de Bourgtheroulde €€€€-€€€

Place de la Pucelle, T02 32 08 32 40 for latest information, hoteldebourgtheroulde.com.
Map: Rouen, p70.
Dating back to 1499, this magnificent late-Gothic and Renaissance mansion (the name is pronounced 'boor-troode') is the city's finest private house of the period. It was a lucky survival after much of its surrounding neighbourhood was destroyed in 1944. Controversially for some Rouennais, it has been transformed into a four-star luxury hotel with its own restaurant, brasserie and spa. It is due to reopen in 2010.

Hôtel du Vieux Marché €€€

33 rue du Vieux Palais, T02 35 71 00 88, hotel-vieuxmarche.com.
Map: Rouen, A4, p70.
The location in a pedestrian street just off place du Vieux Marché is the strong point of this small, very much modernized traditional Best Western hotel within easy walking distance of the sights of Old Rouen. The hotel has its own small pay-to-use car park, a great boon in this quarter. The rooms are comfortable, if some on the small side, in dark-red tones with low lighting. Room rates may be heavily discounted if they are booked online.

Le Dandy €€
93 bis rue Cauchoise, T02 35 07 32 00, hotels-rouen.net.
Map: Rouen, A3, p70.
With some surprisingly grand Louis Quinze furnishings in an otherwise contemporary setting, this friendly and welcoming small hotel has cosy, modernized rooms. It is well placed in a pedestrian street of small shops and eateries that leads to place du Vieux Marché, frequented more by locals than tourists. In the front rooms there may be a little noise from local bars. Rooms at the rear are quieter.

Museums Quarter

Morand Hôtel €
1 rue Morand, T02 35 71 46 07, morandhotel.com.
Map: Rouen, C2, p70.
This is a basic, traditional, family-run hotel, not without charm, on a street corner in a fairly low-key mainly residential part of town. Rooms are a decent size, if perhaps in need of some modernization, and the owners are friendly and helpful. Located just north of the Musée des Beaux Arts and the green square Verdrel, it's outside the busiest part of the tourist area, yet within easy reach of everything.

Near stations

Hôtel Ermitage Bouquet €€€
58 rue Bouquet, T02 32 12 30 40, hotel-ermitagebouquet.com.
Map: Rouen, B1, p70.
This is a pleasant, well-equipped, comfortable hotel in a quiet spot outside the city's historic area. A 19th-century brick building, unusually it's both a member of the upmarket Châteaux et Hôtels de France and the cosier, traditional, family-run Logis de France. It has useful off-street parking and free Wi-Fi. Decor is simple and uncluttered, with plenty of stylish touches including polished wooden floors and chandeliers. The rooms and bathrooms are modern and well equipped, the breakfast good, and staff helpful. It's north of the railway station, on a steep hill, about 15 minutes' walk to the sights of Old Rouen.

Hôtel de Dieppe €€
Place Bernard Tissot, T02 35 71 96 00, hotel-dieppe.fr.
Map: Rouen, C1, p70.
This is a simple, modest, independent hotel right across the road from the railway station. With thoroughly French provincial character, while the hotel may seem in urgent need of modernization, it is better known in the town for its good traditional restaurant – the speciality of the house is the classic local dish, *canard à la rouennaise* (Rouen duck).

Hôtel Andersen €
4 rue Pouchet, T02 35 71 88 51, hotelandersen.com.
Map: Rouen, B1, p70.
Close to the railway station, in a not very appealing backstreet but away from the worst of the traffic noise, the white façade of this basic hotel for low-budget travellers is appealing. The interior is welcoming, with light, pleasant decoration. The public areas have more charm than the bedrooms, which are not particularly large, and some fixtures and fittings seem to need improvement. There's a decent traditional breakfast.

Hôtel Astrid €
11 place Bernard Tissot/rue Jeanne d'Arc, T02 35 71 75 88, hotel-astrid.fr.
Map: Rouen, C1, p70.
This is a very simple, basic, traditional hotel in a corner position right across from the railway station. It can be noisy, both from the street and from neighbouring bedrooms. Rooms are small and bathrooms poky, but for anyone looking to keep expenses down, not fussy about comforts and/or travelling by train, it's ideal. Staff are amiable and helpful and a modest breakfast is available. The sights of Old Rouen are easily reached by bus or on foot.

Riverside north bank

Mercure Champ de Mars €€€
12 av Aristide Briand, T02 35 52 42 32, hotel-rouen-centre.com.
Map: Rouen, E7, p70.
Arguably the best, or at least smartest, of Rouen's hotels, this Mercure is on a busy main road in a riverside setting east of Old Rouen. Behind the hotel is the pleasant Esplanade Champs de Mars. Catering mainly to the business market, with a strongly corporate feel, it's comfortable and well equipped with plush and warm decor, but without being especially luxurious. There's a pub-like piano bar and a good restaurant, sometimes with live jazz.

Suitehôtel Rouen Normandie €€€
Îlot Pasteur, Quai de Boisguilbert, T02 32 10 58 68, suite-hotel.com.
Map: Rouen, A5, p70.
On a rather bleak busy riverside roadway on the north bank of the Seine, about 1.5 km from the sights of Old Rouen, this functional modern white block adorned with balconies offers pleasant, spacious cleverly designed accommodation arranged more like a simple apartment (complete with a small cooking area) rather than a classic hotel room. Decor in the rooms and in the public areas is bright and contemporary, staff are helpful and there is an underground car park.

Hôtel de Paris €€-€
12-14 rue de la Champmeslé, T02 35 70 09 26, hotel-paris.fr.
Map: Rouen, B6, p70.
A classic small family-run hotel of the old style, just off the Seine waterfront, the Paris is a few minutes' stroll from all the sights of Old Rouen. The welcome is friendly and professional, and the hotel appears clean and well kept. There's a decent continental breakfast buffet, and it's useful that the hotel has its own car park. Rooms are simply and pleasantly decorated, unpretentious, not large but very adequately equipped.

Hôtel Arts et Seine €
4-6 rue St-Etienne des Tonneliers, T02 35 88 11 44, artsetseine.com.
Map: Rouen, B6, p70.
South of the cathedral, a block away from the Seine riverside, this hotel is in a post-war commercial area which is perhaps not Rouen's prettiest neighbourhood, but is just a few minutes' walk to all the main sights. Outwardly not very appealing, this is a traditional, modest family-run hotel, friendly, helpful and well managed, with clean, comfortable rooms decorated in pale shades, and offers free Wi-Fi. There is sometimes noise at night from nearby bars.

Ibis Rouen Champ de Mars €
12 av Aristide Briand, T02 35 08 12 11, rouen-centre-hotel.fr.
Map: Rouen, E7, p70.
An inexpensive modern budget chain hotel, this Ibis stands beside a busy main riverside highway east of Old Rouen. It's about 15 minutes' walk to the main sights. Rooms have a pleasing, comfortable simplicity. Behind the hotel, the Esplanade Champs de Mars provides a pleasant prospect. The hotel is an efficient cheap option for both business and leisure travellers, and also has its own car park.

South of the Seine

Rouen Saint Sever €€
20 place de l'Eglise St-Sever, T02 35 62 81 82, hotelrouen-stsever.com.
Map: Rouen, C7, p70.
If you're looking to economize, and are prepared to go without a few creature comforts, this former budget chain hotel beside a commercial centre south of the Seine could be a good choice. The small, functional rooms, each with a little bathroom tacked on, are clean and adequate and the beds are comfortable. Tourists do stay here, but the focus seems to be on one-night business stays and group bookings.

Eating & drinking

Ibis Rouen Centre Rive Gauche €
44 rue Amiral Cécille, T02 35 63 27 27, ibishotel.com.
Map: Rouen, A7, p70.
This reliable, low-budget hotel is opposite a commercial centre about 1 km from Old Rouen. A good cheap option, it's clean, and comfortable. It offers Wi-Fi and also has a car park.

Premiere Classe Rouen Petit Quevilly €
112 av Jean Jaurès, T02 35 72 02 22, premiereclasse.fr.
Map: Rouen, A7, p70.
This budget chain hotel is a plain and simple low-rise on a main road (D3) on the south side of the Seine, about 3 km from Old Rouen. A tram into town passes in front of the door. On offer are small, clean and modern rooms, with minimal service. The location is convenient for getting to town, and there's a basic breakfast to see you on your way.

Suburbs

Auberge de Jeunesse €
Route de Darnetal.
Open 24 hrs a day, 7 days a week.
Map: Rouen, p70.
Housed in a former 18th-century dye manufacturers', right on the banks of the River Robec, northeast of the city centre, Rouen's brand-new, top-of-the-range youth hostel, due to open in 2010, is on a TEOR bus route with access to the central area.

Cathedral Quarter

Brasserie Paul €€
1 place de la Cathédrale, T02 35 71 86 07.
Daily 1200-1500 and approximately 1930-2300.
Map: Rouen, C5, p70.
One hundred years old, full of classic pre-war touches like art deco lamps and polished wood, Brasserie Paul claims to be the longest established brasserie in Rouen and is wonderfully positioned beside the cathedral. Sit under pink parasols and choose from menus of French and Normandy favourites – steaks, *tête de veau*, *andouillette*, *escargots* and fine local cheeses, all at reasonable prices.

Dufour €€
67 bis rue St-Nicolas, T02 35 71 90 62.
Tue-Sat 1200-1345 and 1900-2130.
Map: Rouen, D5, p70.
A wonderfully picturesque four-storey half-timbered building, in a partly pedestrianized shopping street a couple of blocks from the cathedral, is the setting for this charming old atmospheric restaurant, with dark wooden beams, tiles and gleaming white tablecloths. It's touristy, of course, but with excellent traditional Normandy fare for all that, such as the *escalope de veau Vallée d'Auge*.

A La Table Gourmande €
25 rue des Bonnetiers, T02 35 71 87 06.
Daily 0730-2130.
Map: Rouen, D5, p70.
This cheerful brasserie with indoor and outdoor tables near the cathedral is open all day from breakfast to dinner. There's orange and white decor and a café ambience, but decent set menus for lunch and dinner, offering classic French cooking at modest prices.

Brasserie de la Flèche €
12 place de la Calende, T02 35 71 95 61.
Open all day.
Map: Rouen, p70.
There's a green and white colour scheme at this warm and friendly café-bar on the corner of a square right next to the cathedral. Enjoy inexpensive three-course set menus of good simple cooking, served out of doors or inside at tables laid with gingham cloths.

Gros Horloge & Vieux Marché

La Couronne €€€
31 place du Vieux Marché, T02 35 71 40 90.
Daily 1200-1430 and 1900-2230.
Map: Rouen, A4, p70.
A famous name and acclaimed as 'the oldest auberge in France', this picturesque flower and flag-decked Vieux Marché landmark has a dark timber

Pick of the picnic spots

Buy fresh bread, ripe tomatoes, good cheeses or readymade snacks from the food stores along rue de la République (it runs behind the cathedral), from the small covered market in place du Vieux Marché, or if you prefer, at the Super U supermarket at the other side of the square.

Square Verdrel
Facing the entrance of the Musée des Beaux Arts, this lush green square of fine mature trees, flowers, green lawns and paths with benches is a charming haven of repose, ideal for a picnic and a sit-down in the museum quarter. There's a well-equipped children's play area, too.

Jardins de l'Hôtel de Ville
If you buy your food along rue de la République you're just a few minutes' walk from the city centre's quiet, attractive public gardens, spread out behind St-Ouen abbey church. Formerly the monk's private gardens, its rolling green lawn is a good place to relax and appreciate the church's Flamboyant Gothic architecture.

Jardin des Plantes
Take bus no 7 from rue de la République to these extensive, peaceful 17th-century botanic gardens (entrance on rue de Trianon, free of charge), 2.5 km away on the south side of the river. It's a delightful place to wander or sit among tropical greenhouses, an orangery, palm houses, a rose garden, famous collections of fuchsias, an orchard, and even curiosities like carnivorous plants. There are also children's activities, refreshments and more.

façade, plenty of wood beams, plush fabrics, warm lighting and cosy ambience. Classic Norman cooking is served, including a *véritable*, and pricey, *canard à la Rouennaise à la presse*.

Les Nymphéas €€€
7/9 rue de la Pie, T02 35 89 26 69.
Tue-Sat 1200-1400 and 1930-2145, closed Sun and Mon (except national holidays).
Map: Rouen, A4, p70.
Among the top names for Rouen gourmets, this traditional place in Old Rouen has won a Michelin star. Sumptuously furnished, with white napery, flowers and upholstered chairs, it's on two floors of a half-timbered old house in its own courtyard off the Vieux Marché. Menu specialities are hearty French and Norman fare, such as *canard à la rouennaise* and *civet de homard au Sauternes*.

Gill Côté Bistro €€
14 place du Vieux Marché, T02 35 89 88 72.
Daily 1200-1500 and 1930-2300.
Map: Rouen, A3, p70.
In addition to his successful riverside restaurant (see page 93), chef Gilles Tournadre also runs this more informal, low-key alternative on what is unfortunately the least attractive corner of the Vieux Marché. However, the bistro itself is contemporary, stylish and smart, with attractive woods and dark green hues. There's Gilles' same emphasis on local ingredients, but with dishes inspired by all of France and beyond, such as *bœuf bourguignon* with fresh pasta.

Minute et Mijoté €€
58 rue de Fontenelle, T02 32 08 40 00.
Mon-Sat 1200-1415 and 1930-2200, closed part of Aug.
Map: Rouen, A3, p70.
In brasserie-style premises with tables standing among greenery on the pavement, this restaurant not far from place du Vieux Marché serves well-prepared French dishes, both local and from other regions, on monthly changing menus.

Outdoor tables in front of Rouen Cathedral.

Listings

Le Maupassant €€-€
39 place du Vieux Marché,
T02 35 07 56 90.
Daily 1200-1430 and
1900-2230.
Map: Rouen, A4, p70.
Busy and touristy, of course, as it
is on the Vieux Marché, on a
pedestrian section, facing the
Ste-Jeanne-d'Arc church. Service
is generally amiable, and the
cooking competent and good
value for money. There are
French classics on the menu, and
some surprises, such as duck
crumble with chorizo. Finish
with their *moelleux au chocolat*.

Bistrot des Hallettes €
43 place du Vieux Marché,
T02 35 71 05 06.
Tue-Sat 1200-1400 and
1930-2230.
Map: Rouen, A4, p70.
With plenty of red plush and
walls of bare brick, the interior of
this restaurant has a warm
informality. Outside, there's
plenty of seating at tables on the
Vieux Marché cobbles. Food and
wine is generous and hearty,
with fine steaks, kidneys, snails
and *andouillette*.

Brasserie d´Arc €
26 place du Vieux-Marché,
T02 35 71 97 06.
Daily 0900-2400
(Fri and Sat 0200).
Map: Rouen, A3, p70.
This brasserie in the heart of Old
Rouen has indoor and outdoor
tables, and a choice of

inexpensive set menus for lunch.
Classic favourites like *steak-frites*
are the attraction here, along
with a range of salads.

Le Florian €
11 rue de Crosne, T02 35 07 47 17.
Mon-Sat 1200-1400 and
1900-2300.
Map: Rouen, A4, p70.
Trompe l'œil decorates the upper
floors of this pizzeria facing into
place du Vieux Marché, a boon if
you want a good, simple meal at
a low price. Inside, the restaurant
is in an atmospheric old vaulted
basement with tiled floors,
arched white ceilings, and walls
of stone blocks decorated with
intriguing Venetian masks.

Maison Hardy €
22 place du Vieux Marché,
T02 35 71 81 55.
Mon-Sat lunchtime only.
Map: Rouen, A3, p70.
A charcuterie with sausages and
prepared meats, the shop also
has a little restaurant serving
good-value set lunches.

Cafés & bars
L'Euro
41 place du Vieux Marché,
T02 35 07 55 19.
Daily 1500-0200.
Map: Rouen, A4, p70.
A spacious array of outdoor café
tables look on to place du Vieux
Marché, while inside this historic
half-timbered corner building
are three different bars: on the
ground floor a cocktail/lounge

bar ambience; on the first floor a
bar serving French wines with
charcuterie and cheeses; and on
the top floor a livelier show bar
and disco.

Le Vicomte
70 rue de la Vicomte,
T02 35 71 24 11.
Daily 1800-0200.
Map: Rouen, B5, p70.
There's a lot going on in this
popular four-storey bar, with
cocktails and DJ on the ground
level, live music and performers
on the first floor, a billiard room
upstairs, and private events room.

Museums Quarter

Les Petits Parapluies €€€
46 rue Bourg l´Abbé/place de la
Rougemare, T02 35 88 55 26.
Tue-Sun approx 1200-1345 and
approx 1930-2200, closed Sat
lunch and Sun dinner.
Map: Rouen, p70.
This leading Rouen restaurant
specializes in inventive French
cooking with local inspiration,
such as foie gras cooked in cider,
with apple and red onion
crumble. It is sited in a fine
half-timbered building where
once umbrellas were made, and
boasts an art nouveau interior
and stylish decor.

Brasserie des Beaux-Arts €
35 rue Jean Lecanuet,
T02 35 71 02 48.
Daily 1200-1500 and 1900-2100.
Map: Rouen, C3, p70.

You'll spot the yellow chairs and parasols of the outdoor tables of this large corner brasserie by the Musée des Beaux Arts. Inside it's more sober, with polished woods and a pub feel. Choose from three *formules* (fixed-price menus) of popular dishes or select from a salad buffet.

Cafés & bars
Bar de la Crosse
53 rue de l´Hôpital,
T02 35 70 16 18.
Tue-Sat 1000-2200.
Map: Rouen, D4, p70.

This friendly café-bar provides a welcome pause on a traffic-free street that runs from St-Ouen church towards the Musée des Beaux Arts.

Le Diplomate
10 place Foch, T02 35 71 10 80.
Daily, all day.
Map: Rouen, D4, p70.

This unassuming modern little bar with a few pavement tables, across the road from the back of the Law Courts (the former Parlement de Normandie), has a bright interior. It also serves a wide choice of inexpensive set menus of traditional French brasserie fare at lunchtime.

Near stations

Cafés & bars
Le Métropole
111 rue Jeanne d'Arc,
T02 35 71 58 56.
Mon-Fri 0730-1930, Sat 0800-1300.
Map: Rouen, C1, p70.

Perched on a narrow street corner, this 1930s art deco brasserie was the haunt of Jean-Paul Sartre and Simone de Beauvoir. Relaxed and pleasant inside, with Wi-Fi, drinks, snacks and a set *formule* at lunchtime.

Riverside north bank

Gill €€€
8-9 quai de la Bourse,
T02 35 71 16 14, gill.fr.
Tue-Sat 1200-1345 and 1930-2145, closed 1 weekend Apr/beginning May, most of Aug, and Christmas and New Year.
Map: Rouen, B6, p70.

The gastronomic restaurant of renowned chef Gilles Tournadre, on the north bank of the River Seine, is considered the supreme dining experience in Rouen. With two Michelin stars, it has a refined simplicity and elegance in design and in cuisine. Among the menu highlights there is *pigeon à la Rouennaise*, which is a twist on the more traditional duckling *à la Rouennaise*. See also Gill Côté Bistro, page 90.

Le 37 €€
37 rue des Tonneliers,
T02 35 70 56 65.
Tue-Sat 1200-1345 and 1930-2145.
Map: Rouen, B6, p70.

Chic and cheerful in long, narrow premises with a bistro feel, this informal restaurant offers rapid service, set menus and excellent French cuisine. Dishes chalked up on a daily blackboard. Finish with the exquisite *fondant au chocolat*, if it's on.

Tex Mex L´Equateur €
5-7 rue du Bac, T02 35 71 22 16.
Tue-Sat 1145-1400 and 1900-2300 (Fri and Sat 2400).
Map: Rouen, C6, p70.

This bar and restaurant on the Seine north bank is intent on enjoying everything Mexican, from music to drinks to food to upbeat atmosphere. Lunchtime menus are cheap and cheerful.

Cafés & bars
Le Tyrol
36-38 rue de la Champmeslé,
T02 35 71 14 32.
Mon-Fri 0700-1930, Sat 0830-1900.
Map: Rouen, A5, p70.

Open all day for drinks and snacks, with inexpensive set menus at mealtimes, this bright pavement café is just outside the main tourist zone, in the shopping area between Old Rouen and the river.

Entertainment

Shopping

South of the Seine

Les Capucines €€€

16-18 rue Jean Macé, T02 35 72 62 34, bus no 6 from République in the city centre stops at place des Chartreux in Le Petit Quevilly.
Tue-Sun 1200-1400 and 1945-2100, closed Sat lunch and Sun dinner and 3 weeks in Aug.
Map: Rouen, A7, p70.
This solid, reliable gastronomic address occupies a redbrick house in a residential street in the Le Petit Quevilly area south of the river. Decor is stylish and traditional with calm, restful tones, with a pretty terrace outside. Dishes imaginatively combine Norman flavours with classic French cuisine.

Le Catelier €€

134 bis av des Martyrs de la Résistance, T02 35 72 59 90.
Tue-Sat 1200-1400 reopening at about 1900 until 2100, closed most of Aug.
Map: Rouen, C7, p70.
South of the river, in the area of the Jardin des Plantes, this classic, unpretentious good-value restaurant, popular with business travellers, offers a range of well-prepared traditional Normandy dishes. There's a strong emphasis on shellfish and fish fresh from Dieppe and the coast. Madame la patronne is the chef, while her husband – a qualified sommelier – takes care of the wine.

Bars & clubs

Throughout the summer, dozens of city centre bars stay open till late, and many have DJs or live music. In the winter months, it's much quieter. The more hectic nightlife is focused around place du Vieux Marché, and between there and the quays of the River Seine. Irish Pub **Yesterday** (rue Moulinet), more exotic **Shari Vari** (51 rue St-Nicolas) and slicker **L'Euro** (see page 92) are popular late bars in the city centre. Clubbers can get into a Latin American mood at **La Luna** (26 rue St-Etienne-des-Tonneliers).

Music

Opéra de Rouen

Place des Arts, quai de la Bourse, T02 35 98 50 98, operaderouen. com.
Rouen's highly regarded Opéra de Rouen and Théâtre des Arts, set back from the busy Seine quayside closest to Old Rouen, stages a range of dance and music performances.

Zenith

Av des Canadiens, zenith-de-rouen.com, take bus no 7 to Zénith/Parc Expo terminus.
The huge Zenith auditorium stages major rock, pop and other concerts, as well as shows for children and family entertainment. Many of the artists are better known in France than abroad, but some big names also perform here – check what's on during your visit.

Art & antiques

Chasset d'Antiquités

12 rue de la Croix de Fer, T02 35 70 59 97.
Mon 1430-1900, Tue-Sat 1030-1900.
Contains Dinky toys, china, glass and other collectable items.

DnD Antiquités

10 rue Petit de Julleville, T02 35 36 89 86, niaux-d.com.
Tue-Sat 1030-1215 and 1430-1830.
Has a selection of Dieppe ivory work and Asian pieces.

Faïences Saint-Romain

56 rue St-Romain, T02 35 07 12 30, faiences-rouen.com.
Phone to check opening hours.
Makes and sells hand-made ceramic or faience to order.

Fayencerie Augy

26 rue St Romain, T02 35 88 77 47, fayencerie-augy.com.
Tue-Sat 0900-1900.
Sells its newly minted traditional-style faience-ware.

Galerie l'Astrée

10 and 23 rue Damiette, T02 35 70 42 77.
Mon 1400-1900, Tue-Sat 1000-1200 and 1400-1900.
Astrée have several shops between the cathedral and St-Ouen.

Listings

Hire a bike from Rouen's Cy'clic scheme.

Activities & tours

Les Beaux Jours
24 rue St-Nicolas, T02 35 15 53 24.
Tue-Sat 1000-1230 and
1400-1900.
Dolls, teddy bears and other toys
make an appearance.

Clothing & accessories
Galeries Lafayette
25 rue Grand-Pont, T02 35 71 70 53.
Mon-Sat 0900-1930.
For the latest French fashions
and other stylish products.

Hermès
11 rue du Change, T02 35 71 17 58.
Mon 1400-1900, Tue-Sat
1000-1230 and 1400-1900.
Women's luxury accessories
store, with silk headscarves.

Tant Qu'il y Aura des Hommes
79 rue St Nicolas, T02 35 15 14 04.
Mon 1500-1930, Tue-Thu 1000-
1300 and 1430-1930, Fri-Sat
1000-1930.
A French chain with stylish, good
quality clothes and accessories.

Food & drink
Caves Bérigny
7 rue Rollon, T02 35 07 57 54.
Tue-Sat 0930-1230 and
1430-1930, Sun 1000-1300.
This fine wine specialist is also a
good place to browse a wide
choice of Calvados.

Chocolatier Auzou
*163 rue du Gros Horloge,
T02 35 70 59 31.*
Mon 1415-1915, Tue-Sat
0930-1930, Sun 0930-1300.

One of the best known
chocolate makers in town.
Sample their local specialities,
such as *Larmes de Jeanne d'Arc*,
which are almond and nougatine
covered with chocolate.

Comtesse du Barry
4 rue Rollon, T02 35 07 53 35.
Tue-Sat 0900-1300 and
1400-1930.
This gourmet boutique chain,
right beside place du Vieux
Marché, has shelves of preserves,
caviar, fine wines and more.

La Chocolatière
*18 rue Guillaume le Conquérant,
T02 35 71 00 79.*
Daily 0800-1930.
An emporium of chocolate with
a café as well as a shop,
specializing in pralines.

La Fromagerie du Vieux Marché
18 rue Rollon, T02 35 71 11 00.
Tue-Fri 0900-1245 and
1500-1930, Sat 0900-1900, Sun
0900-1245.
Among the diverse array of
shops in this busy street, is this
boutique of a master cheese
maker with a fine selection.

Household
Morin: Tout pour la Pâtisserie
56 rue Jeanne d'Arc.
Mon 1400-1900, Tue-Sat
0900-1200 and 1400-1900.
In a town with many kitchenware
specialists, here's one with a
range of high-quality utensils.

Cycling
Cy'clic
T0800 08 78 00, cyclic.rouen.fr.
Take advantage of the city's
Cy'clic scheme. The 175
help-yourself rental bikes are
available at 17 pick-up points
around the centre. Insert your
credit card and PIN to pick up a
bike. It's free for the first 30
minutes (long enough to go
almost anywhere in town). You
pay €1 for the next 30 minutes,
€2 for the 30 minutes after that.
Charges rack up if you keep a
bike longer than 1½ hours.

Walking
Contact the **Office de Tourisme
de Rouen** (Rouen Tourist Office),
see page 71, for details and
tickets for their varied
programme of all-year-round
guided walking tours, *Laissez-
vous conter Rouen.* Or tour Old
Rouen on your own using an
audio guide available from the
tourist office.

Contents

Upper Normandy

Monet's garden, Giverny.

Introduction

Broad, gently undulating, sparsely populated open country is the characteristic landscape of upper Normandy. The high, rolling chalk plateau of the Pays de Caux reaches all the way from Picardy to the Seine, where in places it plummets down to the river valley in abrupt white escarpments. Here and there are expanses of dense forest that still have the feel of wilderness, especially the Forest of Lyons with picturesque Lyons-la-Forêt at its heart. At Les Andelys, a pretty village nestles beside the Seine at the foot of the white cliffs, while a sturdy Norman castle, Richard the Lionheart's Château Gaillard, stands guard on the heights. On the river's wide estuary, the large industrial port town of Le Havre surprises by its modern artistic heritage – Impressionism was born here. Where the chalk plateau meets the sea, it forms the majestic white cliffs and strange rock formations of the Alabaster Coast. Cut into the coastline, the old port of Dieppe is the main harbour and market town of northern Normandy, as it has been for centuries.

Two *départements* make up the region: Seine Maritime and Eure. The wide, often wooded Seine valley does not quite mark the boundary between them, as Seine Maritime strays to the south bank, and Eure crosses the river above Rouen.

What to see in…

… one day
Monet's house and garden in **Giverny** are a must. Then follow the Seine's north bank (D313) to Les Andelys to admire the white fortress of **Château Gaillard**. Cross the Seine and drive on D135 and N15 to autoroute A13, to bypass Rouen. Leave the autoroute at junction 25 to rejoin D313, and follow it to the riverside village and old abbey of **Jumièges**. Travelling on either side of the Seine, continue on D982 to join A131 into **Le Havre** to see the art museum or on D131 to the beach resort and **Dieppe**.

…a weekend or more
Climb up to **Château Gaillard**, and, having bypassed Rouen, take a detour through the **Brotonne Forest**. After visiting **Jumièges**, pause at **Caudebec-en-Caux** to see its fine Gothic church. Continue into Le Havre, and finish by driving up the **Alabaster Coast**, pausing at its little resorts, to end the second day in **Dieppe**.

Detail of window by Georges Braque, Varengeville-sur-Mer church.

Dieppe

Dieppe's old town lies on a narrow spit of land between the lively, crowded, picturesque harbour with its quaysides on one side, and the 2-km-long pebble beach backed by greensward on the other. Agreeable, traffic-free Grand'Rue, reaching from restaurant-lined Quai Henri IV to place du Puits Salé, is the heart of the old town, and here Dieppe's colourful Saturday morning market is held. Originally an 11th-century Viking port – the name comes from the Norse word for 'deep' – Dieppe became one of the busiest sea ports in France. The imposing Château, overlooking the beach on lofty cliffs behind the town, is a remnant of medieval fortifications. In the 16th century Dieppe was home to Jehan Ango's notorious privateer fleet of 100 ships, but even then it had a recreational quality, and was among the first places in Europe to attract 'tourists'. Henry III visited the town in 1578 to bathe in the sea, laying the foundation of its later reputation. Visits for the same purpose by Queen Hortense of Holland, in 1813, and the influential young Duchess of Berry, every year from 1824 to 1830, gave it the seal of approval for European royalty and high society throughout the 19th century. In the early 20th, it took on a more raffish air. Many artists and writers took up residence, and a community of some 3000 wealthy British expats settled here. No longer so glamorous or fashionable, the town remains lively and attractive, and still attracts crowds of Parisian weekenders.

Château-Musée

Rue de Chastes, T02 35 06 61 99.
Jun-Sep 1000-1200 and 1400-1800, Oct-May
Wed-Mon 1000-1200 and 1400-1700. €3.50, €2
concessions, under 12s free.
Map: Dieppe, p104.

Rising on a cliff at Dieppe's western edge, the
flint-and-sandstone Château dominates the town.
It has been so damaged, repaired, altered and
expanded over the centuries that it's hard to
imagine the original fortress built here in the 10th
century by Richard the Fearless, Duke of Normandy.
The oldest part is the 10th- to 12th-century west
tower; the main structure is largely 15th century,
though its northwest tower dates from the 14th
century and the curtain walls were extended in the
17th century to incorporate the square 13th-
century **St-Rémy Tower**. The structure survived
bombardment by the British in 1694 and 1942, and
is today the town's museum, divided into sections
covering different themes.

The principal exhibition is of 16th- to 19th-
century Dieppe ivories. The town was renowned
for its skilled ivory carvers, whose clever, intricate
work is still a delight to see: statues, model ships,
boxes and miniature portraits, as well as a
multitude of ornaments, tools and household
objects. Several of the finer pieces are copies of
well-known sculptures or popular images of their
day, such as the lovely 18th-century *Four Seasons*.

Other sections deal with the maritime history of
the town, and there are many good paintings,
often on a Dieppe waterfront theme, by artists
who frequented the town, including Renoir, Sisley,
Sickert, Pissarro, Dufy, Courbet and many others,
with a separate section devoted to lithographs by
Georges Braque.

Tip...

Grand'Rue is Dieppe's main street in the old centre of
town. It continues alongside the port as Quai Henry
IV. Running parallel, boulevard de Verdun is the main
avenue for the beach resort and hotels.

Essentials

➊ Getting around The docks, beach, and town
centre of Dieppe all make up a small area that can
be crossed on foot in about 20 minutes. For journeys
further afield, the greater urban area of Dieppe and its
five surrounding suburban villages (Arques-la-Bataille,
Hautot-sur-Mer, Martin-Eglise, Rouxmesnil-Bouteilles
and St-Aubin-sur-Scie) can all be reached on town
buses run by Stradibus. The two principal stops in the
town centre are the railway station and Pont Ango,
between which there are buses every few minutes.
A single journey costs €1.05. A *carnet* of 10 tickets
costs €7.10. Information from **Espace Stradibus**, 56
quai Duquesne, T02 32 14 03 04, infotransports.free.
fr/reseaux/dieppe/informations.htm, Monday-Friday
0800-1200 and 1330-1830, Saturday 0900-1200.
➍ Bus station Boulevard Clemenceau, T02 35 06 69 33.
➎ Train station Boulevard Clemenceau, T02 35 06 69 33.
For details of regional and national services, see page 270.
➒ ATM There are several in the town centre, including
two in Grand'Rue near place Nationale, and two in
place Nationale itself.
➓ Hospital Centre Hospitalier de Dieppe, av Pasteur,
T02 32 14 76 76.
➕ Pharmacy The most centrally located pharmacy is La
Grande Pharmacie, 15-17 place Nationale, T02 35 84 11 20.
➋ Post office 2 boulevard Maréchal Joffre.
➊ Tourist information Pont Jehan Ango, T02 32 14 40
60, dieppetourisme.com. July-August Monday-Saturday
0900-1900, Sunday 1000-1300 and 1500-1800; May,
June, September Monday-Saturday 0900-1300 and
1400-1800, Sunday 1000-1300 and 1500-1800; October-
April: Monday-Saturday 0900-1200 and 1400-1800.

Cité de la Mer

*37 rue de l'Asile Thomas, T02 35 06 93 20,
estrancitedelamer.free.fr.*
Daily 1000-1200 and 1400-1800. €5.80, €4.50
concessions, €3.50 4-16 years.
Map: Dieppe, p104.

Don't imagine a lavish sealife centre – despite the
name, this modest rainy-day museum is mainly
devoted to maritime rather than marine life. Most
exhibits and displays deal with boat building and
fishing, and explain all about tides and sea currents
and their impact on the coast.

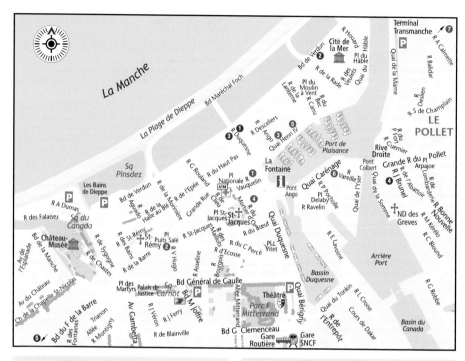

Oscar Wilde's Dieppe

It was to Dieppe that Oscar Wilde fled on being released from prison in 1897. Many old friends and acquaintances were here, including James McNeill Whistler, Walter Sickert and Aubrey Beardsley, and the art critic Robert Ross, to whom he handed the manuscript of *De Profundis*. He perhaps believed he would be welcomed, but it is said that most of the Dieppe community, including many former friends, shunned him, embarrassed by his imprisonment for homosexuality. His favourite haunts were the big and lively Café des Tribunaux that dominates place du Puits Salé, and quiet Café Suisse on the Arcade la Bourse quayside – both are still there. Wilde moved to Berneval-sur-Mer, 10 km away, then an isolated clifftop village, to work on *The Ballad of Reading Gaol*.

Dieppe listings

❶ Sleeping

1 Hôtel Aguado *30 bd de Verdun*
2 Hôtel de l'Europe *63 bd de Verdun*
3 Hôtel de la Plage *20 bd de Verdun*
4 Villa des Capucins *11 rue des Capucins*
5 Villa Florida *24 chemin du Golf*

❶ Eating & drinking

1 Café Suisse *19 arcades de la Bourse*
2 Café des Tribunaux *place Puits Salé*
3 Chez le Gros *35 quai Henri IV*
4 La Marmite Dieppoise *8 rue St-Jean*
5 La Musardière *61 quai Henri IV*
6 Le Bistrot du Pollet *23 rue Tête de Boeuf*
7 Les Voiles d'Or *chemin de la Falaise*

Dieppe raid: Operation Jubilee

On 19 August 1942, more than 5000 Canadian commandos and 1000 British launched a surprise attack on Dieppe and the neighbouring coast between Varengeville and Berneval. With considerable air and navy support, their objective was to breach and destroy German coastal defences, take prisoners, capture German planning documents and gather intelligence. Landing at 0500, they were defeated later the same morning without achieving any useful objectives. By the end of the day more than 1000 of the commandos were dead, over 600 wounded and some 2000 taken prisoner. Their air support lost 106 aircraft, while the Luftwaffe lost 48. Following the catastrophe, the one lesson learned was the strength of German defences on the Channel coast.

Right bank

The animated popular quaysides of Dieppe are on the port's west side – the left bank of the River Arques from which the harbour was carved. Cross the two bridges – Pont Ango and Pont Colbert – to the right bank to reach the little district of **Le Pollet**, a cluster of lanes of old redbrick and flint cottages that make up the fishermen's quarter. Climb up from here to one of the town's most distinctive landmarks, visible from far out at sea – the sailors' small cliff-top chapel, **Notre-Dame de Bon Secours**. This quiet, touching place of prayer, overlooking the harbour, is also a place of remembrance. It contains a memorial to every Dieppe seaman lost at sea since 1876, including whole trawlers missing with all their crew.

It's a fact...

Coincidences of location helped determine Dieppe's destiny as an important fishing harbour, holiday resort and Channel port. It happens to be the nearest port, and the nearest beach, to Paris; and is also the mid-point between London and the French capital.

Eglise St-Jacques

22 rue Boucherie, T02 32 14 63 00.
Usually open during the day, free.
Map: Dieppe, p104.

Dieppe's large parish church, between Grand'Rue and the fishing port, is a striking Flamboyant presence in the town. It has been much damaged and repaired over the centuries, yet remains an attractive example of the evolution of Gothic architecture from the 13th to 16th centuries, and serves as a monument to Dieppe's past prosperity. There's a good rose window over the central doorway. The interior is worn and damaged, but in use. Frescoes of the Stations of the Cross survive on pillars. The high nave of pale stone dates from the origins of the building, while the elaborate side chapels at the eastern end are the final touches. In one of the side chapels, a memorial honours those who died on the ill-fated Dieppe raid in 1942. Out of keeping with the rest is a remarkable Renaissance carved frieze, thought to have been rescued from Jehan Ango's own private palace when it was destroyed by British bombardment in 1694. The carvings show native people of Brazil and the Caribbean, probably encountered by Ango on his voyages.

Côte d'Albâtre

Stretching along the whole length of the Seine Maritime seafront, this coast is called the Côte d'Albâtre (Alabaster Coast) simply because alabaster is so white. The chalky plateau of the Pays de Caux reaches the English Channel in an abrupt, majestic line of soaring white cliffs. Sometimes they jut into the sea, sometimes they are set back behind coves and beaches, and sometimes, where there are deep cuts and breaks in the chalk, fishing ports have prospered. The harbours at the foot of the cliffs were established long ago – Fécamp, for example, has been a busy port since Roman times. Several beach resorts also sprang up along the Côte d'Albâtre more than a century ago and have remained popular, such as Etretat, best known for the way the waves have eaten its chalky rock into curious shapes. On the top of the white cliffs, lush vegetation grows and quiet little villages watch out over the sea. Over the centuries, most have made their living from both farming and fishing, although many also have a long tradition of well-to-do outsiders building fine villas and mansions as tranquil hideaways. Among the grandest of all is the lavish home of 16th-century privateer Jehan Ango at Varengeville.

Manoir d'Ango.

Varengeville-sur-Mer

A pretty wooded cliff-top area of hidden cottages, gardens, footpaths and villas, Varengeville is a delight. Arriving from nearby Dieppe, 8 km east, a sign points from the road into a lane between an avenue of trees, leading to the **Manoir d'Ango,** the grand home of the privateer Jehan Ango, who grew rich by seizing hundreds of Portuguese, English and other merchant vessels (see box, page 109). Although arranged in the form of a traditional Normandy fortified farm enclosure, the building is in 16th-century Italian Renaissance style, with raised arched galleries forming a loggia on one side, and plenty of fine decoration. In black and white stone, it's arranged around an impressive courtyard at the centre of which is a huge dovecote. Only the grounds may be visited (March to November).

Another lane leads through the trees to the **Parc des Moustiers** (T02 35 85 10 02, mid-Mar to mid-Nov, 1000-2000, but ticket office open 1000-1200, 1400-1800, €5 (May-Jun €6), children €2.50), 9 ha of cleverly laid out botanic gardens, with rare trees, flowering bushes and sea views. The park is mostly the work of English landscape gardener Gertrude Jekyll (1843-1932). There's always something in bloom, from March to November. Paths wind among colourful flowering bushes and extraordinary 6-m-high rhododendrons. An unusual mansion at the centre of the park, with curious corner windows and many English country house touches, was built in 1898 by the great Imperial architect Sir Edwin Lutyens.

Perhaps the loveliest sight in Varengeville is the lonely little parish church, **Eglise de St-Valéry**, perched on the edge of a high cliff rising from the seashore. There's a magnificent view of the coast

Veules-les-Roses.

from here. Inside the simple church it's immediately obvious that the building dates from two very different periods, as two naves and two choirs have been stuck together, one 11th-century Romanesque, of pale stone, and one 13th- to 15th-century Gothic, partly in brick. Round arches with strangely carved columns separate the two sections. In the south choir aisle is a beautiful modern stained-glass window depicting *The Tree of Jesse*, by the leading Cubist artist Georges Braque, who lived in Varengeville.

The church is surrounded by its simple **cemetery**, in which Braque (1883-1963) is buried beside his wife. Nearby are several other interesting graves, including that of the composer Albert Roussel (1869-1937).

St-Valéry-en-Caux

After being destroyed during the British retreat to Dunkirk, St-Valéry, 34 km south of Dieppe on D925, was rebuilt and is today a thriving fishing port and marina, overlooked by large modern hotel. The town's new church, built in 1963, has a striking wall of stained glass. The tourist information office is at Maison Henri IV, T02 35 97 00 63.

The coast and countryside nearby are impressive and beautiful. On the beach, magnificent white cliffs rise up, while climbing from the shore in places are pretty villages and lanes, for example at **Veules-les-Roses**. At the roadside in Veules, a memorial commemorates 38 Commonwealth soldiers who died in 1940 during the Dieppe raid.

Jehan Ango

A shipbuilder's son and, at first, a shipbuilder himself, Jehan (or Jean) Ango was born in Dieppe in 1480. He became one of the many great seafaring traders and adventurers of the town, making frequent expeditions to Africa and the Americas. This represented a challenge to the Portuguese, who maintained that they alone had the right to trade off the African coast. Ango built a vast fortune, initially through the piracy of captains he equipped and sponsored, notably Jean Fleury, who seized Aztec treasures being taken from Mexico to Spain.

François I, the French king, wishing to respond to the Portuguese dominance in Atlantic trade, authorized Ango to seize all Portuguese trading vessels he encountered in the Atlantic. Jehan Ango's huge fleet of up to 100 vessels proceeded to terrorize Atlantic shipping, seizing 300 Portuguese trading vessels and their cargo. Ships of other nations, including England and Holland, were also seized. Jehan Ango's fortune increased to royal levels, and the king appointed him Governor of Dieppe. He built two homes, one in Dieppe and one (which survives) in Varengeville. His eminent house guests included François I himself, who made Ango a Viscount. However, the king also felt himself entitled to call on Ango's fortune, and pressed him for such large loans that by the end of his life Ango had little left. He died in 1551 and was buried in Dieppe's Eglise St-Jacques.

Fécamp

Although a busy, industrial fishing port, Fécamp, 30 km north of Le Havre on D940, is also an old resort town, enclosed by white cliffs. It provides the background to several novels by Guy de Maupassant, who was born here. The harbour is the town's focal point, and here a good deal of France's daily catch of fresh cod is landed. The town rises steeply from the waterfront. There's a good market in the town centre on Saturdays, centred on place Bellet.

Fécamp essentials

- **Bus station** 25 rue des Charrettes-Rouen.
- **Train station** Place de la Gare, T02 35 43 50 50.
- **ATM** There are several in the town centre and by the port; for example, at 27 quai Bérigny.
- **Hospital** Centre Hospitalier de Fécamp, rue Henry Dunant, T02 35 10 62 62.
- **Pharmacy** 65 quai Bérigny, T02 35 28 00 68.
- **Post office** 1 place Bellet.
- **Tourist information** 113 rue Alexandre le Grand, T02 35 28 51 01, fecamptourisme.com.

Eglise Abbatiale de la Trinité

Place des Ducs Richard, T02 35 28 84 39.
Approx Apr-Sep 0900-1900, Oct-Mar 0900-1200 and 1400-1700.

Fécamp was put on the map in the early seventh century when pilgrims flocked to see a lead casket, supposedly containing 'drops of the Holy Blood', which had been washed ashore in the hollowed-out trunk of what was said to be a fig tree. A monastery was built to protect the Precious Blood, as it became known. In the 11th century, Richard II of England built the Eglise de la Trinité to house the relic. He also re-founded the monastery as a huge abbey, the first under Benedictine rule. It grew immensely wealthy as vast numbers of pilgrims came to revere the Precious Blood.

The abbey church was later reconstructed in Flamboyant Gothic style, and has been much altered over the centuries, but still contains some lovely vestiges of the original. It is a huge building, its white stone interior tall and soaring in design and, at 127 m, one of the longest churches in Europe. Here you'll find the tombs of both Duke Richard I and Duke Richard II, as well as some superb stone carving and notable artworks, especially the richly detailed 15th-century *Dormition of the Virgin*. Along the length are many side chapels. Even today, pilgrims come here to see the Precious Blood, in the small, carved white marble *Tabernacle du Précieux Sang*.

Palais Bénédictine.

Palais Bénédictine

*110 rue Alexandre le Grand, T02 35 10 26 10,
benedictine.fr.*
Daily 1030-1245 and 1400-1800, slightly longer
hours in summer, €6.50, €3 child, under 12s free.

In the 16th century, Fécamp's Benedictine
community used local wild plants to create their
very own liqueur, and called it, quite simply,
Bénédictine. The abbey's distillery soon became,
and still is, a thriving business, since 1863
unconnected to the monks. Today the distilling
takes place in a wildly ornate 19th-century
mock-Gothic palace called the Palais Bénédictine,
which also houses an eclectic museum on the
history of the Benedictines and their liqueur. In the
museum, astonishing displays include precious
ivories, a 15th-century illuminated Book of Hours,
and several painted panels of the same period,
finely worked silver and gold, priceless alabaster
pieces, ancient manuscripts, a collection of
paintings dating back to the 14th century, and a
gallery of modern art. Afterwards, pop into the airy
tasting room to the right of the entrance for a tot
of rich, sweet, acerbic Benedictine (free with your
entry ticket, or €2 without).

Etretat beach.

Etretat

The great feature of this long-established small
resort, 29 km north of Le Havre on D940, which is
popular with weekenders all year round, is its
green-topped white cliffs, carved into curious
shapes by long millennia of wind and waves. Most
striking, cut out of the chalk of the **Falaise d'Aval** at
the south end of the beach, is a tall offshore needle
of white rock called the **Aiguille**; and the **Porte
d'Aval**, a natural archway that looks like an
elephant's trunk sticking into the water. At the
north end, the charming little 11th- and 12th-
century **Notre-Dame de la Garde chapel** stands
alone on top of the spectacular **Falaise d'Amont**
cliff, which looks like a small open doorway in a
huge white wall in the sea. Clearly marked (but
steep) cliff footpaths allow you to fully appreciate

the beauty and grandeur of the setting. A pleasant
promenade behind the beach runs part of the way
between the two cliffs. South of town, the
Manneport, another curious archway in the sea,
can be reached on a cliff-top path, which is a
section of long-distance footpath GR21.

In the late 19th and early 20th century, Etretat
was one of those thoroughly elegant little
Normandy seaside resorts patronized by the most
distinguished people, its breezy marine freshness
adding to its appeal. While those days are long
gone, the town remains bright and busy, and
preserves a refined air. There's a golf course and a
casino. In town, place du Marché is wonderfully
picturesque, with a wooden former covered
market. There is a tourist information office on
place Maurice Guillard, T02 35 27 05 21, etretat.net.

Well-known artists and writers also came
frequently to Etretat in its heyday. Guy de
Maupassant, who spent his teenage years here, later
took his family for summer holidays at Etretat. Victor
Hugo and Gustave Flaubert both declared how
much they loved the Etretat seaside, and stream of
Impressionists came here to paint, among them
Monet, Courbet, Delacroix and Degas.

Le Havre

Le Havre 100 years ago was a bustling, picturesque sea port and the home of the first Impressionists – some of their views of it can be seen in the important Musée Malraux. Today, thanks to its vast industrial areas, travellers often take the view that Le Havre is a place to get away from rather than go to. Nor is it Le Havre's fault that the 16th-century town was almost completely destroyed by Allied bombing in September 1944 (killing more than 4000 residents in one week) and had to be quickly and cheaply rebuilt. However, the rebuilding was entrusted to Auguste Perret, a 70-year-old follower of the architect Le Corbusier who shared his passion for reinforced concrete. Perret's vision resulted in a Quartier Moderne at the heart of the city laid out as an evenly spaced grid of long straight streets lined with not unattractive but monotonously similar buildings, often the same height along any given street – nearly all five, six or seven storeys high, with a profusion of balconies. There is occasional relief in the form of broad avenues, squares and parks. Le Havre also has a pleasant sand and pebble beach backed by gardens, and a charming, bustling waterfront, close to the main street, avenue Foch. Whether Auguste Perret's Le Havre is a success remains controversial. Nevertheless, in 2005 it was named a World Heritage Site.

Essentials

❶ **Getting around** Within the greater urban area of Le Havre, an extensive public transport network runs from approximately 0600 to 2130, and with six all-night routes, by **Bus Océane** (T02 35 22 35 00, bus-oceane com). If you're planning to make several journeys in Le Havre by bus, ask the driver for a Ticket Ville. This pass is valid for one day, and costs little more than the cost of two ordinary return tickets.

⊜ **Bus station** Gare Routière, boulevard de Strasbourg, T02 35 26 67 23.

⊙ **Train station** Cours Lafayette/Cours République, T02 35 22 35 00.

❾ **ATM** There are four banks around the junction of place des Halles Centrales and rue Bernadin de St-Pierre; all have ATMs.

⊕ **Hospital** (for general emergencies) Hôpital J Monod, 29 avenue Pierre Mendés-France, Montvilliers, T02 32 73 32 32.

✚ **Pharmacy** There are several pharmacies in the town centre, including two in the main square – place de l'Hôtel de Ville – at number 68 (T02 35 41 26 75) and number 26 (T02 35 42 46 78).

↷ **Post office** 62 rue Jules Siegfried, T02 32 92 59 00.

❶ **Tourist information** 186 boulevard Clemenceau, T02 32 74 04 04, lehavretourisme.com, Monday-Saturday 0900-1900, Sunday 1000-1230 and 1430-1800, November-Easter closes 1830 weekdays, mornings only on Sunday.

Musée des Beaux Arts – André Malraux

2 bd Clemenceau, T02 35 19 62 62.
Wed-Sun 1100-1800 (1900 Sat-Sun), closed national holidays. €5, €3 concessions, under 26s free.

Built overlooking the waterside at the very mouth of the Seine, the glass and steel museum – with a large concrete sculpture in front – offers a cool, light-filled space to display a superb collection of Impressionist and Post-Impressionist artworks from some of its greatest names. Other areas are devoted to painting and sculpture from the 16th-20th centuries and contemporary art. The different galleries are linked by walkways like those on a ship. In particular there are over 200 works by Eugène Boudin, as well as several good examples of Monet, Renoir and Pissarro, and other Impressionists. Among Post-Impressionists, another Le Havre native, the Fauvist Raoul Dufy, is very well represented, with numerous paintings and drawings, many inspired by local life. Other Fauvists on display include Van Dongen and Friesz.

It's a fact...

Claude Monet is often credited as the originator of Impressionism. However, he was introduced to outdoor painting, and to techniques of depicting daylight and air, by Eugène Boudin in 1858. Boudin was a fellow artist living and working in Le Havre at the same time as Monet, and the two became friends and collaborators. Monet said of him, "If I became a painter, I owe it to Boudin".

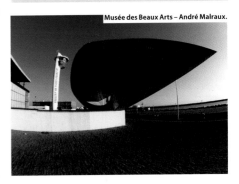

Musée des Beaux Arts – André Malraux.

Around the region

Inside Eglise St-Joseph.

Painters at Le Havre

Some of the world's most famous painters tried to capture on canvas the light and mood of the Seine estuary and Alabaster Coast around Le Havre. Here are the five greatest names and examples of their work in and around Le Havre.

❶ **Claude Monet** *Impression: Sunrise* (painted in Le Havre in 1872), *Pointe de la Hève* (painted at Ste-Adresse, Le Havre in 1864).

❷ **Gustave Courbet** *The Cliff at Etretat after the Storm* (painted at Etretat in 1869).

❸ **Raoul Dufy** *Fête Nautique au Havre* (painted at Le Havre in 1906).

❹ **JMW Turner** *Le Havre: Sunset in the Port* (painted at Le Havre in 1832).

❺ **Eugène Boudin** *L'Avant Port du Havre* and *Bassin du Havre* (1886 and 1887, among many painted at Le Havre in the late 1880s).

Eglise St-Joseph

Bd François 1er, T02 32 74 04 05.
Daily 1000-1800 (except during special ceremonies).

The city's most visible landmark, its distinctive octagonal spire rising to 110 m, has been acclaimed one of Europe's greatest monuments to the post-war reconstruction. This large church, built of concrete and completed in 1957 after Perret's death, is arguably his masterpiece, although whether it can be called beautiful remains debatable. Outwardly the shape resembles a rocket, while the spacious interior seems more like an auditorium than a church. Perret dedicated it to the memory of the victims of the 1944 bombings. He pictured the tall slender spire as a lighthouse – 6500 shards of coloured glass set into the concrete supposedly allowing ever-changing light through the building. This works well on a bright sunny day, which causes a mosaic of colour to be scattered around the angular interior.

Appartement Témoin (the Show Flat)

186 bd Clemenceau, T02 32 74 04 04.
Tours €3, on Wed, Sat and Sun 1400-1700 (tour starts every hour from 1 place de l'Hôtel de Ville) – book at tourist office.

A rare and fascinating exhibit, Perret's Show Flat reveals the humane ambition that lay behind the architect's designs for the new Le Havre. Many of the revolutionary ideas he incorporated into his apartment blocks have now become normal: plenty of light, built-in kitchens, central heating, and chutes in which to throw rubbish. The flat is furnished with the inexpensive but stylish mass-produced furniture of the early 1950s, and all the latest mod cons of the period.

Ste-Adresse

Spread across the sea cliffs north of the city centre, this lofty, airy residential suburb has good views over the port and out to sea. Here the 19th-century Fort de Ste-Adresse – one of several forts built to defend the Seine estuary – has been laid out as an attractive park and botanic gardens called **Les Jardins Suspendus** (Hanging Gardens). Ideal for a rest or stroll, it features a wide variety of rare and exotic plants from around the world.

Les Bains des Docks – thermal baths in Le Havre

As part of a continuing improvement of Le Havre's dockside area, 'Roman' baths designed by leading modern architect Jean Nouvel have been installed. Light-filled, with glass and mosaic decor, the complex has several pools of different temperatures and suites of treatment rooms. See page 144.

Lyons & Bray

On its east side, the wide open fields and occasional copses of Seine Maritime's high chalk plateaux give way to larger, denser wooded areas and more small-scale, varied cultivation. The extensive forests of Eu, Eawy and Lyons are among the most beautiful beech woods in France, cut across with footpaths and bridleways. The Pays de Bray, in Normandy's northeast corner, is a pretty, tranquil region of green fields, orchards, and meadows where cattle are reared for their rich milk, made into the gourmet cheese of Neufchâtel. From Neufchâtel to Gournay a striking depression is carved into the landscape, edged with a chalky ridge, known as the Boutonnière de Bray (the Bray Buttonhole). Among the few towns of any size in this area, Forges-les-Eaux has long been, as its name suggests, both an iron-working centre and a health-giving spa. The Pays de Bray merges and overlaps with the Pays de Lyons (which lies mainly in the Eure *département*), most of which is within the Forêt de Lyons, a 10,700-ha patchwork of ancient beech woods and bright cornfields. Within the forest, you'll find Mortemer Abbey, founded by a king and haunted by a ghostly queen, and the pretty little woodland town of Lyons-la-Forêt.

Abbaye de Mortemer (Mortemer Abbey)

T02 32 49 54 34, mortemer.free.fr.
Exterior open 1330-1800, €6, €4 child 6-16 years;
interior open on guided tours 1400-1800,
May-Sep daily, Oct-Apr weekends only,
additional €3.

The Mortemer Cistercian community was founded
in 1134 on grounds given for the purpose by
Henry I. The monks, charged with maintaining the
Forêt de Lyons as a hunting ground for the Dukes
of Normandy, were responsible for much of its
present-day appearance. They cleared land for
cultivation, built hamlets and laid many tracks
through the woodland. At the time of the
Revolution, the abbey was largely destroyed and
its stonework carted away for reuse.

The ruins of Mortemer are hidden in the woods
just off the road to Les Andelys. Head southwards
out of Lyons-la-Forêt on D2. The third turning on
the left leads to a narrow lane which runs very
steeply down to the valley of the Fouillebroc
stream and a shallow lake created from the waters
of the stream. Beside it stand fragments of
imposing stone walls and arches, what remains of
the original monastery where Henry I had the
fateful dinner of lampreys (similar to eels), which
killed him – he died in Lyons-la-Forêt. Attractive
cloisters survive from the original building.

At a discreet distance stand late 17th-century
buildings erected in an effort to re-establish the
community. These today contain an interesting
museum of monastic life, with deer and ponies
wandering at liberty in the extensive grounds. The
old monastery and its grounds are said to be
haunted by a number ghosts of monks and even of
a cat; the most distinguished ghostly presence is
that of Queen (or Empress) Matilda of England,
granddaughter of William the Conqueror, daughter
of Henry I, mother of Henry II.

Essentials

❶ Tourist information **Forges-les-Eaux**: Rue Albert
Bochet, T02 35 90 52 10, forgeseleseaux-tourisme.fr,
variable opening times. **Lyons-la-Forêt**: 20 rue de
l'Hôtel de Ville, T02 32 49 31 65, paysdelyons.com,
Easter-mid October Tuesday-Saturday 0930-1215 and
1400-1730, Sunday 1000-1200 and 1400-1630; mid
October-Easter Tuesday-Saturday 1000-1200 and 1400-
1700. **Neufchâtel**: 6 place Notre Dame, T02 35 93 22 96,
neufchatel-en-bray.com and neufchatel.fr, Tuesday-
Friday 0930-1230 and 1400-1830, Sunday in high season
1030-1230.

Tip...

Lyons and Bray online:
paysdelyons.com
paysdebray.org

Dovecote of Mortemer Abbey.

Château de Fleury-la-Forêt

About 7 km from Lyons-la-Forêt on D14,
T02 32 49 63 91, chateau-fleury-la-foret.com.
Open 1400-1800 (Jul-Aug daily, other months
Sun only), closed mid-Nov to mid-Mar, €7,
€6 child.

A well-preserved 17th-century grand country
house in elegant grounds, the building has kept its
old wine cellars, chapel, kitchen and laundry, and
today is the setting for a good museum of historic
toys and dolls. In the château, three atmospheric,
grandly furnished rooms are let as unusual and
modestly priced chambres d'hôtes.

Château de Vascœuil – Centre d'Art et d'Histoire

Vascœuil, T02 35 23 62 35, chateauvascoeuil.com.
Apr-Jul and Sep-Nov Wed-Sun 1430-1800,
Jul-Aug daily 1000-1830. €8, €5.50 child/
concessions, €20 family ticket.

This charmingly restored, fortified stone-built
15th-century manor in Normandy style, standing in
its handsome green park, has been an important
contemporary art museum and cultural centre
since 1970. In the grounds there's a large 17th-
century circular dovecote as well as a sculpture
park with some 50 works, including some by
leading names of post-war art, among them Dali,
Vasarely, Braque and Cocteau. The interior of the
building is used from mid-March to mid-November
for three annual contemporary art exhibitions –
Spring, Summer and Autumn. Note that the name,
Vascœuil, is pronounced with a silent 's'.

Close by is the attractive, busy village of **Ry**,
which it is thought served as the model for Yonville
l'Abbaye in Flaubert's *Madame Bovary*.

Forges-les-Eaux

Poised above the Bray 'buttonhole', Forges is in a
lovely part of the Bray countryside. It gets the
Forges of its name from the days when this was a
centre of ironwork, but that ceased centuries ago.

Green Avenue: London–Paris cycleway

A 218-km cycle path, partly open already, is being
laid all the way between St Paul's Cathedral
in London and Notre Dame Cathedral in Paris.
Designated as the Avenue Verte (sometimes locally
known as La Route Verte), it crosses Upper Normandy
via the Pays de Bray, following the route of a former
railway line beside the D1 from Dieppe to Neufchâtel,
continuing to Forges-les-Eaux, then towards
Pontoise and Paris.

Today it's *les eaux*, the waters, which dominate at
this modest country town, with a little spa resort
complex on the south side. Run by casino
operators Partouche, it includes a comfortable and
well-equipped hotel with a wide range of spa
treatments, as well as a casino and a good
restaurant, all in a quiet and attractive setting at
the edge of a park.

Lyons-la-Forêt

Hidden in the middle of the majestic beech woods
of the Forêt de Lyons, romantic Lyons-la-Forêt is
the main town in the Pays de Lyons – though in
reality it is just a simple woodland village with a
population of under 1000. It has had many historic
royal and ducal connections, not least that Henry I
of England died here following a meal of lampreys
– a lamprey is a creature like a blood-sucking eel
– at nearby Mortemer Abbey. Lyons makes an ideal
base for exploring the region. With its old
flower-decked half-timbered houses, especially the
magnificent ensemble around the long, narrow
wooden *halles* (covered market) in the main
square, it is wonderfully picturesque all year round.
Understandably, it attracts a lot of visitors. Perhaps
the best time to visit is in autumn, when leaves
have turned to bright colours and the busloads of
summer daytrippers have departed. The village is
at its quietest on Tuesdays and Wednesdays, when
many of the shops are closed.

Neufchâtel-en-Bray

The capital of the Pays de Bray, though not its largest town (Gournay is larger), Neufchâtel gives its name to the locally produced heart-shaped cheese, which gourmets consider one of the greatest cheeses in France. Neufchâtel is also a centre for other Bray cheeses. Almost destroyed in the war, and rapidly rebuilt, it's not an especially attractive place. Yet it has a pleasant atmosphere, with good markets on Tuesday and Saturday mornings. The town's **Eglise Notre-Dame** (place Notre-Dame) is an interesting old church and, in a 16th-century manor, the **Musée Mathon-Durand** (Grand'Rue St-Pierre, T02 35 93 06 55, Apr-mid Jun and mid-Sep-Oct Sun only 1500-1800, mid-Jun to mid-Sep Tue-Sun 1500-1800, closed Nov-Mar, €2.60, €1.15 child and concessions) is a museum of regional arts taking a thorough look at ironwork, pottery and cider-making.

Neufchâtel makes a convenient starting point for trips into the **Forêt d'Eawy** (the name is pronounced Ee-aa-vee). This extensive mature beech forest lies west of the town, and is crossed by impressive walks and drives. North of Neufchâtel, the small **Basse Forêt d'Eu** and larger **Haute Forêt d'Eu** are similar mature beech woods reaching towards the Picardy border. Just outside Neufchâtel in the direction of Dieppe, the 15th-century **Château de Mesnières-en-Bray** (T02 35 93 10 04, Jul-Aug daily, otherwise Apr-Oct at weekends only – phone to check latest situation, 45-min guided tours only 1430-1830)) was damaged by fire in 2004, and is still being repaired. With its white round towers under black slate roofs, and its fine Cour d'Honneur, it looks like a Loire château placed in the Norman countryside, and is indeed based on the Château de Chaumont on the Loire. The château and its grounds are in use as a college of horticulture and forestry. Just 4 km further on, the church at **Bures-en-Bray** has a twisted octagonal wooded spire. Although the brick façade is a post-war replacement, most of the church is 13th century and it contains 14th- to 16th-century sculpture.

Seine Valley above Rouen

Napoleon declared that Paris, Rouen and Le Havre were "but a single town, whose main street is the River Seine." True, the mighty river, winding and twisting, is navigable all the way from the English Channel into the French capital, but along the way the Seine passes through very different lands, whose ancient differences persist to this day. From Rouen to the eastern edge of Normandy is all part of the Vexin, a historic region divided into two when Normandy came into being with the River Epte as its frontier. On one side of the Epte lay the Vexin Français, with Pontoise as its capital. On the other side of the river was the Vexin Normand, bone of contention between the French and the Anglo-Normans. It's thoroughly peaceful now, and is an interesting, attractive region of woods and farms. Along the north bank of the Seine, chalky white escarpments mark the edge of the river plain. Les Andelys, on the north bank, is the region's main centre. On the other side of the river, Vernon was constructed as a border town by Rollo, founder of the Norman duchy. Cross the Seine again and continue upriver to reach Giverny, home of the great Impressionist, Claude Monet. The village of Giverny, on the eastern border of Normandy, is where Claude Monet, the 'father of Impressionism', made his home after he had become successful.

Monet's house.

Giverny

La Fondation Claude Monet

84 rue Claude Monet, T02 32 51 28 21,
fondation-monet.fr.
Apr-Nov 0930-1800. €6, €4.50 students and
child over 12, €3.50 child 7-12, €3 disabled,
under 7s free.

Claude Monet's house, now a national monument,
is officially known as La Fondation Claude Monet.
He moved here in 1883 and at once began work
creating the exquisite gardens behind his new
home. He acquired an additional piece of land, on
the other side of a lane adjoining the garden, and

Tip...

Monet's house and garden are a major tourist
attraction. To avoid the long queues to get in, book
your ticket in advance at fondation-monet.fr. It's
less crowded first thing in the morning. Better still,
make your visit early or late in the season. On an April
morning, you can have the place to yourself.

this is where the famous lily pond can be found,
subject of dozens of paintings in his latter years.
The interior of the house, simply fitted out and
decorated with the Japanese prints that so
interested Monet, is impeccably preserved and is a
fascinating example of a home in 1926 (the date of
Monet's death). Abandoned after 1926, the house
fell into disrepair and the gardens went to seed for
50 years. In 1977 the Académie des Beaux-Arts
moved in and spent three years restoring Monet's
house and garden to their original condition.

Essentials

ℹ Tourist information Les Andelys: 13 avenue du Général de Gaulle, T02 32 21 08 02, pays-vexin-normand.com. **Vernon**: Maison du Temps Jadis, 36 rue Carnot, T02 32 51 39 60, cape-tourisme.fr, May-September Tuesday-Saturday 0900-1230 and 1400-1800, Sunday 1000- 1200, October-April closes 30 minutes earlier on weekdays and closed Sunday.

Musée des Impressionnismes

9 rue Claude Monet, T02 32 51 94 65, museedesimpressionnismesgiverny.com. Apr-Oct 1000-1800, last admission 1730, check for temporary closures. €6.50, €4.50 students/ teachers/unemployed, €4.50 child 12 and over, €3 child 7-12, under 7s free.

Giverny's former Museum of American Art became (in 2009) the Museum of Impressionisms, a quiet place to enjoy modern painting and a shaded garden. The curious name, with its plural, reflects the intention to explore not just the original Impressionists, but the impact of the movement and the artistic developments that followed it.

Les Andelys

Les Andelys is two separate villages – **Petit Andely** on the bank of the Seine facing an island in midstream, and **Grand Andely** 1 km inland – that have merged to form a single small town. Grand Andely is now mostly modern, while Petit Andely is picturesque and historic.

Château Gaillard

T02 32 54 41 93. Mid-Mar to mid-Nov Wed-Mon 1000-1300 and 1400-1800. €2.50 child 10 and over, under 10s free.

Rising high on the edge of a white riverside cliff next to the Les Andelys, Château Gaillard gives a superb view of the river in both directions. This is the white fortress built (and designed) by Richard the Lionheart in a single year, 1196. The position of the castle, its dashing whiteness, together with the speed with which it was raised, earn it the name *gaillard* – which suggest a bold, stylish swagger. It is reached by a 30-minute steep climb on a footpath from Petit Andely, or by car from Grand Andely. While all that remains is ruins, an impression of how daunting and well-defended the site was quickly becomes clear. The castle's main section stands closest to the cliff edge, while a second section protects the landward approach, and is itself heavily fortified. During Richard's lifetime, it served its purpose in discouraging any French incursions into Normandy. When Château Gaillard passed to King John, the French moved into Les Andelys and began a lengthy siege. They eventually found a way into the castle… the outfall from the latrines. Having taken it, they were free to advance on Rouen. In later years, Les Andelys prospered and was the site of a river toll, a chain stretched across the Seine preventing passage to any vessel that had not paid.

Vernon

On the Seine's left bank, just 4 km downstream from Giverny, Vernon is a pleasant town somewhat overlooked by visitors, originally built as a border defence by Rollo, Normandy's first duke. You can get an attractive view of it from the river bridge, which arrives in the old heart of town. Especially photogenic is the Vieux-Moulin, standing in midstream, relic of an older bridge. The newer part of town is laid out with pleasant avenues.

La Tour des Archives

T02 32 51 39 60.
Apr-Sep Tue-Sun 0915-1215 and 1415-1830,
Sun 1015-1215; Oct-Mar Tue-Sat 0915-1215
and 1400-1730.

La Tour is the remnant of a castle, built after the
French had taken Normandy. It's worth exploring,
and the sentry walk gives another good view.

Musée Poulain

Rue Dupont, T02 32 21 28 09.
Apr-Sep Tue-Fri 1030-1230 and 1400-1800,
Sat-Sun 1400-1800; Oct-Mar 1400-1730.

Vernon's museum covers local prehistory and
art – and surprisingly is the only museum in the
Eure *département* with any Impressionist paintings,
as well as some post-Impressionists. Its highlights
are works by Monet and Bonnard, but there is also

a small Vuillard, and well worth seeing are works by
the daughter of Monet's second wife, Blanche
Hoschedé-Monet (1865-1947). Vernon has an old
church with modern stained glass, and preserves a
few fine half-timbered houses, one of the best of
them being the **Maison du Temps Jadis**, which is
now the tourist office (see box opposite).

Château de Bizy

T02 32 51 00 82.
Apr-Nov 1000-1200 and 1400-1800, €7.80, €5 child.

Just on the edge of Vernon, the Château de Bizy is a
masterpiece of 18th-century neoclassical
architecture, with Regency woodwork and rich
Gobelins tapestries. The château's park, with its
statuary, fountains and ponds, has lovely walks.

Seine Valley below Rouen

Twisting wildly in its wide flat valley, the River Seine continues its erratic journey from Rouen to its estuary at Le Havre. On both banks rise old abbeys and fortresses, evoking the time, almost a thousand years ago, when this waterway was Normandy's main thoroughfare. The gaunt ruins of Norman castles like the Château de Robert le Diable (near Rouen) and Lillebonne (near Le Havre) lend a fairy-tale look to the scene in places. Even the last remnants of the once-great Norman abbey of Jumièges are redolent of the majesty and importance of those powerful monasteries. Another great church stands by the river at Caudebec-en-Caux, beside the graceful Pont de Brotonne, built in 1977. Almost all the towns and sights are on the north bank, as it was easier to harbour boats here. Up to the post-war period, the Seine presented a huge obstacle to land travellers; until the Pont de Tancarville was built in 1959, there was no bridge across the river between Rouen and Le Havre. Much of the way, the river skirts the mature woodlands of the Forêt de Brotonne, now protected as a Parc Naturel Régional. Close to Le Havre, the river broadens to become a vast estuary, and the eye is filled with that space and light which the first Impressionists longed to capture on canvas.

On the Seine's right bank, at the foot of the Pont de Brotonne, the small town of Caudebec was once a thriving river port. For centuries, one of the attractions of Caudebec and the 4 km of riverbank between here and neighbouring Villequier – at the Spring and Autumn equinoxes – was the *mascaret*, or tidal bore, that used to sweep up the Seine from Le Havre, getting higher and higher as the river narrowed. Often catastrophic (Victor Hugo's daughter and son-in-law were among the many who were drowned when they came to observe it), it was eventually brought under control in 1965 and no longer reaches great heights.

Caudebec was renowned too for its wealth of medieval half-timbered houses. When the town centre was set on fire by retreating Germans, almost all were destroyed, although a notable survivor of the flames is the lovely 13th-century **Maison des Templiers** (rue Basin) with its arcaded front. This history is told in the **Musée de la Marine de Seine** (av Winston Churchill, T02 35 95 90 13, Apr-Sep 1400-1830, Oct-Mar 1400-1730, €3.30, €2 child and concessions). Today the town is best known for its 15th- and 16th-century Flamboyant Gothic masterpiece, **Eglise Notre-Dame**. A few paces from the church is place du Marché, where a market has been held every Saturday morning since 1390.

Eglise Notre-Dame

Rue Jean Prévost.
Usually daily 0800-1800.

"The most beautiful chapel in my kingdom," as Henri IV described it, has glorious intricately carved stonework inside and out, especially on the west façade. There is an early 16th-century organ, and superb 16th-century stained glass, including a fine rose window on the west front.

Essentials

❶ Tourist information Information about the lower Seine valley area is available from Office de Tourisme Caux Vallée de Seine, place du Général de Gaulle, Caudebec-en-Caux, T02 32 70 46 32, tourismecauxseine. com, Tuesday-Saturday 1000-1200 and 1400-1800, with other branches at Lillebonne and Bolbec.

Abbaye de St-Wandrille

T02 35 96 23 11, st-wandrille.com.
Daily 0615-1300 and 1400-1915, free.

Standing in the countryside 2 km from Caudebec are the vestiges of the Abbaye de St-Wandrille, originally founded in the seventh century. Almost nothing survives of the Norman and medieval abbey buildings that stood here, except the 14th-century cloisters. However, the Benedictine order returned to the site in the 1930s; the monks' church is a former 13th-century tithe barn brought here from La Neuville-du-Bosc, in the Eure.

On a hilltop behind the villages of La Bouille and Moulineaux, on the Seine's south bank, right beside Autoroute A13, rises the ruined castle of 'Robert the Devil'. Its towers and arches command an immense view over the river and all the Rouen area. There is no entry to the buildings, but the view rewards a climb. There is no historical record of anyone being known by the name Robert the Devil. Many suggestions have been made; the French Ministry of Culture has noted that it may refer to Robert Courteheuse, Duke of Normandy from 1087 to 1096. The existing castle was originally a 13th-century reconstruction, altered again in the 14th century, and largely destroyed in the 15th. It was closed to the public in 2003, damaged by fire in 2007, but is currently being restored. Below the castle, the village of La Bouille is a pretty spot.

Abbaye de Jumièges.

Abbaye de Jumièges

Rue Guillaume-le-Conquérant,
T02 35 37 24 02, jumieges.fr.
Apr-Sep 0900-1830, Oct-Mar 0930-1300 and
1430-1830, change of season dates may vary. €5.

As soon as one steps among the extensive, majestic ruins of this legendary 10th- and 11th-century abbey, it's clear that they give only a hint of how impressive these monumental buildings of white stone must once have been. The abbey's churches were considered among the supreme examples of Norman architecture at its best. Just enough remains to set the imagination working, rebuilding walls and ceiling vaults, and visualizing roofs and doorways and windows that today are missing.

The ruins are of the abbey churches, the older St-Pierre and the principal church Notre-Dame. Many other structures, such as the cloisters, have completely vanished. However, a good deal remains of the west front of Notre-Dame and its two towers, and part of the older St-Pierre, where painted decoration can still be seen. The two churches are connected by a vaulted passage.

The original seventh-century abbey on the site was attacked so often by the Viking raiders, and so comprehensively stripped of its treasures, that it effectively ceased to exist until Rollo promised to repair the damage his people had done in exchange for having a duchy to call their own. The Normans created their own solid but elegant Romanesque style, and Jumièges was rebuilt in the 10th century. It suffered during the Hundred Years War, but it was the French – not the Vikings – who dealt the fatal blow to the abbey and its buildings, during the Revolution in 1789. The whole site was sold at auction in 1793 to a building supplies merchant. The destruction was undertaken systematically, using gunpowder to bring down, for example, the famed lantern tower. In 1852, the site was again purchased by private buyers, the wealthy Lepel-Cointet family, who tried to prevent further damage and preserve what remained, even restoring part of the site. They are credited with preventing the total destruction of the abbey, which they sold to the state in 1946.

Forêt de Brotonne (Brotonne Forest)

Regional Nature Park information: Maison du Parc, Notre-Dame-de-Bliquetuit (on south bank, 4 km from Pont de Brotonne), T02 35 37 23 16, pnr-seine-normande.com/fr/index.php. Apr-Jun and Sep-Oct Mon-Fri 0900-1800, Sat-Sun 1200-1800 (may be closed weekends in Oct), Jul-Aug Mon-Fri 0900-1830, Sat-Sun 1000-1830, Nov-Mar Mon-Fri 0900-1800.

Much of the Lower Seine valley comes within the borders of the Parc Naturel Régional des Boucles de la Seine Normande (formerly the Parc Naturel Régional de Brotonne), which protects the diverse terrains on the riverbanks. The finest feature of the park is the huge Brotonne Forest, which once belonged to the monks at Jumièges Abbey. Most of the forest is a magnificent ancient woodland of beech, oak and pine. Paths and tracks, and roads too, allow for idyllic excursions among the shady trees. The village of **La Haye-de-Routot** on the southern edge of the forest, is a delightful haven of old woodland traditions and crafts.

Breadmaking in Forêt de Brotonne, known for its preservation of rural traditions.

South of the Seine

South of the Seine, the land is almost as flat and open as on the chalky uplands north of the river, with high plains, wide fields and extensive forests. Here, though, the country is more varied, more rustic and with more places great and small that deserve a visit. Almost all lies within the *département* of Eure. Despite industrial pockets, it's a region of appealing down-to-earth rural life, with good traditional cooking. The land is scattered with agricultural towns and villages of interest, ruined castles and monastic sites. Above all, there is plenty of water, with flowing streams and river valleys edged by woods. The wide River Risle flows into the Seine near the estuary, soon after passing through Pont Audemer, where little waterways thread through the town centre. Up the valley from here, the ruined abbey of Le Bec-Hellouin is set above the river, with good views. Another enjoyable river journey is along the little Iton, a tributary of the River Eure, following it as far as Evreux, the local capital much scarred by war. From here yet another river, the Rouloir, skirts the forests of Evreux and Conches to reach the medieval pilgrimage town of Conches-en-Ouche.

Abbaye Notre Dame du Bec-Hellouin (Le Bec-Hellouin Abbey)

T02 32 43 72 60, abbayedubec.com.
Daily Jun-Sep, 1-hr tours at 1030, 1100, 1500, 1600 and 1700 (Sun 1200, 1500 and 1800), Oct-May tours at 1100, 1500 and 1600 (Sun 1200, 1500, 1600), €5, €3.50 concessions, under 18s (or under 26s if resident in France) free.

The early history of this once-vast and wealthy abbey illustrates the close links between Normandy and England. Three abbots of Le Bec-Hellouin also became Archbishops of Canterbury, Lafranc in 1070, Anselm in 1093 and Theobald in 1138. From Le Bec-Hellouin also came bishops of Rochester and abbots of Westminster, Ely, Colchester, Battle, Chester and Bury St Edmunds. Set above the Risle, the abbey once dominated the valley, but today just a few scant remnants stand on the site.

Originally founded about 2 km downriver in 1034, on a little tributary called the **Bec**, the religious community moved to this site in 1060. By then it was already famous, because Lafranc, a leading theologian from Italy, had come here in search of simplicity and seclusion. Here he began teaching, and so established the renown of Le Bec-Hellouin. Lafranc's presence attracted other scholars, most notably Anselm of Aosta.

The abbey flourished and retained through the centuries its early reputation for scholarship and piety. So it remained until the Revolution, when Le Bec-Hellouin was abruptly closed and the community broken up. Soon after, the church and much else was pulled down. The best part of what remains are a great wall of the cloister with a

Conches.

Around the region

14th-century Gothic doorway, and the massive square 15th-century Tour St-Nicolas, which has been restored. In 1948, the land was returned to the Benedictines, who have once more established a community here.

The surviving 17th-century refectory has become the new abbey church. You may walk freely in its grounds, but the abbey is open only for the guided tours. Outside the abbey walls, the little village of **Le Bec-Hellouin** (lebechellouin.fr) rewards a stroll, too, its half-timbered buildings arranged in handsome terraces. Woods and fields climb the slopes to either side.

Conches-en-Ouche

Tourist information: place Briand,
T02 32 30 76 42, conches-en-ouche.fr.

Locally known simply as Conches, this peaceful and agreeable village stands on a long, narrow promontory ringed by the River Rouloir, in a lovely woodland setting. It is a popular centre of hunting, shooting and fishing. Several medieval houses survive along rue Ste-Foy, near the elaborate Gothic **Eglise Ste-Foy** housing the relics of Ste-Foy herself. The remains of this child saint were brought here, seemingly stolen from the magnificent Benedictine abbey church built especially for them at Conques in the Aveyron in southwest France, by the adventuring local lord, Roger de Tosny. He had been exiled from Normandy – it is not known what his crime had been – and went on campaign against the Moors in Spain, where it seems he made

a name for himself as particularly savage. He was eventually granted permission to return to Normandy, and stopped at Conques on the way, taking the opportunity to acquire part of the saint's venerated relics.

The village church in which Roger de Tosny kept the relics was rebuilt in the 15th century, with later additions in the 17th century. Inside is much good sculpture and woodcarving, but its greatest feature is excellent 15th- and 16th-century stained glass, considered some of the best in France. Behind the town hall, gardens lead to stony ruins of the sturdy 11th- and 12th-century **keep** (closed to the public) of the De Tosny family, encircled by a footpath and illuminated at night.

Evreux

Tourist information: Office du Tourisme, 1ter place Général de Gaulle, Evreux, T02 32 24 04 43, grandevreuxtourisme.fr.
20 Jun-20 Sep Mon-Sat 0930-1830, Sun 1000-1230; rest of year Mon-Fri 0930-1815, Sat 0930-1300 and 1400-1800.

The capital of the Eure *département* has been much scarred by war, to the point of being devastated by fire half a dozen times in its history and almost completely demolished by German bombing in 1940 and Allied bombing in 1944. Yet Evreux resiliently rebuilds and carries on. Today once again it is a vibrant town. Its modern centre, around place Général de Gaulle, is bright and pleasant. The nearby **Promenade des Berges de l'Iton** (Banks of the Iton Promenade) is a delightful riverside walk. Anything from the town's long history that did survive the war has been carefully preserved, including the 44-m-high 15th-century **Tour d'Horloge** in the main square, and, most notably, the 12th- to 17th-century **Cathédrale Notre-Dame**. Frequent repairs, in different centuries, have left the cathedral with a combination of architectural styles which is striking and oddly pleasing. There is a fine 16th-century wooden screen, and stained glass, some of which dates to the 13th century.

It's a fact...

Even if it is true that Sir Roger de Tosny stole some relics of Ste Faith, or Ste-Foy, from Conques abbey in the Aveyron, our judgment of him should consider that the monks of Conques very likely acquired them the same way. The original home of the remains of this improbable 12-year-old girl, supposedly beheaded by the Romans, was a fifth-century abbey church at Agen (Lot-et-Garonne *département*). A monk from Conques removed them in the year AD 866.

Tip...

An enjoyable way to see all the sights of Pont-Audemer is to ask the tourist office for their leaflet 'Welcome to Pont-Audemer'. It contains a little self-guided tour, leading you along the prettiest streets to everything of interest in the town centre.

Pont-Audemer

Don't be deterred by the modern development and the traffic encircling this ancient river port town. Its old centre is well preserved, with narrow streets lined with half-timbered houses, many with wrought-iron balconies decorated with flowers; and little canals and waterways, as well as an arm of the River Risle, making their way towards the main river and the old port. Here and there in the old town you'll see former tanneries, as Pont-Audemer was once a centre for high-quality leather goods. Wander the streets on the left bank to the principal church, **Eglise St-Ouen**, which has

Pont-Audemer essentials

🚍 **Bus station** Bus services are daily except Sunday by Le Bus de Pont-Audemer; there are just two lines. There is no bus station, but the terminus is place Victor Hugo.
💲 **ATM** In the main street, rue de la République and across the river in place Verdun.
⊕ **Hospital** Centre Hospitalier de Pont-Audemer, 64 route de Lisieux, T02 32 41 64 64.
✚ **Pharmacy** Several, including two in rue Thiers and one in rue de la République.
✆ **Post office** 15 rue des Carmes, T02 32 20 12 70, Monday-Friday 0830-1800, Saturday 0830-1200.
🛈 **Tourist information** Place Maubert, T02 32 41 08 21, ville-pont-audemer.fr, Monday-Saturday 0900-1230 and 1400-1730. June-September, also open Sunday 1000-1200.

Renaissance stained-glass windows, as well as some vivid modern stained glass by Max Ingrand. Close by, the **Pont sur la Risle** crosses the minor branch of the Risle which passes through the town centre, and gives views of the waterside houses.

Pont-Audemer.

Sleeping

Hôtel Aguado €€
30 bd de Verdun, T02 35 84 27 00, hoteldieppe.com.
Map: Dieppe, p104.
Ideally situated just a moment's walk from the port, the town centre and the beach, this popular, long-established and rather dated three-star straddles a side street. The main attraction is its position, not the amenities. It offers a choice of modest, homely rooms – perhaps a little too well-worn – either facing the beach or facing the town. Friendly and helpful reception.

Hôtel de l'Europe €€
63 bd de Verdun, T02 32 90 19 19, hoteldieppe.com.
Map: Dieppe, p104.
The two-star Europe has an unmissable wood-clad façade. Inside, decor is light and uncluttered, with a beach-resort feel. The spacious, sea-view rooms are smart and comfortably furnished.

Hôtel de le Plage €€-€
20 bd de Verdun, T02 35 84 18 28, plagehotel.fr.st
Map: Dieppe, p104.
Modernized, attractive and pleasant, this low-budget beachfront hotel makes a good base for Dieppe's town centre. Rooms are simple, brightly decorated, and adequately equipped. There's free Wi-Fi throughout.

Chambres d'hôtes
Villa des Capucins €
11 rue des Capucins, T02 35 82 16 52, villa-des-capucins.fr.
Map: Dieppe, p104.
This charming and attractive red-brick cottage in the evocative Le Pollet area is a cosy guesthouse, near to the heart of things yet away from the bustle of the town centre. It has a lovely garden.

Villa Florida €
24 Chemin du Golf, T02 35 84 40 37, lavillaflorida.com.
Map: Dieppe, p104.
Perfect for the golf course, this unusual B&B is a *chambre d'hôte de charme*. It has very comfortable, richly furnished rooms and the proprietor is a keen fan of yoga.

La Terrasse €
Route de Vasterival, T02 35 85 12 54, hotel-restaurant-la-terrasse.com.
Quiet, comfortable, friendly accommodation tucked away in countryside on the cliff top at the western edge of Varengeville, this country-house style hotel has fine views of the sea. Decor is simple and modern. There's a very attractive restaurant with good cooking, see page 137.

Grand Pavois €€€-€€
15 quai Vicomte, T02 35 10 01 01, hotel-grand-pavois.com.
A smart three-star hotel overlooking the harbour, the Grand Pavois has generously sized rooms with plain and simple modern furnishings and decor. Some have a particularly fine view. There's a relaxing piano bar on the ground floor.

Mer €€-€
89 bd Albert 1er, T02 35 28 24 64, hotel-dela-mer.com.
This unpretentious modern two-star is right on the beachfront, with the children's play area next door, and right above a busy brasserie. The casino is not far away. Rooms are simply but pleasantly decorated and adequately equipped, some with sea views and balcony, though the rear rooms have a less pleasant prospect. There's free Wi-Fi.

Hôtel Normandy €
4 av Gambetta, T02 35 29 55 11, normandy-fecamp.com.
Basic and unpretentious modern comfort is on offer for very modest prices in this white-fronted former coaching inn standing beside the church of St-Etienne, on a corner near the port. Some rooms have sea views. Downstairs is the restaurant and brasserie Le Maupassant, see page 137.

Domaine St-Clair – Le Donjon
€€€
Chemin de St-Clair, T02 35 27 08 23, ledonjon-etretat.fr.
Luckily *donjon* means not 'dungeon', but 'keep', rather a grandiose name for this splendid Anglo-Norman country house and belle epoque holiday villa with views across the town to the sea. Rooms are comfortably equipped and very varied; most are large – vast would be a better description in some cases. The hotel stands in its own attractive grounds, and has a heated pool, a library and an elegant gourmet restaurant. There is golf and riding nearby.

Dormy House €€€-€
Route du Havre, T02 35 27 07 88, etretat-hotel.com.
A cliff-edge position with wonderful views adds to the appeal of this handsome 19th-century manor house in its own grounds. Rooms are spacious and comfortable, varying from relatively simple to luxurious, so there's a big price range. Standard rooms look out on the grounds, while superior rooms have a sea view. The hotel has an excellent restaurant, see page 137.

Manoir de la Salamandre
€€-€
4 bd Coty, T02 35 27 17 07, manoirdelasalamandreetretat. com.
This picturesque half-timbered manor house preserves numerous historic touches, exposed beams, polished wood and four-poster beds. Rooms are charming and adequately equipped, very varied in size, some presented as family rooms.

Pasino €€€
place Jules Ferry, T02 35 26 00 00, pasino-lehavre.fr.
Arty, chic and stylish, this comfortable, well-equipped modern hotel is part of the Casino Partouche, and has an atmosphere of self-indulgence and pleasure. Rooms are spacious, staff helpful, and there's free Wi-Fi. In addition to its own casino, the hotel has three restaurants and a luxurious spa (closed Tuesday and Wednesday), where you can go straight from your room in a bathrobe.

Vent d'Ouest €€€
4 rue de Caligny, T02 35 42 50 69, ventdouest.fr.
In a typical Quartier Moderne building well placed near the main shopping area in avenue Foch and close to the waterfront, this quiet, friendly hotel has a bright marine feel. Rooms are

sometimes on the small side, but are comfortably furnished in pine, in an attractive, homely style, especially those equipped with kitchenettes and intended for long stays. The hotel has a useful restaurant and bar.

Art Hôtel €€
147 rue Louis Brindeau, T02 35 22 69 44, art-hotel.fr.
Quirky touches – for example, the elevator made to look like a shower cubicle – enliven the simple, decor at this Quartier Moderne building nearly opposite the entertainment complex Le Volcan. Furnishings are modern, some rooms small, and staff helpful.

Novotel Le Havre Bassin Vauban €€
20 cours Lafayette, T02 35 19 23 23, novotel.com.
With its blue neon sign illuminating the port near the station, the Novotel offers the modern comforts typical of this mid-range, well-priced chain. Interiors are designed to reflect Le Havre's 1950s modernity, and the restaurant aims for a modern style of cuisine.

Terminus €€
23 cours de la République, T02 35 25 42 48, grand-hotel-terminus.fr.
Ideal for a short stopover, this hotel opposite the railway station is functional and straightforward. It's popular with business travellers, with its

reasonable prices, calm atmosphere and soothing, low-key decor. It has its own simple inexpensive restaurant and bar.

Richelieu €

132 rue de Paris, T09 64 39 68 94, hotel-lerichelieu-76.com.
Looking a little out of place in an arcaded row of shops, this little hotel offers small, basic but homely and comfortable rooms, brightly and individually decorated with tiny bathrooms attached. It has a friendly, genuine feel, is clean and well kept, provides free Wi-Fi access and is located in the Quartier Moderne city centre.

Lyons & Bray

Licorne €€€€-€€

27 place Benserade, Lyons-la-Forêt, T02 32 48 24 24, hotel-licorne.com.
This handsome half-timbered former coaching inn has been part of the Lyons scene since 1610. With friendly, genuine and attentive staff, furnishings and decor that combine tradition with elegance, and varied but comfortable rooms in grey tones (with exposed wooden beams), it remains a top place to stay in Upper Normandy. Its restaurant La Licorne Royale (see page 138) is also outstanding.

Forges Hôtel €€€

Av des Sources, Forges-les-Eaux, T02 32 89 50 57, forgeshotel.com.
Prices are for full board: bed, breakfast, and dinner including drinks. The focal point of a complex beside a green park on the edge of town, this modern hotel with dark, stylish, comfortable interiors has swimming pools, lounges and spa treatments. It adjoins a casino with a smart restaurant where meals are included in your stay.

Grand Cerf €€

20 place Isaac Benserade, Lyons-la-Forêt, T02 32 49 50 50, grandcerf.fr.
A comfortable traditional inn that has been here for centuries, Le Grand Cerf reopened at the end of 2009 after being extensively refitted. It's a sister hotel of classier near neighbour Licorne, whose acclaimed young chef Christophe Poirier also oversees the management of the Grand Cerf's restaurant.

Lions de Beauclerc €€-€

7 rue de l'Hôtel de Ville, T02 32 49 18 90, lionsdebeauclerc.com.
Furnished with antiques, but equipped with modern comforts (including free Wi-Fi) and with a home-from-home feel, this brick-built hotel is also an antiques shop – as well as a restaurant and crêperie. Note a €5 price hike for Saturday night stays.

Chambres d'hôtes

Château de Fleury-la-Forêt €€

Near Lyons-la-Forêt, T02 32 49 63 91, chateau-fleury-la-foret.com.
This imposing privately owned 17th-century mansion in elegant grounds is open to visitors, but also has three grandly furnished bedrooms let as unusual and modestly priced chambres d'hôtes. Breakfast is served in the fine historic kitchen.

Auberge du Beau Lieu €

2 route de Montadet, 2 km from Forges-les-Eaux, T02 35 90 50 36, aubergedubeaulieu.fr
Closed Jan and part of Feb, Mon (except for lunch between Easter and 11 Nov) and Tue.
This rustic B&B and restaurant in the midst of Bray country offers three comfortable, simply furnished and attractive bedrooms, in a quiet and peaceful setting. The restaurant serves traditional French cooking, which can be enjoyed on a shady terrace in summer, or by a cheerful fireside in winter.

Seine Valley above Rouen

La Chaîne d'Or €€€-€€

25-27 rue Grande, place St-Sauveur, Petit-Andely, T02 32 54 00 31, hotel-lachainedor.com.
Closed Oct-May Mon-Tue, 3 weeks in Jan and some national holidays.
On the Les Andelys waterfront, this creaky old 18th-century

tollhouse takes its name from the revenues raised from the river tolls which it gathered. It's now a hotel and restaurant of great charm, with greenery cloaking the façade, a riverfront garden and elegant, comfortable bedrooms. The ground floor dining room with beams and a warm, comfortable atmosphere, has river views and delicate, imaginative cuisine.

Evreux Le Relais Normand €
11 place d'Evreux, Vernon, T02 32 21 16 12, hoteldevreux.fr.
A 17th-century mansion that's loaded with historic atmosphere and evocative decor, the Evreux is well placed in the town centre. A traditional, unpretentious family-run small hotel it offers rooms, arranged around an inner courtyard, that are simple, clean and comfortable. Staff are helpful and friendly, and the hotel has its own restaurant.

Chambres d'hôtes
Le Bon Maréchal €€-€
1 rue du Colombier, Giverny, T02 32 51 39 70.
In Monet's day, this was the small bar where he used to enjoy a little drink with friends. Nowadays it's a small and friendly guesthouse with a cottagey feel, and three delightful, simple and uncluttered homely bedrooms. Outside there's an garden and, just a short stroll away, Claude Monet's house.

Seine Valley below Rouen

Le Clos des Fontaines €€€€-€€
191 rue des Fontaines, Jumièges, T02 35 33 96 96, leclosdesfontaines.com.
Closed for 2 weeks over Christmas and New Year.
Very comfortable and well equipped, with many attractive and romantic touches – rich fabrics, four-poster beds, wooden beams, exposed brick – every room in this hotel has its own distinctive character and colour scheme. The smaller rooms have a pleasing neat style, while the pricier junior suites are positively sumptuous. Close to the abbey.

South of the Seine Valley

Belle Isle sur Risle €€€€-€€€
112 route de Rouen, Le Baquet, Pont-Audemer, T02 32 56 96 22, bellile.com.
Open mid-Mar to mid-Nov and for New Year.
Just outside town (in the Rouen direction), standing on an island in the River Risle in its own 2 ha of grounds with lawns, roses and mature trees, this 19th-century manor house now serves as a country-house-style hotel. The bedrooms, all different in size and shape, are decorated in classic style, well equipped and furnished with period furniture. Leisure facilities include sports amenities, indoor seawater

bathing and an outdoor swimming pool. There's a good restaurant (closed at lunchtime on Monday, Tuesday and Wednesday), serving French gastronomic cuisine in a conservatory or in the indoor dining room hung with large paintings and antique mirrors.

Auberge de l'Abbaye €€
12 place Guillaume-le-Conquérant, Le Bec-Hellouin, T02 32 44 86 02, auberge-abbaye-bec-hellouin.com.
Closed Tue, Wed in winter and Dec-Jan.
An 18th-century inn in the centre of this quiet and beautiful village, the Auberge looks over the village green and is replete with old Normandy character and rustic charm, with flower boxes, wooden beams, bare brick and a warm welcome. Rooms are simple, clean, adequately equipped and decorated in pale colours, with a home-from-home feel. The hotel also benefits from a good restaurant.

Eating & drinking

Dieppe

A La Marmite Dieppoise €€€
8 rue St-Jean, T02 35 84 24 26.
Tue-Sat Sun lunch and dinner,
Sun lunch, closed 20 Jun-3 Jul,
21 Nov-9 Dec, 8-16 Feb.
Map: Dieppe, p104.
Tucked away in a little street
between the church and the
port, the restaurant gives its
name to its very own culinary
invention, a rich stew of lobster,
mussels and several kinds of fish
with crème fraîche sauce.
Arguably, it's worth coming to try
it. The rest of the menu, though,
is unremarkable, and prices are
on the high side. The best of the
desserts include a warm apple
tart. Sometimes indifferent
service. Decor, relieved by
romantic touches like candles, is
faux historic, with bare brick, tile
floors and beams.

Tip...
Dieppe specialities include
marmite dieppoise – a rich stew of
fish, shellfish and crème fraîche,
the authentic version must be
made at the restaurant of the
same name; *sauce dieppoise* –
white wine and shellfish sauce;
and *sole dieppoise* – sole cooked
in a sauce of butter, white wine,
mussels and mushrooms.

Les Voiles d'Or €€€
*Chemin de la Falaise, T02 35 84
16 84, lesvoilesdor.fr.*
Wed-Sat lunch and dinner, Sun
lunch, closed 2 weeks end Nov.
Map: Dieppe, p104.
High on the right bank, near the
Notre Dame de Bon Secours
chapel, this modern restaurant is
comfortable and stylish, with
polished pale wood and hanging
voiles d'or – golden sails. There
are two well-prepared set
menus, constantly changing as
they reflect what's best in the
market that day.

Le Bistrot du Pollet €€€-€€
*23 rue Tête de Boeuf,
T02 35 84 68 57.*
Tue-Sat lunch and dinner,
closed 2 weeks in Apr, 2 weeks
in Aug, 10 days in Jan.
Map: Dieppe, p104.
On the island in the harbour, this
convivial little bistro packed with
diners is a top spot for eating out
in Dieppe. Decor is on a seafaring
theme. Cooking is good, with
plenty of hearty traditional
Normandy fare, *dieppoise* sauces,
fresh fish and generous portions.

Chez le Gros €€
35 quai Henri IV, T02 35 82 28 03.
Lunch and dinner.
Map: Dieppe, p104.
Dieppe harbour is packed with
modest fish and shellfish
restaurants attracting tourists
rather than locals. This waterfront
wine bar and bistro looks like a
plain and simple café, but it's

Pick of the picnic spots
The stony beach, 10 minutes'
walk from the town centre, has
magnificent views of the coastal
cliffs. Behind the beach is a wide
promenade with benches. On
Saturday, find a tasty lunch at
the market. On other days, head
to *épiceries fines*, such as C'Royal
in Grand'Rue and Olivier in rue
St Jacques for local Neufchâtel
cheese, ready-to-eat hot dishes,
sausages, bottles of local dry
cider or Loire wine.

quite an exception – authentic
good French cooking that's more
about foie gras and *magret de
canard* than the ubiquitous
moules-frites.

La Musardière €
*61 quai Henri IV, T02 35 82 94 14,
restaurant-lamusardiere.com.*
Feb-Jun and Sep-Dec Wed-Sun
lunch and dinner, daily Jul-Aug.
Map: Dieppe, p104.
Small, brightly lit, here's the
classic cheap and cheerful fish
and shellfish restaurant on the
quayside, with friendly service
and affordable set menus.

Cafés & bars
Café Suisse
*19 arcades de la Bourse,
T02 35 84 10 69.*
Map: Dieppe, p104.
This other one-time haunt of
Oscar Wilde – when he wanted
to get away from the smart
set – survives as a classic, correct

local brasserie, popular with locals. At mealtimes it serves simple traditional fare at modest prices. Outdoor tables are under an arcade.

Café des Tribunaux
Place du Puits Salé, T02 32 14 44 65.
Map: Dieppe, p104.
The tall, attractive, gabled tavern has been the haunt of many great names of art and literature. It's a smart, well-kept place, with a restored pre-war look inside, where stained-glass panels encircle an upper gallery. There are wrought-iron tables and chairs on the little square outside. It remains a lively, atmospheric, dominant presence in the town centre, with a view on to Grand'Rue. Excellent morning coffee, freshly squeezed orange juice and croissants. A painting of the Café des Tribunaux by Walter Sickert, showing the café as it was in 1890, hangs in the Tate Britain in London.

Varengeville-sur-Mer

La Terrasse €€
Route de Vasterival, T02 35 85 12 54, hotel-restaurant-la-terrasse. com.
Daily lunch and dinner.
In the Hôtel la Terrasse (see page 132), this attractive, spacious restaurant, hung with pale fabrics, has lovely views out to sea. The accomplished and

skilful menus focus on fresh local fish and shellfish, with dishes like mussels in roquefort sauce, local specialities such as *sole à la dieppoise*, and favourite desserts such as *tarte tatin*.

Fécamp

Auberge de la Rouge €€
1 rue Bois de Boclon on Route du Havre, 2 km from Fécamp, T02 35 28 07 59, auberge-rouge.fr.
Tue-Sat 1215-1330 and 1915-2100, Sun 1915-2100.
In the pretty, rustic setting of a flower-decked old coaching inn there are plenty of wooden beams and exposed brick. Here good traditional French cooking is served in three cosy dining rooms, using all the best ingredients of the market.

Le Vicomte €€-€
4 rue Président R Coty, T02 35 28 47 63.
Mon-Tue, Thu-Sat for lunch and dinner, closed end Apr and beginning May, 2 weeks in Aug, Christmas and New Year.
Tasty, classic French bistro cooking is served at this busy, appealing little place not far from the port area. What you'll be offered all depends on what's best in the market – menus of the day are written on a blackboard.

Le Maupassant €
4 av Gambetta, T02 35 29 55 11, normandy-fecamp.com.
Mon-Sat all day.
On the ground floor of the Hôtel Normandy (see page 132), this popular restaurant and brasserie serves classic French and Normandy fare, such as foie gras followed by cod in cream sauce, with some well-priced set menus.

Etretat

Dormy House €€€
route du Havre, T02 35 27 07 88, etretat-hotel.com.
Lunch and dinner.
The restaurant in this cliff-edge hotel on the south side of town has magnificent sea views, and a choice of tempting set menus. Dishes are delicate and imaginative, with plenty of fresh fish and local touches, such as fresh cod open ravioli with mushrooms and leeks cooked with cider and shellfish sauce. Desserts include roast apricots with lavender ice cream.

Le Bicorne €€
5 bd Président R Coty, T02 35 29 62 22, hws.fr/lebicorne.
Thu-Mon for lunch and dinner (daily in school holidays).
In a warm and cosy setting of polished timber and wood panels, excellent fish and seafood dishes – and plenty of classic meat dishes as well – are

presented in striking, colourful arrangements. Try the monkfish with *pommeau* sauce. Service is warm and genuine.

La Salamandre €€-€
4 bd Coty, T02 35 27 17 07, lasalamandreetretat.com.
Lunch and dinner.
In a picturesque half-timbered manor house in the town centre, the restaurant of this small hotel has rustic, cosy decor of exposed beams, polished wood and gingham cloths. Everything served is certified organic, or is the fresh catch of the day. Dishes have a simple, natural quality, such as three fresh fish grilled with olive oil, and there's a vegetarian selection.

Le Havre

Jean-Luc Tartarin €€€
73 av Foch, T02 35 45 46 20, jeanluc-tartarin.com.
Tue-Sat for lunch and dinner.
Ambitious gastronomic cuisine has won this acclaimed restaurant a Michelin star. Shellfish is strongly featured. Speciality lobster and young pigeon dishes have striking exotic flavour combinations such as tea, coffee or cocoa. The slick, contemporary decor is in muted pale and dark chocolate tones.

La Petite Auberge €€€
32 rue de Ste-Adresse, T02 35 46 27 32.
Tue-Sun 1200-1330 and 1930-2100, except Sun dinner and Wed lunch. Closed 3 weeks in summer, 1 week in autumn, 2 weeks in Feb.
Towards the heights of Ste-Adresse, this cosy dining room of an old inn has a façade of painted wooden beams, plush decor and furnishing with rich cream and maroon colours and white napery. Fresh market produce is used to make a range of dishes such as rissoles of parma ham and ricotta.

Brasserie Pasino €€
Place Jules Ferry, T02 35 26 00 00, pasino-lehavre.fr, casinolehavre.com.
Daily 1200-2400.
This brasserie with harbour views is one of three eating places in the Casino Hotel Partouche. Affordable menus range from brasserie classics and mixed grills to Normandy specialities.

L'Acrobate €
77 rue Louis Brindeau, T02 35 41 24 42.
Mon-Sat 0900-2300.
This simple and unassuming city centre brasserie attracts locals for a drink or a bite to eat, and serves good simple French classic dishes on a fixed price menu very reasonably.

Cafés & bars
Beer and Billiards
96 rue René Coty, T02 35 42 44 88.
Outside the Quartier Moderne, this pub-like sports bar is on two floors, with a good selection of drinks, 17 billiard tables, and major football matches shown on big TV screens.

Le Chillou
41 rue Chillou, T02 35 41 75 49.
This small, long-established city centre bar can become lively with locals popping in for a drink or a snack. One of its attractions is the patron's warm personality. Another is the daily menu of home-cooked favourites at modest prices.

Lyons & Bray

La Licorne Royale €€€- €€
27 place Isaac Benserade, Lyons-la-Forêt, T02 32 48 24 24, restaurant-lyons.fr.
Lunch and dinner.
In one of the village centre's half-timbered houses, tables are richly laid in white napery, in elegant rooms where in one, for example, framed Brassai photos are spaced around the wall. Imaginative high-quality cooking, including such dishes as a fricassee made with a *poularde* of the Dame Noire breed with girolles mushrooms, have won prestigious national awards for the chef, Christophe Poirier.

Auberge du Beau Lieu €€
2 route de Montadet, 2 km from Forges-les-Eaux, T02 35 90 50 36, aubergedubeaulieu.fr.
Wed-Sun for lunch and dinner (and Mon lunch between Easter and 11 Nov), closed Jan and part Feb.
Good, thoroughly French fare is the order of the day here, featuring such delicacies as foie gras, snails, frogs' legs and a good choice of wines. Eat on the shady terrace in summer, or enjoy cosy fireside dining in the cooler months, at this rustic restaurant in pleasant Bray countryside just outside Forges.

Les Lions de Beauclerc €€-€
7 rue de l'Hôtel de Ville, Lyons-la-Forêt, T02 32 49 18 90, lionsdebeauclerc.com.
Wed-Mon for lunch and dinner.
A comfortable traditional-looking country dining room serving such dishes as soups, snails, salads and fish of the day, it also places the emphasis firmly on crêpes and galettes, which can be eaten as the main course.

Seine Valley above Rouen

La Chaîne d'Or €€€-€
25-27 rue Grande, place St-Sauveur, Petit-Andely, T02 32 54 00 31, hotel-lachainedor.com.
Oct-May Wed-Sun for lunch and dinner, closed 3 weeks in Jan.
On the Les Andelys waterfront, this 18th-century tollhouse is now an utterly charming

riverside hotel and restaurant. There's a fine old dining room with rich fabrics, wooden beams, river views and set menus of clever, tasty and unusual dishes such as roast *magret de canard* with peaches and nectarines and a peach sauce. Lunchtime menus from Wednesday to Friday are especially good value.

Le Relais Normand €€
11 place d'Evreux, Vernon, T02 32 21 16 12, hoteldevreux.fr.
Mon-Sat for lunch and dinner.
A big stone fireplace, with stags' heads displayed on either side, together with white napery, upholstered chairs and wooden beams give charm to this restaurant in the Hôtel d'Evreux, an evocative 17th-century town centre mansion that's now a modest but atmospheric hotel. Good, classic French and traditional Norman cooking is served, and in summer can be eaten in the courtyard.

Baudy €€-€
81 rue Claude Monet, Giverny, T02 32 21 10 03.
Apr-Oct, Mon 1000-1800, Tue-Sun 1000-2130.
This 'historical restaurant', as it is called, with its distinctive patterned pink brick façade, provides lunch and dinner in folksy old-fashioned dining rooms with bare boards, gingham cloths and paintings hanging on the pale walls. It's renowned as a former hotel

where countless well-known artists have stayed. Outside, there's a charming rose garden. Set menus offer classic simple French fare and salads.

Le Bistro des Fleurs €
73 rue Carnot, Vernon, T02 32 21 29 19.
Tue-Sat for lunch and dinner, closed about 1 week in Mar, 3-4 weeks in Jul or Aug.
As the name says, it's a bistro-style restaurant, with a bar, posters on the walls, and classic French dishes of the day chalked on a blackboard. Good cooking at modest prices.

Seine Valley below Rouen

Auberge des Ruines €€€
17 place de la Mairie, Jumièges, T02 35 37 24 05, auberge-des-ruines.fr.
Thu-Mon lunch and dinner except Mon and Thu evenings in winter, closed 2 weeks end Aug, 2 weeks Christmas/New Year, 1 week in Feb.
An utterly charming half-timbered restaurant and outdoor terrace just opposite the abbey, the emphasis is on simple but high-quality gastronomic dining. Try, for example, bass and mushroom oil with garlic-flavoured *crème chantilly*.

Listings

Auberge du Bac €€€-€
*2 rue Alphonse Callais, Jumièges,
T02 35 37 24 16.*
Wed-Sun 1200-1330 and
1900-2100.
Half timbered, with hanging
flower baskets, and inside, a cosy
rustic ambience with old-
fashioned chairs, tiled floor, red
and white cloths and copper
pans hanging on the walls, this
attractive riverside restaurant
offers several set menus of rich
Normandy and French cooking.
There's plenty of fresh fish and
shellfish, and even a between-
courses *sorbet Normand* on
most menus.

South of the Seine Valley

Belle Isle sur Risle €€€€-€€€
*112 route de Rouen, Le Baquet,
Pont-Audemer, T02 32 56 96 22,
bellile.com.*
Mid-Mar to mid-Nov and for
New Year, dinner daily, lunch
Thu-Sun.
This ivy-covered manor house
on a river island just outside
town is a haven in which to enjoy
refined and relatively light
French gastronomic dishes with
intriguing combinations of
flavours; for example, upside
down pear tart with hot foie gras
and *cassis* vinegar. Vegetarians
are catered for. Choose between
the conservatory or the indoor
dining room hung with large
paintings and antique mirrors.

La Gazette €€€
*7 rue St-Sauveur, Evreux,
T02 32 33 43 40,
restaurant-lagazette.fr.*
Mon-Fri for lunch and dinner, Sat
for dinner, closed most of Aug.
Stylish and contemporary-
looking inside and out, with
intriguing soft lighting, soft
colours and soft music in a
building with exposed timbers,
this elegant place is pricey but
serves wonderfully imaginative
good French cooking, such as
trout in a potato-bread crust
with spinach and herb cream.

Auberge de l'Abbaye €€
*12 place Guillaume-le-
Conquérant, Le Bec-Hellouin, T02
32 44 86 02, auberge-abbaye-
bec-hellouin.com.*
Wed-Mon for lunch and dinner
(Thu-Mon Oct-Mar), closed
Dec-Jan.
It's no surprise that locals come
from all the surrounding towns
and villages to eat at this rustic,
charming 18th-century
restaurant, with beams, low
ceilings and bare brick, in the
pretty village centre. Cooking is
traditional and reaches a high
standard. Among the highlights
is its *tarte au pommes*.

Le Canterbury €€-€
*3 rue de Canterbury, Le Bec-
Hellouin, T02 32 44 14 59.*
Wed-Mon for lunch and dinner
except Sun dinner.
Virginia creeper drapes the
half-timbered house where, in a
more modern interior, this
good-value restaurant serves
traditional yet imaginative
French and Norman seasonal
dishes without fuss. Prices are
modest, and set weekday
lunches especially good value.

Restaurant de la Tour €€-€
*1 place Guillaume-le-
Conquérant, Le Bec-Hellouin,
T02 32 44 86 15.*
Fri-Wed for lunch and dinner,
except Wed dinner, and Mon
dinner in winter.
In the pretty heart of the village,
this is an inexpensive place to
enjoy a friendly welcome and a
choice of quick, simple dishes
and classic French and Norman
cooking, such as *cuisse de canard
au cidre* (leg of duck braised in
cider). In fine weather, eat
outdoors on the terrace.

Le Cygne €
*2 rue Guilbaud, Conches-en-
Ouche, T02 32 30 20 60,
lecygne.fr.*
Tue-Sat for lunch and dinner.
Old wooden beams, tiled floors
and rustic decor in different
dining rooms give atmosphere in
this good classic local restaurant
specializing in foie gras and a
selection of traditional French
and Normandy dishes, well
prepared and presented.

Entertainment

Bars & clubs

Grand Casino Dieppe

*3 bd de Verdun, T02 32 14 48 00,
casino-dieppe.fr.*
Mon-Thu 2100-0300, Fri
2100-0400, Sat 2000-0400,
Sun 1600-0300.
Near the sea at the foot of the
château, Dieppe casino has slot
machines and simple, modern
gaming tables. It's far from
glamorous, but also has two
restaurants, a piano bar and
show theatre with occasional
cabaret or entertainment.

Festivals & events

Kite festival

*Ask the tourist office for the latest
festival information, or visit
dieppe-cerf-volant.org.*
Filling the sky with scores of
curious shapes and wild colours,
Dieppe Kite Festival is held in
September in even-numbered
years, and attracts kite-flying
experts from all over the world.

Theatre & cinema

Théâtre

*1 quai Bérigny, T02 35 82 04 43,
dsn.asso.fr.*
Tue-Sun 1400-1830.
At the end of the harbour, this is
the principal venue in Dieppe for
arts events, stage shows, world
music concerts, drama, modern
dance and a full programme of
arts performances and family
entertainment. There's also a
cinema showing a wide variety
of new art and popular films as
well as cinema classics. If you
want to see English-language
films, note that 'VO' means a film
is shown in its original language.

Etretat

Bars & clubs

JOA Casino

*1 rue Adolphe Boissaye, T02 35
27 00 54, joa-casino.com/
Nos-casinos/JOACASINO-Etretat.*
Daily from 1000.
With a pub-like feel, Etretat's
casino has slot machines, some
simple gaming tables, a bar
and restaurant, as well as a
programme of evening
entertainment like a disco or
jazz. The best feature is its
position on the beach, with
views towards the arch cliffs.

Le Havre

Bars & clubs

A fast-changing dance club
scene provides late-night
entertainment all week. Most
clubs are in the docks area, by
the Bassin du Commerce.

Lounge Bar Pasino

*Place Jules Ferry, T02 35 26 00 00,
casinolehavre.com/fr/Lounge-
Bar-Le-Havre.html.*
Fri and Sat 2000-0200.
This rather glamorous clubby
cocktail bar at the casino is the
place to relax with a drink and be
entertained by DJs or live music
from jazz to rock.

Music

Le Volcan – Le Havre National Stage

*Oscar Niemeyer, rue de Paris,
T02 35 19 10 10, levolcan.com/.*
Brilliant arts complex inside two
volcano-shaped structures, the
work of architect Oscar Niemeyer
(who, like Auguste Perret, is fond
of concrete). They stage
performances of modern dance
and classical music.

Seine Valley below Rouen

Festivals & events

Fête du Cidre du Pays de Caux

Caudebec-en-Caux.
End of Sep – not every year.
At apple harvest time, the big,
jolly Cider Festival takes over
Caudebec for a day. There's cider
making and tasting, as well as
traditional craftsmen and
women making and selling their
wares, processions, puppet
shows and local folk music.

Shopping

Music
L'Abordage
1 av Aristide Briand, Evreux, T02 32 31 86 80, abordage.net.
A short distance west of Evreux town centre, by the Cora commercial centre, this is the place to hear a good selection of live rock, pop and indie bands and performers from around the world.

Pub Mac Léod
45 rue Jean Jaurès, Evreux, T02 32 33 00 09.
Adorned with fireplace, beams and a choice of beers, packed at times, with a lively young atmosphere, this popular spot has an agreeable terrace at the back and hosts live gigs that attract big crowds. Happy hour Tuesday-Friday 1700-1900.

Tip...

Be wary of buying carved ivory in Dieppe. It is illegal to import ivory products into the UK, US or Canada unless they are over 100 years old, with accompanying documentation to prove their age and provenance. However, modern ivory carvers now at work in Dieppe generally use synthetic ivory or bone instead of the real thing.

Food & drink
Epicier Olivier
16 rue St-Jacques, T02 35 84 22 55, epiceriefine-olivier.fr, Tue-Sat 0800-1230 and 1400-1915, Sat no lunchtime closing, Mon afternoons in Jul-Aug.
This respected *épicerie fine* with its traditional tiled façade specializes in the best of fine foods. Cheeses are a speciality, but you'll find here too butter sold off the block, *fromage blanc* and crème fraîche ladled from tubs, as well as coffees, teas, Calvados and local produce. Service is brisk but helpful.

Market
Dieppe's traditional Saturday market attracts shoppers from across the region. Stalls run the length of Grand'Rue into place du Puits Salé, place Nationale, place St-Jacques, rue St-Jacques and the side streets. You'll find fresh produce from farms and fishing boats, fine displays of farm-made butter, charcuterie and cheeses (especially the local treat, Neufchâtel), baked goods, farm cider and apple juice, flowers, and stalls selling cooked dishes, especially hot roasted free-range chicken. Many of the fruit and vegetables are *bio* (organic). Other stalls offer honey and conserves, leather goods, kitchenware, CDs, souvenirs and clothes.

Food & drink
Palais Bénédictine
110 rue Alexandre le Grand, T02 35 10 26 10, benedictine.fr. Daily 1030-1245 and 1400-1800, slightly longer hours in summer.
The Benedictine distillery has its own boutique selling bottles of the liqueur at €25 for a litre, and a selection of unusual treats and delicacies filled or flavoured with it, such as 12 chocolates filled with Benedictine, for €8.

St-Vincent area between St-Roch public park and the beach is packed with classy little shops selling haute couture, gourmet specialities, jewellery, art and antiques.

Market
The big, bustling street market in avenue Réné Coty is held every Monday, Wednesday and Friday.

Shopping centres
Centre Commercial Grand Cap
Av du Bois au Coq, T02 35 54 71 71, grandcap.fr. Mon-Sat 0930-1930, except Auchan: Mon-Sat 0830-2130.
For shopping under one roof, head to the Grand Cap mall on the northern edge of the city. There's an Auchan hypermarket, and much else besides.

Espace Coty
Av René Coty, T02 32 74 86 87.
The area around avenue Foch, rue de Paris and avenue René Coty is full of chic fashion, accessories and jewellery stores, as well as top-quality gourmet food specialists, including a branch of Chocolatier Auzou. Coty shopping mall has 80 shops on three floors, as well as restaurants and cafés, plus a post office and a supermarket.

Lyons & Bray

Antiques
Antiquités Boulange
7 rue de l'Hôtel de Ville, Lyons-la-Forêt, T02 32 49 18 90, antiquites-lyonslaforet.fr.
Wed-Mon.
Adjoining the Hotel-Restaurant Les Lions de Beauclerc, this shop is crammed with antique furniture, silver and jewellery, paintings and other art, and more.

Markets
Most towns and villages throughout the region have street markets at least once a week. The local produce market is still held in the historic wooden Halles in the centre of Lyons-la-Forêt every Thursday, Saturday and Sunday morning. In the Bray country, Forges-les-Eaux holds its market on Thursday and Sunday mornings, while at Neufchâtel-en-Bray the market is on Saturday morning.

La Boutique des 4 Fermières
22 bis rue de l'Hôtel de Ville, Lyons-la-Forêt, T02 32 49 1973,
Mon 1000-1200 and 1430-1830, Thu-Fri 0930-1230 and 1430-1830, Sat 0930-1230 and 1430-1900, Sun 1000-1200.
At this store four lady farmers sell local gourmet products and farm produce.

South of the Seine

Art & antiques
Le Bec-Hellouin Ceramics and Crafts
Les Ateliers du Bec, Abbaye Notre-Dame du Bec-Hellouin, T02 32 43 72 60.
When not at prayer, the monks of Bec-Hellouin spend their hours in workshops producing delicate, high-quality hand-made ceramics, porcelain and faience with elegant, striking designs

and decoration. In particular, they make dinner services and chinaware, lamps, vases and candleholders. Everything is for sale in their boutique at the abbey. Prices reflect the beauty and high quality, with dinner plates at about €20 or salad bowls from €22.50. Also on sale in the shop are unusual candles, CDs of liturgical music and books.

Food & drink
Chocolatier Auzou
34 rue Chartraine, Evreux, T02 32 33 28 05.
Tue-Sat 0930-1230 and 1400-1900.
This is a favourite spot for wonderful hand-made chocolates and mouth-watering soft *macarons* as well as an array of their own imaginative confections like *zouzous d'Auzou* and *pommes Calvados* (real Calvados inside!), and traditional local treats like *Caprice des Ursulines*. All should be sampled.

Activities & tours

Dieppe

Fishing

Quayside firms run fishing trips and sea cruises. Ask at the tourist office for latest details.

Golf

Golf de Dieppe-Pourville, 51 route de Pourville, T02 35 84 25 05, golf-dieppe.com.
Daily all year 0900-1800.
This renowned high-quality 18-hole golf course was established as long ago as 1897. Considered a fairly challenging course, it hosts competitions from March to October.

Petit Train tour

Petit Train Touristique de Dieppe, quai Henri-IV (beside tourist office), T02 35 04 56 08.
Easter-end Sep, 1030-1930. €7, €5 child (4-10).
All aboard for a fun ride around town. The tour lasts about an hour and takes in the beach and town centre sights.

Thermal baths
Les Bains des Docks
Quai de la Réunion, T02 32 79 29 55, vert-marine.com/les-bains-des-docks-le-havre-76.
Sep-Jun Mon and Wed 0900-2100, Tue, Thu and Fri 1200-2100, Sat-Sun 0900-1900; Jul-Aug daily 1000-2000. €5, €4 child 8-12. Aqua-gym is open only for certain periods during the day Mon-Sat.

This beautiful gleaming white dockside public baths was designed by a leading modern architect, Jean Nouvel. It has several indoor and outdoor pools of different temperatures, including a heated outdoor Olympic pool, as well as sports and play areas, an 'aqua-gym' for fitness sessions in the water and treatment rooms.

Côte d'Albâtre

Boat tours

Tourisme et Loisirs Maritimes 15 rue Vicomté, Fécamp, T06 16 80 24 10.
€13.50, €9.50 child.
See the coast and port on a guided tour aboard a 63-seater boat. The outing takes 1½ hours.

Golf

Golf d'Etretat, route du Havre, Etretat, T02 35 27 04 89.
Apr-Aug 0830-1900 daily (except as affected by special events and competitions), Sep-Oct Wed-Mon 0900-1800, Nov-Mar Wed-Mon 0900-1700.
On top of high chalk cliffs beside Etretat, with their dramatic arches stepping into the waves, is spread the green expanse of the town's golf course. Founded in 1908, it soon became prestigious: many of its members were British aristocrats. It is still highly rated, in a remarkable setting, and the clubhouse has an excellent restaurant.

Le Havre

Cultural tours

Le Havre Ville d'art et d'histoire, 186 bd Clemenceau, T02 35 21 27 33, ville-lehavre.fr.
Prices may vary slightly depending on the tour. Approx €5, €3 students, €3 child 12-18, under 12s €3 during summer school holidays, under 12s free at all other times, unemployed free. Visit to the Appartement Témoin €3, free for under 26s.
Le Havre city council and tourist office run a full programme of guided visits to Le Havre's cultural and architectural attractions. Each tour lasts 1-1½ hours and focuses on a single site or aspect of the city. There are also tours to the Hanging Gardens and Le Volcan arts centre. The tourist office can provide information and make bookings.

Petit Train tour

Office de Tourisme, 186 bd Clemenceau, T02 32 74 04 04, le-havre-tourism.com.
Runs during school holidays only, usually needs to be booked in advance, €5.50, €3 child 5-12 years, €14 family ticket.
The 'little train' snakes through the city to the sights on a choice of itineraries: for example, Le Havre World Heritage Site (one hour), or Le Havre Ste-Adresse (45 minutes).

Le Volcan arts centre, Le Havre.

Contents

Brasserie in Deauville, Le Pays d'Auge.

A t the heart of Normandy lies Calvados. This one *département* possesses in abundance all that the duchy has to offer. In Calvados are told the great stories of the Norman Conquest and of the Normandy landings. To learn more about either of these, visit Caen and Bayeux, historic towns not far from the coast. Along the Calvados seashore are five of the six Landing Beaches where on D-Day 1944 the English-speaking world returned, in an act of immense self-sacrifice, to rescue France. By contrast with that dramatic shore, travel along the waterfront of the Côte Fleurie, in the other direction from Caen, to find a string of swish beach resorts – especially Deauville – which have fond memories of the elegant belle epoque a century ago.

Inland, a profound rusticity prevails. In the Pays d'Auge, arguably the loveliest and most picturesque part of Normandy, quiet lanes thread through a green landscape of lush pasture, grazing cows, orchards laden with blossom in spring and apples in autumn. To either side are thatched village houses and half-timbered manor houses. This is the country that produces many great names of the cheeseboard, as well as good Normandy cider and the finest Calvados.

What to see in...

...one day
In Caen, focus on the majestic church of William the Conqueror, **Abbaye aux Hommes**. Drive to **Beuvron-en-Auge** in **Pays d'Auge**. Continue on to D37 for the Orne river crossing at Pegasus Bridge, said to be the first place liberated in 1944. Travel to **Arromanches-les-Bains**, on Gold Beach, brimming with evocative D-Day sights. D516 leads to **Bayeux**, where the **Bayeux Tapestry** is the top priority. Return to Caen on N13.

...a weekend or more
Add the **Mémorial de Caen** to your Caen must-sees. Take D79 to the **Landing Beaches**, following the coast to **Arromanches**. Turn inland into **Bayeux**. Cut through west of Caen to Thury-Harcourt, at the edge of the hilly Suisse Normande. Turn east to **Falaise**, William's birthplace, and **Château de Vendeuvre** into the **Pays d'Auge**. Stroll in **St-Pierre-sur-Dives**, and head to **Beuvron-en-Auge**. Join D765 to return to Caen.

Dotted with apple orchards, Pays d'Auge is well known for its cider and Calvados.

Caen

Caen needs time to be thoroughly explored. Fortified by William the Conqueror, this city became his new capital of Normandy. The former capital of Rouen was, he felt, too vulnerable to attack from the Franks. The mighty rampart of his château is still the centre of the city, while the main shopping streets, the Vaugeux restaurant district and Quai Vendeuvre leisure area are all at its foot, extending away from the south side of the castle walls. Several of Caen's other principal sights ring the edges of the city centre. Each one of them deserves unhurried attention, and you should allow plenty of time too for the journey from one to the other. The church of the Abbaye aux Hommes, for example, the Men's Abbey where William the Conqueror's tomb lies in front of the altar, stands at a very proper distance from the Abbaye aux Dames! Both are unmissable works of Norman architecture, built as part of the penance undertaken by William and his wife Mathilde for their incestuous marriage. For a moment's quiet repose, the lovely Jardin des Plantes lies north of the central district. It's on the way to Le Mémorial, a museum complex on the northern ring road dedicated to honouring those who died in the Second World War, providing a record of the conflict and explaining its background.

Le Château de Caen

Main entrance is accessed from rue Poissonnerie, in front of Eglise St-Pierre, chateau-caen.eu.
Free access.
Map: Caen, p152.

Climb the grass-covered slope and cross a dry moat to enter William the Conqueror's castle walls, which still dominate the city centre. A drawbridge and fortified gateway allow entry through Porte St-Pierre (opposite Eglise St-Pierre in the city centre) or the massive Porte des Champs (on the east side) into the heavily defended enclosure. The surprise inside is how little remains of the ducal buildings. The destruction of the original castle keep began at the Revolution and continued until the 19th century. There was further damage during the war. Instead the ramparts enclose a vast space broken up by a few small structures. The partly rebuilt, mainly 15th-century Eglise St-Georges once served the 'parish' living and working within the castle walls. The 17th-century Governor's Lodge, built against the southern ramparts, now houses the

Le Château de Caen.

Essentials

◐ Getting around A fast modern city transport system of 25 bus routes and two tram lines is operated by Twisto (T02 31 15 55 55, twisto.fr). Maps at the stops show which bus or tram you need to reach other parts of the city or to reach the sights. A single ticket costs €1.20, while a pass for 10 journeys costs €10.60. The 24-hour pass is a bargain at just €3.55. Tickets can be bought on the bus, or using ticket machines at the stops, or from the two Boutiques Twisto shops in Caen: 15 rue de Geôle, T02 31 15 55 55 and Théâtre, boulevard Maréchal Leclerc, T02 31 15 55 50, Monday-Friday 0715-1830, Saturday 1000-1645.

◐ Bus station Place de la Gare (no telephone enquiries). See page 273 for regional bus travel.

◑ Train station Place de la Gare, T02 31 83 70 47. See page 271 for regional rail travel.

◑ ATM There are several in the town centre; for example, in rue Strasbourg near the Château, on the corner of rue St-Pierre and in place Bouchard.

⊕ Hospital CHU de Caen, avenue de la Côte de Nacre, T02 31 06 31 06.

⊕ Pharmacy One of the most centrally located pharmacies is the **Grande Pharmacie du Progrès**, 41 rue St-Pierre, T02 31 27 90 90.

◑ Post office There are 16 post offices in Caen. The most centrally located is at 50 quai Vendeuvre, T02 31 27 16 70 61, Monday-Friday 0830-1830, Saturday 0830-1200.

❶ Tourist information Office de Tourisme, 12 place St-Pierre, T02 31 27 14 14, tourisme.caen.fr. April-June and September Monday-Saturday 0930-1830, Sunday 1000-1300, July-August Monday-Saturday 0900-1800, Sunday 1000-1300; October-March Tuesday-Saturday 0930-1300 and 1400-1800.

Musée de Normandie. The low, partly underground Musée des Beaux Arts was built against the eastern ramparts in the 1960s. Over on the west side, beside the ruins of the keep, stands one impressive remnant of the ducal period, the 12th-century **Salle de l'Echiquier** (Exchequer Room). Despite the name (which was given in the 19th century), this was the dukes' two-storey Great Hall, with kitchens on the ground floor and lavish banqueting chamber above.

Around the region

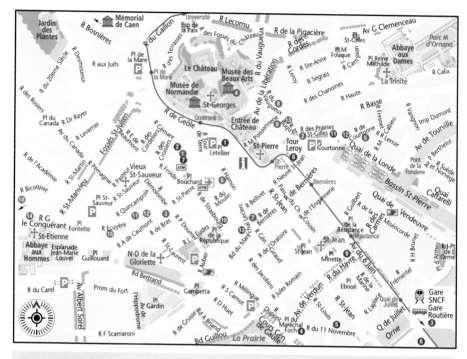

Caen listings

Sleeping
1 Central Hôtel *23 place Jean Letellier*
2 Dauphin Best Western *29 rue Gémare*
3 Etap Hôtel Caen Gare *16 place de la Gare*
4 Holiday Inn Caen Centre *4 place Maréchal Foch*
5 Hôtel Bristol *31 rue du 11 Novembre*
6 Hôtel de France *10 rue de la Gare*
7 Hôtel des Quatrans *17 rue Gémare*
8 Hôtel du Château *5 av du 6 Juin*
9 Hôtel du Havre *11 rue du Havre*
10 Hôtel Kyriad Caen Centre *1 place de la République*
11 Ibis Port de Plaisance *6 place Courtonne*
12 Mercure Port de Plaisance *1 rue de Courtonne*
13 Moderne Best Western *116 bd Maréchal Leclerc*

Eating & drinking
1 ArchiDona *17 rue Gémare*
2 Brasserie Martin *1 rue des Prairies St-Gilles*
3 Café Latin *135 rue St-Pierre*
4 Café Mancel *Musée des Beaux Arts, Le Château*
5 Incognito *14 rue de Courtonne*
6 La Maison d'Italie *10 rue Hamon*
7 La Normande *41 bd Maréchal Leclerc*
8 Le Bistrot *12 rue du Vaugueux*
9 Le Bouchon du Vaugueux *12 rue Graindorge*
10 Le Pressoir *3 av Henri Chéron*
11 Le Vertigo *14 rue Ecuyère*
12 Lounge Café *2 place Malherbe*
13 Maître Corbeau *8 rue Buquet*
14 Pain et Beurre *46 rue Guillaume le Conquérant*
15 Rose & Grey *27 rue Ecuyère*

Rent a bike from the V'eol hire stand.

Tip...

If you're staying a while, sign up for V'eol (T0800 20 03 06, veol.caen.fr), the town's bicycle-hire scheme. Once you have an account, a bike can be picked up (using your credit card) at stands all over town. The first 30 minutes are free; second, third and fourth 30-minute periods cost €1 each. Thereafter, it's €2 for each 30 minutes.

Musée des Beaux Arts (Caen Fine Arts Museum)

Le Château, T02 31 30 47 70, ville-caen.fr/mba.
Wed-Mon 0930-1800. Free.
Map: Caen, p152.

In an unobtrusive modern building of Caen stone just inside the Château entrance is the Fine Arts Museum. In a series of rooms, a wide range of artworks focuses mainly on 16th- to 17th-century French, Italian and Flemish painting, including pieces by Tintoretto, Breughel the Younger, Rembrandt and a good collection by minor figures. Among earlier periods, one of the museum's greatest possessions is Rogier van der Weyden's *Virgin and Child.* In downstairs rooms devoted to modern art, there are numerous pictures depicting Normandy scenes and landscapes, including lesser works by some of the greatest names, among them Dufy, Monet, Boudin, Bonnard, Vuillard, Corot and Courbet. Paintings showing pre-war Caen are especially interesting. The museum also hosts temporary exhibitions.

Musée de Normandie (Normandy Museum)

Le Château, T02 31 30 47 60, musee-de-normandie. eu.
Daily 0930-1800 (closed Tue Nov-May).
Permanent collection free, seasonal exhibitions €5.20, €3.20 concessions, children free.
Map: Caen, p152.

Interesting diverse collections all about Normandy include geology, archaeology, farming, history, folk culture, and how the region's traditional arts and crafts gave rise to its modern industries. There are also summer-long temporary exhibitions.

Tip...

Available at the tourist office, Caen Pass Tourisme is a little book of vouchers giving valuable discounts at numerous sights, attractions, shops and restaurants. The price? It's absolutely free.

Abbaye aux Hommes by night.

Eglise St-Pierre

Place St-Pierre.
Daily.
Map: Caen, p152.

Standing close to the main south entrance of the Château, St-Pierre is the highly decorated parish church of Caen city centre, a remarkable survivor of the wartime assault. Its rebuilt 75-m spire provides an easy-to-spot landmark. The building, constructed over a 300-year period starting in the 13th century, is a fine example of late Gothic, with an apse incorporating rich Renaissance ornamentation. Inside there is good stained glass, notably the rose window on the west front. Notice the amazingly detailed carved allegorical figures on some of the capitals. A display of photographs shows how the church looked immediately after the Allied bombing in 1944. What also makes the church especially interesting is that, following the damage caused in 1944, it is being painstakingly restored to its original condition. The result is newly carved Flamboyant and Renaissance white exterior stonework, giving an impression of how such churches looked when they had just been built.

Abbaye aux Hommes (Men's Abbey)

Esplanade Jean-Marie Louvel, T02 31 30 42 81.
Guided tours of the monastic buildings (town hall) daily at 0930, 1100, 1430 and 1600, with additional tours in Jul-Aug. €2.20, €1.10 concessions, children free.
Map: Caen, p152.

Although the Men's Abbey was founded by William the Conqueror (see box, opposite), most of what can be seen today dates from later centuries.

Death of a king

Not only was the birth of William 'the Bastard' disreputable, requiring him to fight rivals for the titles of Duke of Normandy and then King of England, but his death too was unseemly. At 59 and terribly overweight, William the Conqueror led a savage raid on the town of Mantes across Normandy's border with France. During the attack, he fell from the saddle and injured himself. He was rushed back to Rouen, but was beyond help. In his dying hours he sent money to Mantes to rebuild the churches he had just destroyed and on 9 September 1087 he died, with none of his family present. At once, according to Orderic Vitalis, those in attendance looted whatever they could carry from the body and from the room, and his corpse was unceremoniously abandoned, naked and unattended for days. As disputes raged over the inheritance

of his titles, the corpse began to decay. Eventually William was taken to the abbey church of the Abbaye aux Hommes in Caen, where he had wished to be buried. People gathered in Caen to watch the funeral procession, but a fire broke out, causing the crowds and the funeral cortege to rush away in terror. When at last they arrived at the church the service began, but was stopped by a man named Asselin, who claimed that he had never been paid for the land on which the church stood. After a wrangle about price, it was purchased from him there and then. As the service resumed, the rotting, obese corpse burst open. The mourners and congregation fled the stench and sickening spectacle, leaving monks to complete the rites and close the grave over William the Conqueror.

While much survives of the original abbey church (see Abbatiale-St-Etienne below), the monastic buildings themselves date mainly from as recently as the 18th century, when they were entirely rebuilt. Only the grand 14th-century Gothic hall known as the Salle des Gardes predates the reconstruction. The new abbey briefly served its intended purpose in the decades before the Revolution. Since 1965 they have been used as the **Hôtel de Ville** (town hall), with very attractive formal gardens laid out in front. Parts of the building can be visited on guided tours, which reveal a lovely cloister and exceptionally beautiful and elegant interiors containing the finest craftsmanship, especially in the oak-panelled former refectory.

Abbatiale St-Etienne

Daily 0815-1200 and 1400-1930. Free.
Map: Caen, p152.

Begun in 1067 and supposedly completed by 1081, the abbey's St-Etienne church is considered to be among the great buildings of Europe. Constructed in haste because William the Conqueror wished to be buried in the church (which in fact he was just six years after it was 'completed'), much more work remained to be done, and continued for some 200

years. The curious blend of 11th-century Norman Romanesque in its purest form with 12th and then 13th-century Norman Gothic construction is unexpectedly harmonious and serene. There is a sense of great size, with little adornment yet delicate proportions. In front of the altar lies a marble slab to mark William's tomb. The original tomb was destroyed in the Wars of Religion, and even the replacement was destroyed, in the Revolution. It is said that just a single thigh bone of the Conqueror remains buried in his grave.

It's a fact...

Caen was a prime objective for the Allied forces making their way inland from the Landing Beaches. However, Panzer tank divisions effectively protected the city. To wrest Caen from German hands, on 7 July 1944 Allied planes dropped 2500 tons of bombs on the city. Fighting for control of Caen continued until 22 August, by which time 75% of its buildings had been destroyed and thousands of its citizens killed.

What the author says

Call me a hedonist, but one of the things I *most* like about Normandy is the sense of abundance. This was always a productive land, a land of plenty and of quality. It is a Norman tradition to eat well – so well, indeed, that family meals could last hours, and it became necessary to pause between main courses for a *trou Normand,* literally the Norman opening or gap, filled with a tot of Calvados. Nowadays that way of eating is preserved only in the best restaurants or for celebration dinners, and the *trou Normand* is more likely to be a sorbet than a drink. Nevertheless Normandy remains a prolific region. You'll see it in the markets. Normandy's markets, with their cornucopia of produce from land and sea, are surely among the best in France. Arriving at the huge Sunday morning market in Caen for the first time was overwhelming. At once rustic and sophisticated, it fills the large central place Courtonne and runs – four aisles wide – down quai Vendeuvre beside the water. Here are farm-made Normandy cheeses and cream, stacks of strange looking *andouilles* and sausages, bottles of local cider and *poiré* (cider made from pears), the best of just-gathered vegetables, some of them enormous, oysters and other shellfish on ice, potted meats, eggs, flowers, breads and cakes and pastries, mountains of seasonal fruit, grapes by the kilo, piles of plaited strings of garlic, more kinds of olives than you knew existed, and much, much more – and that's without mentioning stalls selling ready-to-eat hot dishes to take away. And I noticed that while I wandered around dazed by the spectacle, matter-of-fact locals came briskly with their shopping baskets, perfectly accustomed to such a feast of quantity and quality.

Abbaye aux Dames (Women's Abbey)

Place Reine Mathilde, T02 31 06 98 98.
Church daily about 0900-1800, may be closed 1200-1400. Free. Former convent guided visits daily 1430 and 1600. Free.
Map: Caen, p152.

The penance required of William and Mathilde by the Pope for their incestuous union (they were cousins) was to found four hospitals and two abbeys. William decided that all should be in Caen. His Abbaye aux Hommes was matched by Mathilde's Abbaye aux Dames a mile away. Both were rebuilt in the 18th century, neither is still an abbey, but at both the church is an impressive survivor from the time of the Dukes. Now the Basse-Normandie Conseil Régional (Regional Council), the Women's Abbey suffered from some unsuccessful 18th- and 19th-century restorations. However, Mathilde's simple church in creamy stone, **Eglise de la Trinité** – much smaller than William's – remains a fine example of Norman Romanesque architecture, incorporating 12th- and 13th-century early Gothic developments. Inside, Mathilde lies beneath a slab of dark marble in the chancel. Narrow steps lead down to an atmospheric crypt packed with pillars. The neighbouring former convent buildings (guided tours only) include delightful three-sided cloisters, an oval lavatorium (washroom) and a spacious Hall with a twin staircase.

Abbaye aux Dames.

Le Mémorial de Caen

Esplanade Général Eisenhower, T02 31 06 06 45,
memorial-caen.fr.
Mar-Dec daily 0900-1900 (Tue-Sun 0930-1800
during approximate period 12 Nov-5 Feb). Ticket
desk closes 1 hr 15 mins before museum. €17.50
(€17); €15 (€14.50) children over 10, students,
over 60s and unemployed; free for under 10s,
war veterans and unemployed. Prices in brackets
for Oct-Dec 2010. Many more concessions
available; see website. Family pass €45
(for 2 adults and at least 1 child 10-18 years).
Temporary exhibitions may have a separate
entry charge, or may be free.
Map: Caen, p152.

A sombre memorial to those who died as a result
of the Second World War, Le Mémorial is also a
museum about the development of modern
warfare in relation to the social and political
background, progress and eventual conclusion of
that war. A large section is devoted to the French
experience, and another to the experience of the
world as a whole. In addition, it has taken on a
broader mission to oppose war and conflict. To

some extent, the task is too vast, with the result
that some aspects of the Second World War are
dealt with too sketchily. Others are examined with
impressive thoroughness.

Descend the spiral staircase at the start of the
exhibition which leads down, step by ominous
step, past posters and photographs and news
media of the period marking all the significant
dates, from 9 November 1918 down into the
growth of Nazism in Germany, the acquiescence of
other nations, and the eventual world war. There
the exhibition expands to track the political,
military and social course of the war, with a vast
amount of authentic historical material, including
such items as Nazi flags, the outfit worn by inmates
of death camps, military maps and genuine
weaponry. Important letters on display include one
from Albert Einstein to President Roosevelt
suggesting that nuclear fusion could form the basis
of a bomb. There are also wartime letters from
soldiers – including Germans – to their families.
Films using newsreel of the period are devoted to
key periods in the war, including a poignant and
fascinating account of the Battle of Britain.

Côte Fleurie

Between the estuaries of the Seine and the Orne, the sandy Calvados coast has been attracting high-class holidaymakers since the 19th century. A century ago the beach resort of Deauville was synonymous with fashionable elegance. Facing it across the River Touques, neighbouring Trouville catered for those respectable people who couldn't quite afford Deauville, and the smaller beachfront communities along the wide sandy seafront made every effort to capture something of the same style. Nowadays, on the Côte Fleurie just as everywhere else, there's a good deal less aristocratic refinement and a more everyday working-town atmosphere. Yet the old glamour has not quite gone, with plenty of well-dressed tourists strolling Deauville's wooden promenade in the short, busy summer season, visiting for a breath of sea air and a flutter at the races.

Strictly speaking, the cliffs east of Trouville belong not to the Côte Fleurie but to the Corniche Normande. At its northern and eastern tip, the picturesque, arty old harbour of Honfleur is one of just two places on this Calvados shore with any great history. The other, on the River Dives at the other end of the Côte, is Dives-sur-Mer. It was from the ancient port of Dives that William the Conqueror set sail to claim the throne of England.

Pretty-as-a-picture fishing harbour and much-loved haunt of the Impressionists, Honfleur is also a port with a considerable history. From here Samuel Champlain set sail in 1608 with a party of local men to colonize Canada. The centrepiece of the town is its charming **Vieux Bassin** (Old Harbour), alive with boats tied up against the cobbled quays, busy waterside bars and restaurants, *salons de thé* and art galleries, and all enclosed by tall, narrow buildings dark with slate. At the fortified harbour entrance stands **La Lieutenance**, the sturdy 16th-century Governor's House. Turn the corner into equally picturesque place Ste-Catherine with the fascinating **Eglise Ste-Catherine** at its centre. Constructed in Gothic style, but all of timber, not stone – and by shipwrights, not masons – it was built to thank God for the departure of the English at the end of the Hundred Years War. There's some exquisite wood carving inside.

It's a delight to wander the attractive streets of the old town centre, with their cobbles and small half-timbered dwellings. **Rue Haute** is especially attractive; the imaginative comic artist, writer and composer Erik Satie (1866-1925) was born at No 90, which now houses an entertaining museum about him and his work, known as the **Maisons Satie** (entrance is on the other side of the building at 67 bd Charles-V, T02 31 89 11 11, Wed-Mon 1100-1800, 1000-1900 in summer).

Essentials

ℹ Tourist information Quai Lepaulmier, T02 31 89 23 30, ot-honfleur.fr, Monday-Saturday 0930-1230 and 1400-1830 (1700 July-August, 1800 October-Easter), Sunday 1000-1230 and 1400-1700 (no midday closing July-August, Sunday mornings only October-Easter).

Honfleur harbour.

On the Beach by Eugène Boudin.

Musée Eugène Boudin

Place Erik Satie, T02 31 89 54 00.
15 Mar-30 Sep Wed-Mon 1000-1200 and
1400-1800, 1 Oct-14 Mar Wed-Mon 1430-1700,
Sat-Sun 1000-1200. €4.80 (€5.50 Jul-Sep); €3.30
students, children 10-18, over 60s (€4 Jul-Sep);
unemployed, professional artists, under 10s free.

A surprising museum for such a small town,
though a fitting one for a place so influential in the
development of modern art, the Boudin Museum
is renowned for its 19th and 20th-century
collections with a local emphasis. Here are works
by Monet, Jongkind, Courbet, Vallotton, Marais,
Dufy and a vast number by Boudin himself, who
was born in Honfleur and lived here as a child. In
addition, the museum displays interesting
contemporary Honfleur artists. An ethnographic
section is devoted to Normandy's historic regional
costumes, furnishings, toys and everyday objects.

Côte de Grace

The modern artists who gathered in Honfleur at
the end of the 19th century – among them
Pissarro, Cézanne, Corot, Courbet, Sisley, Monet
and Boudin – used to climb this slope with their
easels to paint, talk and enjoy a simple meal and
home-made cider at Mère Toutain's tavern (now
the luxury hotel **Ferme St-Siméon**). From Mont Joli,
on the way, views extend over the town and along
the Seine. At the top of the Côte de Grace hill a vast
panorama opens up, reaching right across the
immense estuary. However, things have changed
since the 19th century: a large crucifix now
dominates the hill, and the view takes in the
petrochemical refineries and industry on the far
side of the Seine. Close by, the little chapel of
Notre-Dame de Grace, originally 11th century, was
rebuilt in the 17th century.

Norman house on the seafront, Trouville.

Trouville

Tourist information: Office de Tourisme, 32 quai Fernand Moureaux, T02 31 14 60 70, trouvillesurmer.org.
Daily Nov-Mar 0930-1800, Apr-Jun and Sep-Oct 0930-1830, Jul-Aug 0930-1900.

Although established several years earlier, Trouville eventually lost ground in the 'class' hierarchy to Deauville, its neighbour across the River Touques. That distinction remains to this day, Trouville having a more popular appeal and workaday feel with its busy harbour and fishing quays where *fruits de mer* and the fresh catch are sold. It also has an all-year-round existence, making it perhaps the more agreeable out of season. The centre of activity, close to the quayside beside the River Touques, extends from the beach to the Pont des Belges, which crosses to Deauville. Grandiose

19th-century seaside villas ranged along the seashore, some designed as mock chateaux, give a flavour of the town's early years. The old wooden boardwalk still lends traditional charm to the wide beach. Near the promenade you'll find the town's casino and a very modest aquarium. More interesting is the **Arts and Ethnography Museum, Musée de Trouville Villa Montebello** (64 rue du Général Leclerc, T02 31 88 16 26, Wed-Mon, €2), housed in one of the old villas. Here is memorabilia

It's a fact...

Eugène Boudin's paintings of bourgeois holidaymakers on Trouville and Deauville beaches between 1865-1895 were revolutionary in their day, showing middle-class women at leisure in the open air, the wind catching at their hair and crinolines. They were also among the first ever paintings of families holidaying at a beach resort. It is striking that everyone on the beach, including the children, was fully clothed.

Beach at Deauville.

of the resort's heyday, as well as an entertaining collection of the colourful post-war French advertising posters of Raymond Savignac (1907-2002). It also hosts numerous temporary art exhibitions. The museum has a separate art gallery on the port quayside, the Galerie du Musée (32 bd Fernand Moureaux, T02 31 14 92 06, Wed-Mon, €2).

Deauville

Tourist information: Office de Tourisme de Deauville, place de la Mairie, T02 31 14 40 00, deauville.org.
Mon-Sat 1000-1800, Sun 1000-1300 and 1400-1700, except Jul-Aug and film festival Mon-Sat 0900-1900, Sun 1000-1800.

The long, wide boardwalk of wooden slats lying on the sand – called Les Planches – gives a lot of old-fashioned charm to Deauville's immense beach. Once frequented by the royal families of Europe, over 100 years later the resort can still claim a certain cachet. It has few must-see sights, but people-watching is the thing here. There's genuine money on display, especially at the top hotels and the gleaming casino, the racecourse and the yacht marina with its jostling boats. A number of

Tip...

The 15-km journey from Honfleur to Trouville on D513 takes a pretty route through woods and small villages and gives some lovely sea views. In summer it can be crowded on this little road, but in spring and autumn it's at its best.

It's a fact...

Deauville was laid out as a more refined alternative to Trouville at the suggestion of the Duc de Morny, half-brother of Napoleon III, after he visited the village of Dosville in marshes on the other side of the River Touques, in 1858. His spacious new town was an immediate success.

The covered market at Dives-sur-Mer.

prestigious summer events are held in Deauville – international polo championships, golf tournaments and a horse fair. The **Festival du Cinéma Américain** (American Film Festival) in early September brings Deauville's summer to a close, but not without excitement as it's not unusual for Hollywood stars to make an appearance.

West of Deauville

The coast road skirts long sandy beaches backed by woods, and passes through the well-kept, sedate resorts of **Villers-sur-Mer** and **Houlgate**, where mock-medieval pre-war holiday villas adorn the seafront. Between the two towns, the road heads inland to avoid the steep, dark slopes of the sea-facing **Vaches Noires** hills, cut into rugged ravines and cliffs noted for their profusion of fossils.

Dives-sur-Mer, the only place along this shore that predates the 19th century, is a historic and picturesque harbour town near the mouth of the River Dives. During the Middle Ages it flourished as a large and important port serving Caen, and there are still some 15th and 16th-century buildings, notably the handsome wooden **Halles** (covered market). From Dives harbour William the Bastard, Duke of Normandy, set sail with 1000 ships on the voyage that turned him into William the Conqueror, King of England.

Cross the river to enter **Cabourg**, a smart, purpose-built resort laid out in the middle of the 19th century alongside the wide sandy beach. It follows an interesting plan, with a semi-circle of boulevards radiating from the seafront public gardens, casino and **Grand Hotel**, which together form the focal point of the town. Although he was quite scathing about the resort, Cabourg is proud

of its association with Marcel Proust (the waterfront promenade is named after him), who holidayed here every year from 1907 to 1914.

West of Cabourg, the preserved **Batterie de Merville** (place du 9ème Bataillon, Merville-Franceville, T02 31 91 47 53, batterie-merville.com, 15 Mar-15 Nov, €5) was one of the formidable gun emplacements and bunkers of Hitler's Atlantic Wall. It controlled the Orne estuary and could fire directly on to Sword Beach. In an operation costing hundreds of lives, it was seized and put out of action by British bombers and paratroops during the night before the D-Day Landings. Part of the bunker, Casemate 1, has been immaculately restored, and is the setting for a noisy, alarmingly realistic re-enactment of the battle several times an hour.

Le Pays d'Auge

Taking up a large part of eastern Calvados (and crossing the border into the Orne *département*), the historic heart of the Pays d'Auge lies between the Touques and Dives rivers. Around its edges are old country towns and marketplaces, notably Pont l'Evêque, St-Pierre-sur-Dives and Orbec. This profoundly rural, gently hilly region of apple orchards, contented cows, stud farms, winding lanes and picture-book villages contains some of Normandy's richest and most satisfying countryside. Here are cottages of heavy timbers, grand old manor houses that local gentry once called home, and traditional little farms and farmyards. Some of France's best known gourmet cheeses come from here, among them Pont l'Evêque, Livarot, Pavé d'Auge and (in the Orne), best known of them all, Camembert. With all those apple orchards, it's no surprise that the Auge is known as well for cider and Calvados. Farm gate signs beckon passersby to sample their home-made products, and for those with time to spare, two marked routes can be followed through the region, the Route du Cidre (cider route) and Route du Fromage (cheese route).

Pont l'Evêque

Tourist information: 16 bis rue St Michel, T02 31 64 12 77, blangy-pontleveque.com.

Though extensively damaged in 1944, Pont l'Evêque has a bustling, congenial air and an attractive setting at the meeting of rivers. It gives its name to one of the most famous of Normandy's strong, creamy cheeses, made and sold here for 900 years, and is known too for its Calvados. Despite the damage of 1944, the old town has a few handsome half-timbered houses as a reminder of its pre-war appearance, for example along the rue St-Michel (the main street) and its continuation rue de Vaucelles. A side turn leads to the fine Flamboyant Gothic **Eglise St-Michel**. Along here too you'll find the grand brick and stone 18th-century **Hôtel de Brilly**, now housing the town hall and tourist office. At their distillery in town, Calvados-makers Père Magloire run the charming

Musée du Calvados et des Métiers Anciens (Museum of Calvados and Old Crafts, route de Trouville, T02 31 64 30 31, calvados-pere-magloire. com, €3).

Lisieux

Tourist information: 11 rue d'Alençon, T02 31 48 18 10, lisieux-tourisme.com.

The administrative centre for the Auge country, and its largest town, Lisieux is busy, relatively charmless and untypical of the region. It makes a good shopping centre, though, with a busy Saturday market, and does have remnants of its pre-war appearance, including an impressive

Tip...

To see the Pays d'Auge at its best, leave the main roads and main towns and venture along the country lanes to explore the small villages and farm country. See also page 170.

Basilique de Ste-Thérèse, Lisieux.

12th-century Norman Gothic cathedral. More remarkably, Lisieux attracts more than a million pilgrims annually to the hilltop **Basilique de Ste-Thérèse** (Ste-Thérèse Basilica), a huge white church in modern neo-Byzantine style. They are devotees of Thérèse Martin (1873-1897), a young and pious middle-class girl from Alençon, who entered a Carmelite convent in Lisieux at the age of 15, and died there of TB at the age of 24. Her eloquent chronicle of despair, depression and determined struggle to keep her faith, and above all her desire to love and be loved, published as *The Story of a Soul*, has become one of the most popular classics of Catholic writing. Thérèse, known to millions as the Little Flower of Jesus, was canonized in 1925 and, because of the power of her writing, in 1999 was declared a Doctor of the Church.

Orbec

Tourist information: 6 rue Grande, T02 31 32 56 68, mairie-orbec.fr.

On the eastern limits of the Pays d'Auge, but one of its most appealing small towns, ancient Orbec is a picturesque but unpretentious market town, and home of cider-makers and the large Auge cheese-makers, Lanquetot. The town's landmark is the Renaissance church belfry, standing a little incongruously atop an older defensive tower. Standing beside the rushing River Orbiquet, whose medieval mills and tanneries made a fortune, Orbec is noted for its fine 15th- to 16th-century half-timbered tradesmen's houses. In the main street, the **Vieux Manoir** (107 Grand'Rue, T02 31 32 58 89, €1.50) now serves as an eclectic local museum, but is most worth visiting for the chance to see the interior of this magnificent, heavily timbered 16th-century house.

Camembert cheese maturing at a dairy, St-Pierre-sur-Dives.

Tip...

Cheese from all over the world may be called Camembert. To make sure it's the real thing, look for the letters VCN – it means *Veritable Camembert de Normandie.*

St-Pierre-sur-Dives

Tourist information: rue St Benoist, T02 31 20 97 90, mairie-saint-pierre-sur-dives.fr.
15 Oct-15 Apr Mon-Fri 0930-1230 and 1300-1730, 16 Apr-14 Oct Mon-Fri 0930-1230 and 1330-1800, Sat 1000-1230 and 1430-1700.

Pleasantly positioned not far from the right bank of the River Dives, St-Pierre is the place where most of Normandy's light wooden cheese boxes are made. The town dates back to the founding of its Benedictine abbey in the 11th century. Partly rebuilt over the centuries, the beautiful, light and spacious **Eglise Abbatiale** (abbey church), originally consecrated in 1067 in the presence of William the Conqueror, combines Romanesque with glorious Gothic stonework. Curiously the north and south of the building are not aligned, and notice the metal strip in the floor which marks the town's meridian line – the position of the sun at noon. The neighbouring chapter house has some of the best Gothic work, including a 13th-century floor of glazed brick. It is used in part as a museum about the making of Livarot cheese. The town has long been known for its busy Monday morning market, where all the finest farm produce of the Pays d'Auge is for sale at (and outside) a magnificent 11th-century stone and timber **Halles** (covered market), which was painstakingly restored using the original techniques after wartime damage and is one of the most impressive in Normandy.

Some 5 km outside town, **Château de Vendeuvre** (Vendeuvre, T02 31 40 93 83, vendeuvre.com, May-Sep daily 1100-1800, €7.50-€9.50) is a luxurious 18th-century residence in immaculate formal gardens, and still with its original furnishings. Its lovely vaulted Orangery has been turned into a curious and fascinating Musée du Mobilier Miniature (Museum of Miniature Furniture), where an amazing array of exquisite hand-made small-scale items is displayed. Many are delicately inlaid with precious jewels or ivory or decorated with miniaturized paintings. All were made by apprentices as part of their examination for admission to the guilds of master craftsmen.

Detail from the Bayeux tapestry.

Falaise

Between the rolling Pays d'Auge and steeper slopes of the Suisse Normande lies the flatter plain of Falaise plateau. Here the fortress town of Falaise stands on a steep-sided spur between two rivers, the Ante and the Marescot. Such magnificent natural defences attracted the Dukes of Normandy, who chose this site in the very middle of their duchy for one of their first stone fortresses. An early resident of the castle was Duke Robert the Magnificent. Legends tell that Robert was visited in his chamber by a local tanner's daughter, Arlette. She had two children by him – Adelaide and Guillaume. When Guillaume was seven years old, Robert died. He had named Guillaume as his successor but, after his death, Robert's barons rejected his choice of an illegitimate child. When Guillaume was only 15, he recaptured the castle and reclaimed the title. He was already on the way to becoming Guillaume le Conquérant – William

Falaise essentials

ℹ Tourist information 54 boulevard de la Libération, T02 31 90 17 26, falaise-tourisme.com, May-September Monday-Saturday 0930-1230 and 1330-1830 (also 22 June-15 September Sunday 1030-1230 and 1400-1600), October-April closes at 1730.

the Conqueror. Falaise remained an important town throughout the Middle Ages, and until 1944 its centre was filled with medieval half-timbered buildings. Then in the space of five days in August of that year, most of it was destroyed in the Battle of Falaise Pocket, the most decisive and bloody defeat of German occupation forces in Normandy.

Five of the best

Places to discover William the Conqueror

❶ **Château de Falaise** Birthplace of William, son of Robert the Magnificent and Arlette, tanner's daughter.

❷ **Château de Caen** William's fortress is still the centre of the city he built to be his capital.

❸ **Dives-sur-Mer** In 1066, William set sail from this port to claim the throne of England.

❹ **Bayeux Tapestry** This embroidery graphically depicts William's conquest of England in 1066.

❺ **Abbatiale St-Etienne** William died in 1087 and was buried in the church of his Abbaye aux Hommes.

Château de Falaise

Place Guillaume le Conquérant, T02 31 41 61 44, chateau-guillaume-leconquerant.fr.
Daily 1000-1800 (Jul-Aug 1900). €7, concessions €5.50, €3 child.

The castle where William the Conqueror was born and spent his early childhood was demolished and replaced by his son, Henry I, and much altered in subsequent centuries. The present château remains the pre-eminent example of the substantial, robustly defended fortress of the Dukes of Normandy. Its three keeps and their massive round towers, especially the huge Tour Talbot (Talbot Tower), dominate the town. The restoration commissioned in the 1980s and 1990s remains contentious for the use of modern materials incompatible with the original, but is evocative and effective. The place offers a visual treat for children, with a continuous audiovisual show about the Anglo-Norman dukes.

Musée Août 44

Le Musée de la Bataille de la Poche de Falaise, Chemin des Roches, T02 31 90 37 19, normandie-museeaout44.com.
1st weekend in Apr-11 Nov Wed-Mon (daily Jun-Aug) 1000-1200 and 1400-1800. €6, €2.80 child.

With an impressive collection of original vehicles and heavy equipment, the museum below the château explains the crushing defeat of the Germans in the Battle of Falaise Pocket, a critical stage at the end of the Battle of Normandy. The exhibits include models of Allied soldiers in action during the liberation of Falaise.

Automates Avenue

Bd de La Libération, T02 31 90 02 43, automates-avenue.fr.
Apr-Sep 1000-1230 and 1330-1800 (Jul-Aug no midday closing), Oct-Mar weekends and school holidays (except Dec open daily, and 4 weeks Jan-Feb completely closed). €6, €4.50 child.

This 'museum' arranged as an old-style Paris street displays the fairytale world of the animated mechanical Christmas window displays of the Parisian department stores of the 1920s-1950s.

Great days out

This is a rural ride through one of the loveliest parts of Normandy. The starting point is Pont l'Evêque, one of the little towns that lie around the edges of the Pays d'Auge. It can be reached from Caen (40 km on autoroute A13 or main road D675), or from the Côte Fleurie (8 km from Deauville, 17 km from Honfleur).

Take the smaller rural road (D48) heading upriver on the left bank of the River Touques (in the direction of Lisieux). At the village of **Coquainvilliers**, Calvados Boulard's distillery **Moulin de la Foulonnerie** is open to visitors in summer. Turn right on to D270, left when you reach D45, right again on to D270A at Manerbes. This leads into the heart of the Pays d'Auge. When you reach the former abbey **Abbaye du Val Richer**, transformed into a château in the 19th century, turn right on to D59. Pass another country house, **Château de Roque Baignard**, and follow the D117. Reaching D16, turn left and right towards **Clermont-en-Auge**.

Just 3 km away is **Beuvron-en-Auge**, a picture postcard of a place with its streets of timber-framed cottages. Turn south on D49 (and on to D50), until you reach a left turn for the village of **Cambremer**. Come back and continue (on D101) to **Crèvecœur-en-Auge**, where there is an example of a small well-preserved **medieval château**.

Take D16 to **St-Pierre-sur-Dives** to see its Gothic church and chapter house and covered market place. On a Monday, the town is crowded because of its market. Now turn back towards Lisieux on D511.

One of the attractive features of Pays d'Auge is its old *manoirs* and châteaux of timber, stone and patterned brick. Most of these date from the 16th century. Continue to St-Julien-le-Faucon, where two examples lie just off this road, on the left at **Grandchamp-le-Château**, where the moated château is a fortified house, and on the right at **Coupesarte**, where the manor and its grounds are now a farm. Both are private houses. Continue to Lisieux, the capital of the Pays d'Auge. Avoid the town centre by taking the ring road (D613, D406), following signs back to Pont l'Evêque and the Côte Fleurie, or turn left on D613 if you are going towards Caen.

Driving through Le Pays d'Auge

Bayeux

One of Normandy's most pleasing country towns, and with more historical significance than most, Bayeux is a place to stroll, explore and linger. It has good restaurants, especially on and around the main street rue St-Martin and its continuation rue St-Jean. Its cobbled shopping streets and riverside walks, the wealth of centuries-old half-timbered houses, and the picturesque area around the Norman Gothic cathedral all come as a surprise so close to the Landing Beaches – for which it makes an ideal base. During the Second World War the Germans deployed most of their troops defending Caen and were unable to put up strong resistance at Bayeux and as a result, it was the first French town to be liberated, and largely kept its pre-war appearance. On the ring road, the Battle of Normandy Memorial Museum records the events of the invasion and the neighbouring Bayeux War Cemetery is the largest Second World War British Commonwealth war grave in France. Most of the dead fell during the landings on Gold Beach.

The name of Bayeux is, of course, synonymous with its greatest possession – the fascinating 900-year-old Bayeux Tapestry, beautifully displayed in the town centre. This single strip of cloth superbly illustrates the long and close association between Normandy and England.

Musée de la Tapisserie de Bayeux (Bayeux Tapestry Museum)

Centre Guillaume le Conquérant, rue de Nesmond, T02 31 51 25 50, tapisserie-bayeux.fr.
15 Mar-15 Nov 0900-1830 (May-Aug until 1900), 16 Nov-14 Mar 0930-1230 and 1400-1800, except Mon-Fri in 2nd week of Jan, last entry 45 mins before closing. €7.80, €2.80 concessions, €3.80 child.

As an artwork no less than as a historical document, the Bayeux Tapestry is a phenomenal and unique object, a 900-year-old seamless embroidery telling the tale of one of the most important events in European history. Its full length (70 m) is displayed so that you can study each of its 72 scenes in turn, as they show with Latin captions how William's inheritance of the throne of England was disputed, his setting out to claim it, the battle at Hastings in which Harold was killed, and William's eventual conquest. It is uncertain, but probable, that the tapestry (technically an embroidery) was commissioned by the 11th-century Bishop Odon of Bayeux and made for him in England. However, it seems it remained in storage until 1476, when it at last decorated the nave of Bayeux Cathedral.

Detail from the Bayeux Tapestry.

Essentials

ℹ **Tourist information** Pole Touristique du Bessin, Pont St-Jean, Bayeux, T02 31 51 28 28, bayeux-tourism. com, July-August Monday-Saturday 0900-1900, Sunday 0900-1300 and 1400-1800; September-October and April-June daily 0930-1230 and 1400-1800; November-March Monday-Saturday 0930-1230 and 1400-1700.

Musée Mémorial de la Bataille de Normandie (Memorial Museum of the Battle of Normandy)

Bd Fabian Ware, T02 31 51 46 90.
Oct-Apr 1000-1230 and 1400-1800, May-Sep 0930-1830, last admission 1 hr before closing. €6.50; €3.80 child over 10; €2.80 students; under 10s and veterans free.

With masses of authentic equipment, artefacts, plans, photographs and documentation of the period, with tableaux and models, and a 25-minute film using archive footage, the museum tells the story of the dramatic Battle of Normandy, which started with the D-Day Landings and ended in victory for the Allies on 29 August 1944.

Bayeux War Cemetery

Bd Fabian Ware.

This is the largest British Commonwealth wartime cemetery in France, with the graves of 4144 British dead and more than 500 others, mainly German. Across the road, the Bayeux Memorial bears the names of over 1800 other British Commonwealth troops missing in action whose bodies were not recovered. Most of the dead were killed as they arrived on Gold Beach or in the first days of the liberation.

Tip...

It is difficult to park outside the Bayeux War Cemetery, but nearby chemin des Marettes generally has space.

Les Plages du Débarquement (Landing Beaches)

The Allied invasion of Nazi Europe started early one summer morning with the surprise appearance from the sea of 160,000 soldiers along on the wide sandy beaches of western Calvados and the eastern Cotentin. It was one of the most thrilling, astounding and shocking events in the history of warfare. Codenamed Operation Neptune, the landings took place over a 80-km stretch of coast, divided into five separate areas of attack, codenamed (west to east) Utah, Omaha, Gold, Juno and Sword. The Americans took on Utah and Omaha, British forces landed on Gold and Sword beaches and Canadian troops went ashore at Juno. As they surged from their vessels into the water and waded towards the gunfire, large numbers of the young conscripts were mown down in their first steps. It remains difficult to grasp the magnitude of what the men endured, the greatness of what they achieved, and the vastness of the profligate destruction which ensued, of whole towns and villages, cathedrals and cottages, livelihoods and lives, that were lost before the final victory. Today the Landing Beaches are simply wide airy sands fringed in places with the promenades of little holiday resorts and fishing ports, yet all along this shore numerous memorials honour those who died here, and those who lived, on 6 June 1944.

Sword Beach

Map: Les Plages du Débarquement (Landing Beaches), G2, p176.

About 8 km long and centred on the small resort of Lion-sur-Mer, Sword stretched from the Riva Bella beach near Ouistreham harbour on the Orne estuary almost to St-Aubin-sur-Mer. Today, almost its whole length is a ribbon development of holiday towns, protected by a sea wall and fronting on to wide flat sands under big skies. A few remnants of German beach defences are still in place.

The plan for the British troops who came ashore here on D-Day was to travel inland and meet up with the men of the airborne division who had already successfully taken control of the bridges over the Caen canal (Pegasus Bridge) and Orne river, and proceed from there to Caen. Resistance on the beach was lighter than anticipated, and the men made their way cautiously towards the bridges.

The village of Colleville-Montgomery, just inland, was the site of a German underground bunker, signal centre and gun emplacement (restored, and can be visited). Soldiers of the Suffolk Regiment went into action and proceeded to capture it. Later, the village adopted the name of the commander of the British forces to show gratitude.

Further inland though, the British troops were stopped in their tracks by Panzer tank divisions who put up a powerful defence and prevented the British advance to Caen.

It's a fact...

The phrase 'D-Day' (Jour-J in French) does not refer specifically to the Normandy Landings. It is military parlance for the day on which a major operation is planned to start. The phrase 'H-Hour' is used for the exact time. The intended start date for Operation Neptune was 5 June, not the 6th, but it was held up by the weather. So the landings took place on 'D-Day plus one'.

Essentials

❷ **Getting around** Although there are some local bus services in the Landing Beaches area, they are impractical for touring. It's best to join an organized minibus tour, for example with Battlebus in Bayeux (battlebus.fr) or Le Mémorial in Caen (memorial-caen.fr), or pre-book a rental car to be collected on your arrival.

❶ **Tourist information** Arromanches-les-Bains: 2 rue Maréchal Joffre, T02 31 22 36 45, ot-arromanches. fr. **Carentan (Manche département):** boulevard de Verdun, T02 33 71 23 50, ot-carentan.fr. **Courseulles-sur-Mer:** 5 rue du 11 Novembre, T02 31 37 46 80, courseulles-sur-mer.com. **Grandcamp-Maisy:** 118 rue Aristide Briand, T02 31 22 62 44, cc-isigny-grandcamp-intercom.fr. **Isigny-sur-Mer:** 16 rue Emile Demagny, T02 31 21 46 00, cc-isigny-grandcamp-intercom.fr. **Lion-sur-Mer:** place du 18 Juin 1940, T02 31 96 87 95, mairie-lion-sur-mer.fr. **Luc-sur-Mer:** rue du Docteur Charcot, T02 31 97 33 25, luc-sur-mer.fr. **Ouistreham-Riva-Bella:** Jardins du Casino, T02 31 97 18 63, ville-ouistreham.fr. **Port-en-Bessin-Huppain:** quai Baron Gérard, T02 31 22 45 80, bayeux-bessin-tourism.com. **St-Aubin-sur-Mer:** Digue Favreau, T02 31 97 30 41, tourisme-saintaubinsurmer. fr. **St-Laurent-sur-Mer (Omaha Beach):** kiosk at village bus stop, T02 31 51 39 52, oti-omaha.fr. **Ste-Mère-Eglise (Manche département):** 6 rue Eisenhower, T02 33 21 00 33, sainte-mere-eglise.info.

Cannon in a bunker, Longues Sur Mer.

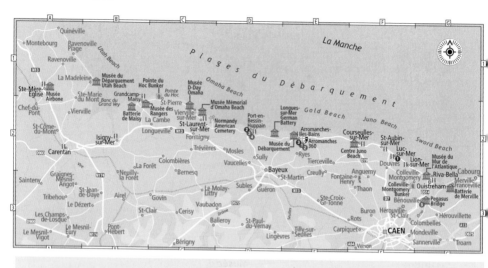

Les Plages du Débarquement (Landing Beaches) listings

❶ Sleeping

1 Camping Municipal 'La Capricieuse'
av l'Ecuyer, Luc-sur-Mer **F2**

2 La Chenevière *on D6,*
Port-en-Bessin **D2**

3 La Marine *1 quai du Canada,*
Arromanches-les-Bains **E2**

❶ Eating & drinking

1 La Marine *1 quai du Canada,*
Arromanches-les-Bains **E2**

2 Le Bistro d'Arromanches
23 rue du Maréchal Joffre,
Arromanches-les-Bains **E2**

3 Le Bistrot d'à Côté
12 rue Michel Lefournier,
Port-en-Bessin-Huppain **D2**

4 Le Vauban *6 rue Nord,*
Port-en-Bessin-Huppain **D2**

5 Pegasus Bridge Café Gondrée
12 av Commdt Kieffer, Bénouville **G3**

Pegasus Bridge.

Pegasus Bridge

Map: Les Plages du Débarquement (Landing Beaches), G3, p176.

On the busy main road (D515) from the city of Caen to its seaport at Ouistreham, a turning (D514) crosses on to the bridge over the Caen canal. This small bridge saw the first action of the Normandy Invasion, and became known as Pegasus Bridge in honour of the British troops of the Oxfordshire and Buckinghamshire Light Infantry (Ox and Bucks) Airborne – their insignia is the mythical winged horse Pegasus. Under the command of Major John Howard, some hours before dawn on 6 June 1944 they landed in three gliders almost beside the bridge. Their mission was to capture the bridge intact, while another group took the nearby River Orne crossing. This was successfully achieved in just 10 minutes, though with loss of life. The men then used the premises of the **Café Gondrée**, next to the bridge, to tend to their wounds. The bridge itself was replaced in 1994. The original Pegasus Bridge can now be seen outside the museum of the **Mémorial Pegasus** (av du Major Howard, Ranville, T02 31 78 19 44, normandie1944.fr, Feb-Nov, approx 0930-1830, €6, €4.50 child and concessions), just across the canal.

Musée du Mur de l'Atlantique (Atlantic Wall Museum)

Av 6 Juin, Ouistreham, T02 31 97 28 69, musee-grand-bunker.com.
Apr-Sep 0900-1900, Oct-Mar 1000-1800. €7, €5 6-12 years, under 6s free.
Map: Les Plages du Débarquement (Landing Beaches), G3, p176.

With impressive authentic and original interiors, and a sweeping view of Sword Beach, this museum occupies the immaculately restored 17-m-tall concrete German HQ which commanded the River Orne defences.

Tip...

The Landing Beaches resorts have more to offer than wartime memories. The bright, airy and unspoiled Calvados coast west of the River Orne is also known as the Côte de Nacre (Mother-of-Pearl Coast). It markets itself as Campagne-sur-Mer (Countryside-on-Sea), and has its own tourist information website, cotenormande.com.

It's a fact...

The massive German gun emplacements and batteries along the Normandy coast were part of the Atlantikwall. The Germans realized early in their occupation of Europe that the Channel coast was vulnerable to a sea-borne attack and in 1942 Hitler ordered that a continuous line of fire be put in place, reinforced by impenetrable defences, along the continent's entire western coastline. The one weakness in this colossal fortification was that defences were especially focused around ports, as it was thought to be impossible to launch a full-scale attack on Nazi Europe without a harbour to unload men and equipment.

Juno Beach

Map: Les Plages du Débarquement (Landing Beaches), F2, p176.

Canadians had already suffered demoralizing losses on the Normandy coast in the ill-fated Dieppe Raid of 1942. For Operation Neptune, under British command, they were given the 6 km from **St-Aubin-sur-Mer** to **Courseulles-sur-Mer**. In the event, despite a difficult approach among offshore rocks and mines, they quickly overcame the German defenders and progressed inland. By 16 June 1944 the area was safe enough for King George V and Prime Minister Winston Churchill to make a brief visit, when they inspected **Graye-sur-Mer**, adjoining Courseulles. Today, the area is popular for sailing, surfing, horse riding and the sport of *char à voile* – sail-powered go-karting on the flat sands. At low tide, seafood enthusiasts can gather their own shrimps and crabs.

Centre Juno Beach

Voie des Français Libres, Courseulles-sur-Mer, T02 31 37 32 17, junobeach.org.
Apr-Sep 0930-1900, Mar and Oct 1000-1800, Feb, Nov and Dec 1000-1700. €6.50, €5 child and concessions.

Located on the extreme western end of Juno Beach, this is the only specifically Canadian museum and memorial on the Landing Beaches. It pays tribute to the French and English Canadians who took part in D-Day, including those who had behind-the-scenes roles. It also explores Canada's Anglo-French (and First Nation) culture and history.

Gold Beach

Map: Les Plages du Débarquement (Landing Beaches), E2, p176.

The centre of attention for most British visitors now, Gold was an 8-km length of coast from near Courseulles-sur-Mer to the rockier shore just west of Arromanches-les-Bains, a resort village on a lightly curved section of beach close to a small rocky headland. Still visible in the water and lying on the beach at **Arromanches** and **Le Hamel** about 1 km east are the remnants of the **Mulberry Harbour** – a fully functioning port assembled on the spot by the Allied forces with ready-made sections towed from England. It was in use just three days after D-Day. After securing the shore and constructing the harbour, the Allies were able to bring ships here from England loaded with soldiers, weapons, equipment and supplies. A beachside **D-Day Museum** in the heart of busy little Arromanches, right beside these great slabs, explores the story of the Landings and the role and construction of the Mulberry. The best overview of the layout of the huge harbour is from the specially constructed viewpoint on the hill rising behind the little town. Signposted '**Belvédère**', it is close to the Arromanches 360 cinema.

The coastline remains little developed to this day, and gives a sense of what the British troops

It's a fact...

The Mulberry Harbour at Arromanches was not the only one. Two of the ready-made ports, constructed of hollow concrete breakwaters, were towed in sections across the Channel from 6-7 June and were ready for use by 9 June. 'Mulberry A' was assembled at Omaha Beach and served its purpose for just 10 days until broken up by a violent storm on 19 June. 'Mulberry B' at nearby Arromanches survived the storm and became known as Port Winston. During a 10-month period it was used to bring over two million soldiers and half a million armoured vehicles to Normandy, together with all their supplies.

themselves saw on the morning of 6 June 1944. Here they were set down with the order to take control of Arromanches, and disable the German gun battery at nearby **Longues-sur-Mer**. Tanks and armoured vehicles were driven directly on to the beach. An unlikely spot for an invasion, the Arromanches coast was not especially well protected. Although offshore defences had caused damage, on land the German divisions tasked with defending it were not crack troops, while some turned out to be forced labour from Russia and Poland, who had no wish to help their masters. A unit trained to respond to an invasion were unprepared and were in Bayeux. On the coast at Le Hamel, the Germans were not in bunkers but in fortified beach houses that were destroyed by naval bombardment before the troops came ashore.

By the end of that day 25,000 British soldiers had landed on this beach, and the troops had reached several kilometres inland where they met with the Canadians coming in from Juno Beach. In the other direction, they had taken the gun battery at Longues and reached the road above Port-en-Bessin in an effort to aid the Americans battling on a blood-soaked Omaha Beach.

Arromanches 360

Chemin du Calvaire, Arromanches les Bains, T02 31 22 30 30, arromanches360.com.
Jun-Aug 0940-1840, Apr-May and Sep-Oct 1010-1740, Feb and Dec 1010-1640, Mar-Nov 1010-1710. €4.20, € 3.70 concessions (veterans free), under 10s free. You also have to pay €2 to park in the car park.
Map: Les Plages du Débarquement (Landing Beaches), E2, p176.

On a hill behind the town, this unusual cinema-in-the-round shows a film called *The Price of Freedom*. Splicing vivid contemporary D-Day footage with

Around the region

Port-en-Bessin.

modern film of the locations it powerfully brings home the events of D-Day and a sense of its purpose and accomplishment.

Musée du Débarquement (D-Day Museum)

Place du 6 juin, T02 31 22 34 31, musee-arromanches.fr.
Feb and Nov-Dec 1000-1230 and 1330-1700, Mar-Apr and Oct 0900-1230 and 1330-1800, May-Aug 0900-1900, Sep 0900-1800 (except Sun, opens at 1000), apart from Easter weekend 0900-1900. €6.50, €4.50 child and concessions.
Map: Les Plages du Débarquement (Landing Beaches), E2, p176.

Dominating the little main street beside the beach, and with real armaments and weaponry standing outside, the museum is right in front of pieces of the Mulberry harbour lying on the sand. Inside, photos, film footage and authentic mementos are displayed, and an extensive scale model shows the scene on D-Day. Audio-visual presentations (in English and other languages) give an insight into the strategy behind D-Day and the engineering feat involved in creating the artificial harbour.

It's a fact...

Airborne troops who landed inland during the night of 5-6 June prepared the way for the D-Day invasion the following morning. The most famous examples are the taking of the bridge over the Caen canal (Pegasus Bridge), inland from Sword Beach, the capture of Ste-Mère-Eglise, inland from Utah Beach, and the attack on the Merville Battery, within range of Sword and Juno Beaches.

Longues-sur-Mer German Battery

Signposted from Longues-sur-Mer.
Free.
Map: Les Plages du Débarquement (Landing Beaches), D2, p176.

A key element in the German defences of the Calvados coast was this massive gun emplacement behind the coast just west of Arromanches, complete with an observation post set into the cliffs. Its four powerful 150-mm guns were able to hit targets not only at sea but also on both Gold Beach and Omaha Beach. In the run-up to D-Day, a British warship engaged it in a determined exchange of fire. Although damaged, it was still in action on the morning of D-Day, but was taken later in the day. The guns are still in place and parts of the bunker are well preserved.

Port-en-Bessin

In between Gold and Omaha beaches, Port-en-Bessin rewards a visit. More correctly called Port-en-Bessin-Huppain (it's administratively joined to neighbouring Huppain), it is known locally simply as Port. A semicircle of granite jetties shelters this charming little fortified fishing village between the cliffs, where there's a daily auction of fresh fish. The village has some good places to eat or to stay. On D-Day, the Americans on Omaha and British on Gold were supposed to meet up at Port-en-Bessin. They managed it on 8 June – two days after the landings.

Map: Les Plages du Débarquement (Landing Beaches), C/D2, p176.

The focus of the American attack was the coast between **Vierville-sur-Mer** to a point east of **Colleville-sur-Mer**. Today, at low tide locals stroll the shore calmly gathering shellfish. The rustic Bessin countryside inland is a dense patchwork of small fields and mature hedges. All is utterly peaceful. Yet as soon as you see the layout of Omaha Beach, the problems become clear: the wide, flat beach is hemmed in by a sea wall and cliffs. To leave it requires a steep climb.

The whole of the 20-km stretch of Calvados coast between Port-en-Bessin and the mouth of the River Vire was robustly defended by the Germans, with concrete gun emplacements and smaller gun bunkers. Many can still be seen, dug into the ridge of rocky cliffs rising up and overlooking the seashore. Despite the pounding they received and the passage of time since, some of these concrete structures seem little damaged. From these vantage points the Germans trained their guns on to the wet sand as the American soldiers emerged from their landing craft.

Omaha Beach was bound to be a tough fight and the Americans offered to take it on. But it was even tougher than expected. Delayed after a rough crossing in which most of their armoured vehicles had been lost, they were subjected to a ceaseless torrent of gunfire as they struggled to wade ashore. Many were killed on the spot. Those who reached the cliffs had to climb them with rope ladders. Any who survived the climb found themselves surrounded by landmines. They continued towards the German gun bunkers, which eventually were overrun and silenced. By the evening of the day, the Americans had landed 34,000 men and suffered 2400 casualties, but they had taken control of the awesome German gun emplacement at **Pointe-du-Hoc**, and at Vierville they held the coast road (D514) to Grandcamp-Maisy in one direction and Port-en-Bessin in the other.

American Military Cemetery, Omaha Beach.

The area remains deeply marked by the immense American self-sacrifice. Its most affecting sight is the tranquil and neatly kept **Cimetière et Mémorial Américains de Normandie (American Military Cemetery and Memorial)** (signposted, 1 km off D514 between St Laurent-sur-Mer and Colleville-sur-Mer, T02 31 51 62 00, abmc.gov/cemeteries/cemeteries/no.php, daily 0900-1800 (1700 from 16 Sep to 14 Apr) except 25 Dec and 1 Jan), set back from the beach at the centre of the battlefield. On land given by France to the United States, it holds 9387 graves. In pristine white rows stand the thousands of white crosses, and some Stars of David, laid out before a dignified semi-circular memorial wall on which are inscribed the 1557 names of the missing.

Around the region

Normandy American Cemetery Visitor Center

American Military Cemetery and Memorial, near St Laurent-sur-Mer, T02 31 51 62 00.
Same times as cemetery. Free.
Map: Les Plages du Débarquement (Landing Beaches), C2, p176.

Within the grounds of the cemetery, in a wooded area close to the memorial wall and garden, the centre is one of the most powerful of the D-Day museums. It provides a gripping and vivid view of Operation Overlord, the events of D-Day and what led up to them, and the experience of those who took part, with authentic personal stories, photos and film.

Musée Mémorial d'Omaha Beach (Omaha Beach Memorial Museum)

Les Moulins, av de la Libération, St Laurent-sur-Mer, T02 31 21 97 44, musee-memorial-omaha.com.
15 Feb-15 Mar 1000-1230 and 1430-1800, 16 Mar-15 May and 16 Sep-15 Nov 0930-1830, 16 May-30 Jun and 1 Sep-15 Sep 0930-1900, Jul-Aug 0930-1930. €5.80, €4.50 child 16-18 and up to 25 in full-time education, €3.30 child 7-15, under 7s free.
Map: Les Plages du Débarquement (Landing Beaches), C2, p176.

Set back 100 m from the beach, the museum displays large collections of authentic D-Day weapons and vehicles, uniforms, personal possessions, maps, photos and more.

Musée D-Day Omaha (Omaha D-Day Museum)

Route de Grandcamp-Maisy, Vierville-sur-Mer, T02 31 21 71 80, dday-omaha.org.
Jun-Aug 0930-1830, Apr-May and Sep-Oct shorter hours may apply. €5.50, €3 child and concessions, under 7s free.
Map: Les Plages du Débarquement (Landing Beaches), C2, p176.

This fascinating small collection of original military material, housed in and around a wartime beachside hangar, includes landing craft and a steel observation dome. Close by, on the same theme, are remnants of the ill-fated Omaha Beach Mulberry Harbour.

Grandcamp-Maisy

Map: Les Plages du Débarquement (Landing Beaches), B2, p176.

This quiet little fishing port and yacht harbour about 10 km along the coast from Omaha Beach was a focal point for German defences around the **Banc du Grand Vey** bay, a huge area of sandflats between the Calvados coast and the Cotentin peninsula covered at every tide. Two large bunkers complete with underground offices and stores and powerful gun batteries were dug into the coastal cliffs nearby. They could fire on to both Omaha and Utah beaches. One of them, east of Grandcamp-Maisy on the lofty **Pointe du Hoc** headland (about an hour's walk from the road), was taken by the elite US Rangers force after a ferocious fight on D-Day. On 9 June the Rangers captured the huge underground complex southwest of Grandcamp-Maisy at the **Batterie de Maisy** (route des Perruques, T06 78 04 56 25, maisybattery.com, Mar-Sep 1000-1800, Oct-Apr 1000-1600, €5), which was left abandoned after the war; it was rediscovered and uncovered almost intact by a British enthusiast, Gary Sterne, as he researched the area almost 60 years later. In the village, the **Musée des Rangers (Rangers Museum)** (quai Crampon,

---

Tip...

For a realistic dramatization of the landings at Omaha Beach, see the opening sequences of Steven Spielberg's film *Saving Private Ryan*.

Grandcamp-Maisy, T02 31 92 33 51, daily 0930-1300 and 1430-1830 excluding Mon mornings (winter: Tue-Sun afternoons only), €4, €2 child and concessions) tells the story of the US Rangers and their hair-raisingly difficult and dangerous assaults on the German bunkers.

Utah Beach

Map: Les Plages du Débarquement (Landing Beaches), B1, p176.

Unlike the other Landing Beaches, Utah Beach is not in Calvados but across the Banc du Grand Vey on the Cotentin Peninsula. By sea, it is 20 km from Omaha Beach.

D-Day really began not at dawn, but at 0230 on 6 June, and the invasion came not by sea but from the air. That's the moment when thousands of men of US 101st Airborne descended on the village of Ste-Mère-Eglise, to prepare the way for troops who would be reaching Utah Beach later in the morning. At Ste-Mère-Eglise (see page 213), the events of that night are brought to life at the Musée Airborne. One of the American parachutists was caught on the church tower in the village centre. He is commemorated to this day by a dummy and parachute still hanging there. The Allies needed to move through the Cotentin to capture the port of Cherbourg as soon as possible, and that was the mission of the American soldiers put ashore on Utah Beach. Unlike the tragedy of Omaha Beach, here things went relatively well for the invaders.

Today, the long straight Utah Beach, edged by a low sea wall, is wide, sandy, sparsely inhabited, and remains almost completely undeveloped. Cotentin locals drive here to enjoy the open spaces, for seashore horse riding and sand-karting. Some German defences are still in place. At the southern end of the beach stands a memorial and monument to those who took part in the Landings. You'll notice the KM00 milestone, too, marking the start of the **Voie de Liberté** (Liberty Trail), which continues 1446 km all the way from here to Bastogne, in Belgium.

Monument at Utah Beach.

Musée du Débarquement Utah Beach (Utah Beach Landing Museum)

La Madeleine, Ste-Marie-du-Mont, T02 33 71 53 35, utah-beach.com.
Apr, May, Oct 1000-1800, Jun-Sept 0930-1900, Feb, Mar, Nov 1000-1730. €6, €4.50 concessions, €2.50 child.
Map: Les plages du débarquement/landing beaches, B1, p176.

Located right next to the sand at one end of Utah Beach, beside the Navy memorial, this museum uses authentic artefacts, archives and personal memorabilia to recall the Utah Beach landings. In front of the museum stands an original US landing craft. That alone brings home something of what the troops endured.

Tip...

The two best bases for a tour of the Landing Beaches are Caen and Bayeux. Both are easily accessible by train from Paris (Caen about 90 minutes, Bayeux two hours). If you are including Utah Beach on your trip, choose Bayeux.

Sleeping

Dauphin Best Western €€€
29 rue Gémare, T02 31 86 22 26, le-dauphin-normandie.com.
Map: Caen, p152.
In a city without any accommodation above the three-star level, this comfortable, pleasant hotel in a converted former priory near the Château, close to the pedestrianized shopping streets, is a contender for the best place in town. Moderately sized, well-equipped rooms, attractively decorated in pale colours and modern style, but with genuine old beams. Useful free parking in the hotel's (cramped and hard to use) car park. There's also a restaurant.

Holiday Inn Caen Centre €€€
4 place Maréchal Foch, T02 31 27 57 57, caen-hotel-centre.com.
Map: Caen, p152.
This hotel may suit some as it is off the usual tourist beat, beside Caen's racecourse, several minutes' walk from the city centre and main sights. Occupying a large corner building fronting on to a square with a war memorial, it has a dated feel. Bedrooms are varied, mainly with muted chocolatey tones. Choose an 'executive' room – some 'standard' bedrooms are rather poky.

Moderne Best Western €€€
116 bd Maréchal Leclerc, T02 31 86 04 23, hotel-caen.com.
Map: Caen, p152.
Looking on to a square close to pedestrianized shopping streets and a few minutes' walk from the main sights, this comfortable city centre three-star hotel has reasonably spacious, if rather dated rooms in smart, sober colours with polished wooden furnishings. There's also useful private parking.

Mercure Port de Plaisance €€€-€€
1 rue de Courtonne, T02 31 47 24 24, mercure.com.
Map: Caen, p152.
An attractive modern low-rise close to place de Courtonne in the heart of Caen, and looking on to the Port de Plaisance, this reliable, well-run chain hotel offers among the best of three-star comfort and amenities. Public areas are spacious and plush. Varied bedrooms have simple, calm colour schemes.

Hôtel de France €€
10 rue de la Gare, T02 31 52 16 99, hoteldefrance-caen.com.
Map: Caen, p152.
South of the River Orne, this two-star is on a main road close to the railway station. Well-kept rooms in rose and pastel colours have wooden furnishings, are double glazed, adequately equipped and popular with business travellers. Tram and bus routes outside provide a quick link to the centre.

Hôtel des Quatrans €€
17 rue Gémare, T02 31 86 25 57, hotel-des-quatrans.com.
Map: Caen, p152.
A classic two-star with well-kept, small and simple but comfortable rooms in rich, dark tones, the hotel stands on the edge of the pedestrianized shopping area close to the Château. Free Wi-Fi is available. Downstairs is the hotel's excellent ArchiDona restaurant (see page 188).

Hôtel du Château €€
5 av du 6 Juin, T02 31 86 15 37, hotel-chateau-caen.com.
Map: Caen, p152.
It's on a busy street just a few moments from the Château and the Port de Plaisance, and beside the tramline, yet this basic and inexpensive two-star is quiet and comfortable. It's six storeys high (there's a lift), with bright and colourful decor, has Wi-Fi access and its own pay-to-use car park.

Ibis Port de Plaisance €€
6 place Courtonne, T02 31 95 88 88, ibishotel.com.
Map: Caen, p152.
A branch of the familiar Ibis chain is well located in the heart of Caen close to the Château and the Port de Plaisance. Rooms are

plain and simple, highly functional and admittedly charmless, but adequately equipped and affordable. The hotel has its own restaurant, and a bar open day and night.

Hôtel Bristol €€-€
31 rue du 11 Novembre, T02 31 84 59 76, hotelbristolcaen.com.
Map: Caen, p152.
North of the River Orne, but close to the railway station (and the racetrack, if that's of interest), this modestly priced family-run hotel has small, simple but attractive rooms in pale tones, with fabrics in warm colours. There's a homely bar/*salon*, and a decent buffet breakfast is served.

Central Hôtel €
23 place Jean Letellier, T02 31 86 18 52, centralhotel-caen.com.
Map: Caen, p152.
Some of the lowest prices in town are charged for these traditional, and perhaps rather dated, simple bedrooms in a basic building with few facilities. The location is its best feature – near the Château and main shopping streets.

Etap Hôtel Caen Gare €
16 place de la Gare, T08 92 68 09 05, www.accor.com.
Map: Caen, p152.
This Etap is south of the River Orne, right next to Caen railway station. For those unfamiliar with Etap's budget formula, every room is identical, modern and

tiny, with blue and white decor. Facilities are cleverly functional yet adequate, and prices could hardly be lower. Buffet breakfast is available.

Hôtel du Havre €
11 rue du Havre, T02 31 86 19 80, hotelduhavre.com.
Map: Caen, p152.
Straightforward and functional, decorated in warm colours, this simple but adequate city centre backstreet accommodation in an unpretentious modern building is excellent value for money and is not without homely charm. Wi-Fi is included.

Hôtel Kyriad Caen Centre €
1 place de la République, T02 31 86 55 33, hotel-caen-centre.com.
Map: Caen, p152.
Rooms are small and simple, but modern and decent, at this city centre low-budget chain hotel. There are a few pleasant little extras, such as free Wi-Fi, and free coffee and biscuits in every room.

Honfleur

La Ferme St-Siméon €€€€
Rue Adolphe-Marais, T02 31 81 78 00, fermesaintsimeon.fr.
In its former existence as a modest hostelry run by Mère Toutain, this small hilltop hotel was assured a place in the history of modern art when its regular clientele began to include such artists as Corot, Courbet, Boudin

and Monet. Today it is a luxurious country-house-style hotel of tremendous charm and panache, with wood panelling, beams and rich fabrics. It has a pretty garden, dazzling estuary views, traditional comfortable rooms and an excellent restaurant. Facilities include a spa.

La Ferme de la Grande Cour €€
Côte de Grâce, T02 31 89 04 69, fermedelagrandecour.com.
This simple, family-run two-star hotel with wooden beams and rustic decor is well placed near the Notre-Dame de Grâce chapel outside Honfleur. Stairs climb to varied, traditional, functional but adequately equipped bedrooms. It has calm and attractive grounds, a restaurant emphasizing fish dishes and the flavours of Normandy, and pleasant outdoor summer dining in the shade of trees.

Chambres d'hôtes
La Petite Folie €€€
42-44 rue Haute, T06 74 39 46 46, lapetitefolie-honfleur.com.
An unusual chambre d'hôte occupying two picturesque old houses in this delightful street, the 'Little Madness' has a sumptuous high-life feel, with quirkily original furnishings, masses of flair and very comfortable, well-equipped rooms. B&B in one house, self-catering in the other.

Deauville & Trouville

Normandy €€€€
38 rue Jean Mermoz, Deauville, T02 31 98 66 22, lucienbarriere. com.
A superlative example of turn-of-the-century mock-medieval Norman beach-resort architecture, this is a veritable palace of towers and tiles and green-painted timbers, steep roofs and dormer windows. Inside, the Normandy has a smart country-house feel, with every comfort and convenience. Rooms are very richly furnished and decorated. An interior courtyard accommodates the tables of the grand belle epoque restaurant. A covered walkway connects the hotel to the casino.

Royal €€€€
Bd Cornuché, Deauville, T02 31 98 66 33, lucienbarriere.com. Open approx Mar-Oct and 30-31 Dec.
This creamy palace with red highlights is the grandest hotel in Deauville, and one of the grandest in France. The bedrooms and suites are opulently furnished and decorated, with luxury wallpapers and carpets, rich drapery and fine furnishings. Its two restaurants have earned a Michelin star.

Flaubert €€€
Rue Gustave Flaubert, Trouville, T02 31 88 37 23, flaubert.fr. Mid-Feb to mid-Nov.
It's possible to stay right on the beachfront at Trouville, in this pleasant and traditional hotel in a 1930s mock-medieval villa, well placed just a few minutes' walk from the town centre. Rooms are comfortable and attractive, with pale colours, pictures and antiques. Facilities deserve more than the two-star rating.

Chantilly €€
120 av de la République, Deauville, T02 31 88 79 75, 123france.com/chantilly.
Deauville on the cheap? No, it's not *that* cheap, but this comfortable, pleasant little hotel is excellent value. It's close to the racecourse and the main shopping streets.

West of Deauville

Grand Hôtel €€€€
Les Jardins du Casino Cabourg, T02 31 91 01 79.
The famed seafront Grand Hôtel de Cabourg, beside the casino and gardens at the centre of the resort, was once one of the Côte Fleurie's masterpieces of belle epoque style. That glamour has faded into memory, but there are still spacious rooms, sea views and helpful service. Choose the sea-facing side – the other rooms are less pleasing.

Pont l'Evêque

Le Lion d'Or €€€-€€
8 place du Calvaire, T02 31 65 01 55, leliondorhotel.com.
Right in the centre of the little town, this attractive well-run family-owned small hotel has character and charm and offers comfortable, well-equipped rooms of a good size and decorated with simple, elegant taste. The 'duplex' rooms are like home-from-home apartments. There's free Wi-Fi, breakfast is good value, and the hotel also has its own little spa area with a variety of relaxation treatments.

Lisieux

La Coupe d'Or €€-€
49 rue Pont Mortain, T02 31 31 16 84.
A solid, traditional family-run two-star hotel restaurant on a corner in the city centre. With correct service, traditional local and French cooking and plain no-nonsense decor, the Coupe d'Or has been a reliable address in the town for many years.

Beuvron-en-Auge

Chambres d'hôtes
Le Pavé d'Hôtes €€
At the edge of Beuvron-en-Auge, T02 31 39 39 10, pavedauge.com.
Run by the acclaimed Pavé d'Auge restaurant (see page 192) in the village, this small guesthouse sets out to offer 'the

comfort of today with the charm of yesterday', with simple, stylish, thoroughly comfortable and well-equipped bedrooms and a generous breakfast.

Bayeux

Lion d'Or €€€-€€
71 rue St-Jean, T02 31 92 06 90, liondor-bayeux.fr.
This three-star handsome old former coaching inn is a calm, family-run Relais du Silence with a plush, luxurious feel for a moderate price. Arranged around a courtyard, the bedrooms are mainly on the small side, traditional and comfortable, and pleasantly decorated in classic taste. Choose a suite for more space. The hotel has an excellent restaurant.

Hôtel Churchill €€
14-16 rue St-Jean, T02 31 21 31 80, hotel-churchill.fr.
Centrally located in an attractive stone building on a cobbled shopping street near place de Québec, this well-run three-star is a good base for visiting the town or exploring further afield. Rooms are moderately sized, but well equipped and attractively decorated and furnished. Those at the back are quieter. Staff are helpful.

Argouges €€-€
21 rue St-Patrice, T02 31 92 88 86, ohotellerie.com/dargouges.
In a pair of rather grand 17th-century buildings set back from the street, some bedrooms and public areas at this inexpensive two-star hotel have period features and almost a château feel. The setting is surprisingly peaceful for such a convenient location in the city centre. Breakfast might be considered overpriced.

Family Home – Auberge de Jeunesse €
39 rue Général de Dais, T02 31 92 15 22, www.bayeux-familyhome.com.
With a range of basic hotel rooms as well as shared rooms and cheaper dormitory accommodation if you prefer, this popular youth hostel has plenty of charm with its paved courtyard, clean and unpretentious amenities, free breakfast and low-cost dinner.

Les Plages du Débarquement (Landing Beaches)

La Chenevière €€€€
On D6, Port-en-Bessin, T02 31 51 25 25, lacheneviere.com.
May-Nov.
Map: Les Plages du Débarquement (Landing Beaches), D2, p176.
This sumptuous mansion in a setting of lawns and gardens started as an 18th-century manor house, became grander in the 19th century, and was beautifully restored in the 1980s. Today it has elegant, richly furnished rooms combining antique furnishings with contemporary, and with all modern comforts. There is also a good restaurant.

La Marine €€
1 quai du Canada, Arromanches-les-Bains, T02 31 22 34 19.
Map: Les Plages du Débarquement (Landing Beaches), E2, p176.
There's bright, fresh decor and plenty of blue and white contrasts at this very well-placed traditional waterside hotel at the heart of the tiny resort. It's just a few paces from the D-Day Landings Museum.

Campsites

Camping Municipal 'La Capricieuse' €
Av l'Ecuyer, Luc-sur-Mer, T02 31 97 34 43.
Map: Les Plages du Débarquement (Landing Beaches), F2, p176.
This four-star campsite in the thriving little resort of Luc-sur-Mer, close to the sands of Sword and Juno beaches, has chalets and mobile homes as well as camping sites. There are adequate facilities, as well as entertainment in season.

Eating & drinking

Caen

Incognito €€€
14 rue de Courtonne, T02 31 28 36 60, www.stephanecarbone.fr.
Lunch and dinner Mon-Sat (closed Sat midday).
Map: Caen, p152.
Caen's most highly rated restaurant, right in the city centre, has contemporary decor in warm colours, with views into the kitchen. Refined imaginative dishes are elegantly presented (including a menu devoted to lobster), but prices are high.

Le Pressoir €€€
3 av Henri Chéron, T02 31 73 32 71, ivanvautier.com.
Tue-Sun lunch and dinner. Closed Sun dinner, Sat lunch and 2 weeks in Aug.
Map: Caen, p152.
At some distance from the centre, just off the ring road on the southwest side of town, this gastronomic address in a former coaching inn is worth the journey. Well known to locals, it's a chic, contemporary setting for French regional variations on Normandy cuisine, using the best seasonal ingredients.

Tip…

All the classic Normandy cheeses are made in similar style, as small, dense, shallow, shaped cheese with a washed rind, packed into light wooden boxes. They are ready to eat when soft.

Brasserie Martin €€
1 rue des Prairies St-Gilles, T02 31 44 18 06, brasserie-restaurant-martin.com.
Daily 1130-2400.
Map: Caen, p152.
Lively, popular, centrally located, this brasserie off place Courtonne is the place for a drink, snack or a full meal any time from breakfast to dinner. Sit indoors or at tables on the pavement. A long menu features all the familiar French brasserie favourites like snails, steaks and salads, along with some distinctively Norman flavours, like turbot in a cider cream sauce.

Café Mancel €€
Musée des Beaux Arts, Le Château, T02 31 86 63 64, cafemancel.com.
Tue-Sat lunch and dinner, Sun lunch.
Map: Caen, p152.
A useful place for a drink or snack (including such satisfying things as bread and cheese) or a full meal of classic French dishes when you're visiting the Château, this smart, contemporary café at the Fine Arts Museum is worth returning to for live music evenings across the range from jazz to classical.

La Maison d'Italie €€
10 rue Hamon, T02 31 86 38 02.
Lunch and dinner daily.
Map: Caen, p152.
Bright, brisk and popular child-friendly eatery serving up pizzas, pasta and other Italian classics. Nothing Norman in sight, but good-value dining in a pedestrian street near the Château.

Maître Corbeau €€
8 rue Buquet, T02 31 93 93 00, maitre-corbeau.com.
Tue-Fri 1145-1330, Mon-Sat 1900-2230. Closed for about 2 weeks in winter and 3 weeks in summer.
Map: Caen, p152.
Cheese mad and decorated with a chaotic assortment of knick-knacks, cheese boxes, labels and anything cow related, this fun little restaurant proudly offers La Cuisine au Fromage. No surprise, then, that the emphasis is firmly on dairy produce, with meat in cheese sauces, cheese salads and a big choice of cheese fondues. Enjoy a chocolate fondue for dessert.

ArchiDona €€-€
17 rue Gémare, T02 31 85 30 30, archidona.fr.
Tue-Sat 1200-1400, 1900-2200.
Map: Caen, p152.
A lively and popular yet refined, rather smart eating place near the Château, the ArchiDona has a thoroughly modern ambience, pale wicker and white decor and ever-changing menus of tasty and original Mediterranean-oriented cuisine. Excellent value menu for early diners.

Pick of the picnic spots

Jardin de l'Hôtel de Ville
In front of Hôtel de Ville.
Free access.
These immaculately tended gardens with imaginative flowerbeds are laid out in front of the former Abbaye aux Hommes, right beside its abbey church. It's a good place to unwrap a snack or simply have a rest on one of the benches before or after visiting the church.

Jardin des Plantes
5 place Blot, T02 31 30 48 38.
Daily 0800-dusk (1000 on Sat-Sat). Free.
Pick up your picnic at one of the street markets or *traiteurs* and bring it to this pretty botanic garden. There are leafy paths and greenhouses, as well as a public park with benches, a children's play area and toilets.

La Normande €€-€
41 bd Maréchal Leclerc, T02 31 30 10 40.
Lunch and dinner except Sun evening.
Map: Caen, p152.
This comfortable modern Parisian-style brasserie on different floors has chandeliers and pre-war touches, and attracts a well-to-do crowd for brasserie cooking served in several rooms with different atmospheres.

Pain et Beurre €€-€
46 rue Guillaume le Conquérant, T02 31 86 04 57.
Tue-Sun 1230-1400 and 1930-2200 except Sat lunch and Sun dinner.
Map: Caen, p152.
You'll find more than bread and butter at this tempting bistro on different floors over by the Abbaye aux Hommes. It's adventurous, enjoyable and diverse fusion cooking based on what's best at the market.

Le Bistrot €
12 rue du Vaugueux, T02 31 93 20 30.
Lunch and dinner daily.
Map: Caen, p152.
With so many hungry tourists wandering up and down the delightful traffic-free streets in Caen's tiny 'old quarter' – a fragment near the Château that remained unscathed after the destruction in 1944 – it's wise to choose carefully. With its blue-painted exterior timbers, comfortable pub-like interior and tempting outdoor terrace tables, this place is popular with locals and stands out for traditional brasserie-style cooking at an affordable price.

Le Bouchon du Vaugueux €
12 rue Graindorge, T02 31 44 26 26.
Tue-Sat 1200-1400 and 1930-2230, closed Aug.
Map: Caen, p152.
On the corner of an 'old quarter' backstreet, this unpretentious spot is one of the best-value little eating places in town. Following the tradition of a typical *bouchon* in Lyon (where the word means a good, simple bistro specializing in local dishes), there's a menu of the day with seasonal local fare at a very modest price. It's small, so reservation is advisable.

Rose & Grey €
27 rue Ecuyère, T02 31 85 20 96.
Mon-Sat 1200-1430, 1900-2230.
Map: Caen, p152.
Lovely name, and this inexpensive little restaurant popular with students does indeed have appealing contemporary rose, silver and grey decor. At first sight a simple salad bar, it also serves tasty *galettes*, crêpes and classics like grilled meats or mussels and fries.

Café Latin, Caen.

Cafés & bars

Café Latin
135 rue St-Pierre, T02 31 85 26 36.
Mon-Sat 0830-0100.
Map: Caen, p152.

Always busy, from morning coffee to late-night drinks. The gaudy exterior draws you into this Spanish-oriented café and bar with atmospheric bare stone and wooden beams. Simple inexpensive meals are available; for example, Spanish omelette and fries.

Le Vertigo
14 rue Ecuyère, T02 31 85 43 12.
Mon-Sat 1000-0100
Map: Caen, p152.

Tiny, packed and trendy, with wooden benches and stone walls, relaxed atmosphere, rock music, their own jug cocktails and amiable service.

Lounge Café
2 place Malherbe,
T02 31 36 04 04.
Daily all day.
Map: Caen, p152.

A small, relaxed place with cool young style inside, and tables outside on the attractive little triangular square where rue St-Pierre meets rue Ecuyère. Popular with students.

La Ferme St-Siméon €€€
Rue Adolphe-Marais, T02 31 81 78 00, fermesaintsimeon.fr.
Lunch and dinner.

About 120 years ago artists met at this Côte de Grace inn for plain and simple fare with a glass of cider. Today it's a prestigious restaurant, with its massive old timbers and brickwork, where traditional local flavours are an important part of the inspiration for refined cooking. Shellfish is the speciality. The *carte des vins* includes some of the grandest wines in France.

Sa Qua Na €€€
22 place Hamelin, T02 31 89 40 80, alexandre-bourdas.com/ saquana/
Mon, Tue, Wed, Fri for dinner only, Sat-Sun for lunch and dinner.

The name is (broadly) Japanese for 'fish', and that's the speciality of this tranquil, refined Michelin-starred establishment. Under chef Alexandre Bourdas, skilful preparations like a piece of sea bream lightly cooked in coconut and lime oil are prepared with delicacy and finesse. The uncluttered ivory and charcoal decor with pale wooden tables enhances the zen-like simplicity. A meal here is a first-rate gastronomic experience. Book well ahead.

Bistro des Artistes €
14 place Pierre Berthelot, T02 31 89 95 90.
Thu-Mon (and Wed in season), closed Jan.

Enjoy simple, cheerful eating at this arty little quayside restaurant on several floors just off place Ste-Catherine (the third floor looks on to the port). On offer is a choice of tasty prepared salads all freshly made when ordered, delicious home-made bread, fresh oysters or a cooked dish of the day. Decor lives up to the name, with art books to peruse.

La Tortue €
30 rue de l'Homme-de-Bois, T02 31 81 24 60, restaurantlatortue.fr.

Good-value Normandy eating is served here in one of the town centre's appealing old half-timbered houses. Its different rooms are cosy and attractive with pale wooden floors, painted beams, walls adorned with pictures and white napery on tables that are set close together. There's a choice of wines by the glass to accompany straightforward fish and meat dishes usually well prepared.

Listings

Trouville & Deauville

Royal €€€
Bd Cornuché, Deauville, T02 31 98 66 33, lucienbarriere.com.
Mar-Oct, and 30-31 Dec, Mon-Fri dinner, Sat-Sun lunch and dinner.
The two opulent and old-fashioned restaurants of this white palace have earned it a Michelin star. The Etrier specializes in modern cuisine, while the Côté Royal, draped in luxury, offers substantial traditional French set menus.

Bistrot Les Quatre Chats €€
8 rue d'Orléans, Trouville, T02 31 88 94 94.
Mon-Fri 1930-2130 and also Fri-Sun 1200-1330.
With its immaculate 1950s decor, this popular and lively brasserie could almost pass for an old cinema, except, of course, for the little tables, snack-bar bench seating, simple traditional French cooking and well-stocked bar.

Les Vapeurs €€
160 quai Fernand Moureaux, Trouville, T02 31 88 15 24, lesvapeurs.fr.
All day.

Tip...
At Trouville's daily fish market on the quayside, you can buy ready-to-eat takeaway plates of oysters and other *fruits de mer*, complete with sliced lemon.

On the Trouville quayside among several other popular brasseries, Les Vapeurs is a pre-war establishment complete with original fittings. It can be too lively and crowded for comfort, but fresh local fish and shellfish are on the menu, with creamy Normandy sauces, and there's a selection of Normandy cheeses too. Prices are reasonable. During Deauville's film festival, you may see some famous faces.

Cafés & bars

Dupont avec un Thé
134 bd Fernand Moureaux, Trouville-sur-Mer, T02 31 88 13 82, and 20 place Morny, Deauville, T02 31 88 20 79, patisseriedupont.com.
This most luxurious of *pâtisseries salons de thé* is a feature of the Côte Fleurie, with a branch on both sides of the River Touques. Sit down and enjoy fine chocolate, fruit and almond indulgences or tender *macarons*.

West of Deauville

Dupont avec un Thé
42 rue Gaston Manneville, Dives-sur-Mer, T02 31 91 04 30, and 6 av Mer, Cabourg, T02 31 24 60 32, patisseriedupont.com.
The Côte Fleurie's favourite *pâtisserie salon de thé* has tender *macarons* and delicious treats of chocolate, fruit and almond. There's a branch in both these main towns at the western end of the coast.

Orbec

Au Caneton €€€
32 rue Grande, T02 31 32 73 32.
Tue-Sat lunch and dinner, Sun lunch only.
A really very pretty old building with its ivy and flower-boxes, and with two traditional, comfortable dining rooms, this is a good place to tuck into tasty and well-presented classic French cuisine.

St-Pierre-sur-Dives

Auberge de la Dives €€
27 bd Colas, T02 31 20 50 50.
Wed-Sun lunch and dinner (winter Sun lunch only), Mon lunch only.
With a terrace facing the River Dives, this simple unpretentious 'restaurant with rooms' surprises with its good quality cooking of classic Normandy fare.

Beuvron-en-Auge

Le Pavé d'Auge €€€€
Village centre, T02 31 79 26 71, pavedauge.com.
In the former covered market at the heart of the village, the long-established, Michelin-starred Pavé stands out as one of the top restaurants in the Auge region. Inventive, refined, luxurious cooking of fine local and worldwide produce, with plenty of Normandy lamb and seafood, creates fresh, clean flavours, beautifully presented.

Le Pommier €€€-€€

30-40 rue des Cuisiniers, T02 31 21 52 10, restaurantlepommier. com.
Daily 1200-1400 and 1900-2100 (Nov-Mar closed Sun), closed 3 weeks Dec-Jan.

As if the name didn't say it all, the apple-themed decor and colours make sure there's no mistaking the speciality of this stylish restaurant near the cathedral. Normandy's traditional dishes are imaginatively prepared and attractively served in an atmospheric setting of beams and bare stone. Tables are a little close together. There's also a vegetarian menu, if preferred.

Lion d'Or €€€-€€

71 rue St-Jean, T02 31 92 06 90, liondor-bayeux.fr.
Lunch and dinner.

Traditional and plush decor in this old inn provide the civilized setting for well-prepared classic French cuisine. Work through the *menu régional*, with Normandy specialities in every course.

Café Inn €

67 rue St-Martin, T02 31 21 11 37.
Mon-Sat 0900-1830.

This little *épicerie*, coffee shop and *salon de thé* is just the place to relax with a coffee and pastry, and also makes a good choice for inexpensive snacks, salads and omelettes at very modest prices.

La Marine €€

1 quai du Canada, Arromanches-les-Bains, T02 31 22 34 19,
Map: Les Plages du Débarquement (Landing Beaches), E2, p176.

A great place to enjoy fresh fish and seafood platters at bay windows or open-air tables right beside the seashore at Gold Beach, within a few minutes' walk of the D-Day Museum.

Le Bistro d'Arromanches €€

23 rue du Maréchal Joffre, Arromanches-les-Bains, T02 31 22 31 32, le-bistro.fr.
Wed-Sun.
Map: Les Plages du Débarquement (Landing Beaches), E2, p176.

There's simple, relaxed and cosy decor and good hearty eating of *fruits de mer* and fish dishes, and a good selection of salads, and pizzas, all at reasonable prices, as well as a choice of beers.

Le Bistrot d'à Côté €€

12 rue Michel Lefournier, Port-en-Bessin-Huppain, T02 31 51 79 12, barque-bleue.fr.
Map: Les Plages du Débarquement (Landing Beaches), D2, p176.

There's a seaside feeling at this bright and cheerful bistro near the beach, serving generous, well-prepared traditional fresh fish and seafood dishes with plenty of local flavours.

Le Vauban €€

6 rue Nord, Port-en-Bessin-Huppain, T02 31 21 74 83, restaurant-levauban.com.
Thu-Mon 1200-1345 and 1900-2045, Tue 1200-1345.
Map: Les Plages du Débarquement (Landing Beaches), D2, p176.

This simple local restaurant, decorated in pale colours with traditional table settings, offers good *fruits de mer*, fresh fish dishes and cuisine based on what's best in the market.

Pegasus Bridge Café Gondrée €

12 av Commdt Kieffer, Bénouville,T02 31 44 62 25.
Map: Les Plages du Débarquement (Landing Beaches), G3, p176.

When the British paratroops landed, they discovered a simple café-bar right beside the Caen canal bridge (on the Allied side on the canal). The café, flag-draped, is still run by the same family. Ordinary bar fare of drinks, snacks and light meals is served. Inside, it is a veritable museum dedicated to the wartime events. The original Pegasus Bridge can be seen in the nearby Mémorial Pegasus.

Entertainment

Bars & clubs

Le Carré
32 quai Vendeuvre, T02 31 38 90 90, caenbynight.com/carre.
Tue-Sun from 2230.
Smart dress and over 27s only (20 on Wednesday and Thursday) allowed at this crowded rock and retro club by the Port de Plaisance. The French Café is upstairs.

Le Chic
19 rue des Prairies St-Gilles, place Courtonne, T02 31 94 48 72, www.lechic.fr.
Tue-Sun 2230-0500.
Upbeat crowded disco with a 1980s feel and very varied music with the emphasis on dance rhythms. Caribbean nights Tuesday and Thursday. In the city centre close to the waterside.

Le French Café
32 quai Vendeuvre, T02 31 50 10 02, caenbynight.com/french.
Tue-Sun 1800-0300. Tue: singles. Wed: rock.
A good place to start your evening, or finish it, this relaxed, fun cocktail bar is on the theme of a café in Provence, complete with a plane tree and even a little second-hand shop. Almost all the music is French.

Children

Festyland
Route de Caumont, Bretteville-sur-Odon, T02 31 75 04 04, festyland.com.
Good old-fashioned family fun is on offer at this large leisure park on the southwestern edge of the city. It's themed around a fanciful version of Normandy's history, with simple rides and entertainments based on Vikings, William the Conqueror, pirates and the Middle Ages. There's a picnic area and four family-friendly restaurants, too.

Music

Comédie de Caen
1 square du Théâtre, Hérouville St-Clair, T02 31 46 27 29, comediedecaen.com.
Sep-May Mon-Fri 1400-1800 (and Sat 1500-1800 in Sep-Oct), usually €18, €14 concessions, €8 children 11 and over, €4 children 4-11.
Located in Hérouville, a suburban 'new town' on the city's northeast, the Comédie de Caen is a major host for cultural events in Normandy. Its main venue is the Théâtre d'Hérouville, a 700-seat theatre staging a wide variety of traditional and modern works across the range from dance to concerts to circus. It has a second venue in Caen city centre, the 300-seat Théâtre des Cordes (32 rue des Cordes).

Le Cargo
9 cours Caffarelli, T02 31 86 79 31, lecargo.fr.
Ticket office Tue-Sat 1400-1900.
You can catch up with a whole spectrum of live new bands and latest sounds at this concert venue and packed dance club, located across the water where the Port de Plaisance meets the River Orne.

Orchestre de Caen – Grand Auditorium de Caen
1 rue du Carel, T02 31 30 46 86 (for tickets), caenlamer.fr/orchestre_de_caen.
Ticket desk Mon-Fri 1000-1800, Sat 1000-1230, closed during school holidays.
Resident orchestra performing a wide variety of high-quality concerts from baroque to contemporary classical composers, as well as choral music and even jazz.

Théâtre de Caen
135 bd du Maréchal Leclerc, T02 31 30 48 00, theatre.caen.fr.
Tickets from €5 to €55, with a variety of reductions and concessions depending on the performances. There are no performances in July and August. The 1000-seat auditorium of Caen's city centre theatre is the venue for an extensive programme of modern and classical music, opera, dance and arts performances. In addition there are other stage entertainments like acrobats and

comedians, and in summer, when the theatre is closed, free events in the square outside.

Zénith
6 rue Joseph Philippon, T02 31 29 14 38, zenith-caen.fr.
Caen's 7000-seat auditorium hosts major stage performances by local, French and international names. There are shows in all genres, from ballet to world music, but the emphasis is on rock and pop.

Honfleur

Bars & clubs
Le Vintage Café
8 quai des Passagers, T02 31 89 05 28.
All day until late, food served Wed-Sun all day till 2400.
Convivial, laid-back atmosphere, food, wine and an evening of jazz till late are the mix that makes this one of Honfleur's most popular spots for visitors and locals. It's open for snacks and meals during the day too.

Trouville & Deauville

Bars & clubs
Casino Barrière de Deauville
2 rue Edmond-Blanc, Deauville, T02 31 14 31 14, lucienbarriere. com.
Sun-Thu 1000-0200, Fri 1000-0300, Sat 1000-0400. Gaming tables from 1600. Over 18s only – ID required.

Deauville has one of the grandest casinos in Europe, a glorious belle epoque palace belonging to the Lucien Barrière group (which owns several of the town's classiest addresses). Inside, in sumptuous pre-war gilded settings of chandeliers, marble and rich fabrics, there are slot machines and gaming rooms, three restaurants, three bars and a nightclub (Régine's – see below), a cinema and a show theatre with a wide spectrum of entertainment. The dress code is reasonably smart, with no sportswear allowed.

Casino Barrière de Trouville
Place du Maréchal Foch, Trouville-sur-Mer, T02 31 87 75 00, lucienbarriere.com.
Sun-Thu 1000-0200, Fri 1000-0300, Sat 1000-0400. Over 18s only – ID required.
If you'd like a flutter but don't want to risk losing a bundle among Deauville's high-rollers, try your luck in Trouville instead. Maybe something of a poor relation to Deauville's casino, nevertheless Trouville's grandiose waterfront landmark has many bars and restaurants, more than 200 slot machines and two gaming tables.

Le Régine's
Casino Barrière de Deauville, T02 31 14 31 96.
Summer daily, out of season Fri-Sat and national holidays only 2300-0500.

Dark, art deco designs create the opulent, hedonistic mood of this smart disco and nightclub at Deauville's Casino. Beware: the cheapest drinks on the menu start at €20 a glass (€120 for a bottle).

Les Planches
Domaine du Bois-Lauret, Blonville-sur-Mer, Deauville, T02 31 87 58 09, lesplanches.com.
Daily in summer, out of season Fri-Sat 2300-0500. Variable entry fees, sometimes free.
Some 7 km along the seafront, this is one of the resort's top spots for a night of upbeat music (mostly house), provided by a resident DJ and often celebrity guest DJs. There is a huge glitzy main space and several other areas including a pool, all right beside the beach.

Children
Natur'Aquarium
'Les Planches' Promenade Savignac, Trouville, T02 31 88 46 04, natur-aquarium.com.
Easter-All Saints 1000-1200 and 1400-1830 (except Jul-Aug 1000-1900), All Saints-Easter 1400-1800 (and 1000-1200 in part of school holidays). €7, €5 child/concessions.
This modest beachside aquarium may amuse young children for an hour with its collections of fish, insects and snakes.

Shopping

Children
Parc Zoologique Lisieux
*Cerza, Hermival-les-Vaux, T02 31
62 17 22, cerza.com.*
Jul-Aug 0930-1900, Apr-Jun and
Sep 0930-1830, Feb-Mar and
Oct-Nov 1000-1730, last entry
(all year round) 1600. €16, €9
4-10 years, under 4s free.
Get up close and personal with
over 600 species of wild animal
at this innovative zoo just outside
Lisieux, where you can travel
around by 'Little Train' between
the spacious animal enclosures,
meet certain creatures
face-to-face, and even spend the
night at the zoo with family
accommodation in chalet-style
'safari lodges'.

**Les Plages du
Débarquement
(Landing Beaches)**

Bars & clubs
Casino de Luc-sur-Mer
*20 rue Guynemer, Luc-sur-Mer,
T02 31 97 32 19.*
Daily 1000-0300, except
gaming tables Wed-Sun
2100-0300.
It's a surprise to find cabaret and
dancing on the Landing Beaches.
Unwind with dinner and a show
at the bars, theatre and gaming
tables of the seafront casino in
this busy little resort.

Caen

Clothing
Galeries Lafayette
*108 bd Maréchal Leclerc, T02 31
39 31 00, galerieslafayette.com.*
Mon-Sat 0930-1930.
Browse latest French style and
quality at this upmarket fashion
and furnishings department
store in the heart of the city
centre shopping district.

Food & drink
Charlotte Corday
*114 rue St-Jean, T02 31 86 33 25,
chocolat-corday.fr.*
Mon-Sat 0930-1230 and
1430-1900 (Mon morning
closed in winter).
This treasure house of
confectionery and hand-made
chocolate indulgences offers a
wide selection of local
specialities and delightfully
inventive treats, to eat now or in
smart gift packs.

Stiffler Pâtissier Traiteur
*72 rue St-Jean, T02 31 86 08 94,
stifflertraiteur.com*
Wed-Sat 0900-1300 and
1430-1930, Sun 0800-1800.
Top-quality pastries are the
speciality here, and you can sit
down and sample them on the
premises, which are also a *salon
de thé*. In addition, the shop sells
ready-prepared meats, salads
and savoury dishes to take away.

Caen market

There's a produce market
somewhere in Caen every day
of the week. The city's biggest
market is on Sunday morning
(0730-1330), when hundreds
of stalls fill place Courtonne
and neighbouring streets and
run four rows deep along quai
Vendeuvre. This huge gathering
of local producers and market
traders attracts buyers and
browsers from the whole city and
outlying areas. Not only is there a
huge array of high-quality food,
fresh farm produce and farm-
made *andouilles*, cheeses and
cider, but also whole sections
devoted to hats and clothes,
shoes and leather goods, carpets
and kitchenware, books and toys
and all sorts of arts and crafts.

Honfleur

Markets
The town centre around place
Ste-Catherine has an excellent
street market on Saturday
mornings, with a tempting array
of all the best of Normandy's
food and drink.

Activities & tours

Trouville

Markets

There's a daily indoor fish market at the Poissonnerie, on the waterfront. On Wednesday and Sunday, a busy market runs along the quayside from the Poissonnerie to the Pont des Belges.

Le Pays d'Auge

Markets

Lisieux
Wednesday and especially Saturday morning.

Orbec
Wednesday morning.

Pont l'Evêque
Monday morning.

St-Pierre-sur-Dives
Monday morning.

Caen

Cultural

Caen tourist office tours
Information and reservation T02 31 27 14 14, tourisme.caen.fr.
End Jun-end Aug, Tue-Sat. €6, €4.50 concessions, under 10s free.
Caen tourist office runs a range of guided city tours on summer afternoons, including a tour of the Château (starting 1400 and 1630), a walk to the Abbaye aux Dames (1430) and a walk to the Abbaye aux Hommes (1530). Tours last from one hour 15 minutes to one hour 30 minutes, and are in French only.

Caen Tourist Office dramatized tours
Information and reservation T02 31 27 14 14, tourisme.caen.fr.
Approx 8 Jul-23 Aug. €13, €9.50 concessions, under 10s free.
For French speakers, actors bring history to life on walking tours of the Château (Wed, Fri and Sat 1700) or to the Abbaye aux Dames (Thu and Sat 2100).

Petit Train
Leaves from place St-Pierre, opposite the tourist office, T06 16 37 01 45.
Jun-Sep, 1000-1800, approx hourly departures. €5, €4.50 child.
Board the 'Little Train' for a gentle trip through the city centre to all the main sights. Commentary is in French and English.

Food & wine

Ferme de Billy
29 bis rue de l'Eglise, Rots, T02 31 97 32 04, ferme-de-billy.com.
Daily 1 Apr-8 Nov, otherwise Mon-Sat.
About 7 km from Caen, heading northwest from the city, drop in at this interesting 17th-century mixed farm with 10,000 apple trees. Watch apple juice, ciders, *pommeau* and Calvados being made – and enjoy a free taste.

Racing

Hippodrome de Caen
La Prairie, T02 31 85 42 61.
For lovers of horseracing, Caen's famous 2-km track La Prairie borders the south side of the city centre, beside the north bank of the River Orne. There are about 30 races every year.

Trouville & Deauville

Literary walking tours

Trouville tourist office, 32 quai Fernand Moureaux, T02 31 14 60 70, trouvillesurmer.org.
May-Sep. French only.
Trouville tourist office puts on varied guided walking tours of Trouville – for example, *Promenades Littéraires* or *Sur les pas de Proust* – to discover the resort's many literary connections and visit the homes of famous 19th-century writers who lived or holidayed here, notably the writers Alexandre Dumas, Gustave Flaubert and Marcel Proust.

Racing

Deauville-Clairefontaine

Route de Clairefontaine, Deauville, T02 31 14 69 00, hippodrome-deauville-clairefontaine.com.

Though apparently oriented to holidaymakers and family visits, even encouraging picnickers to its pretty setting, this track is also serious about racing, with steeplechase and other events as well as flat racing every few days throughout July and August.

Deauville-La Touques

45 av Hocquart de Turtot, Deauville, T02 31 14 20 00, france-galop.com.

Deauville's prestigious main racecourse, almost in the town centre, attracts serious and wealthy racing enthusiasts as well as holiday crowds, especially to its mid-August yearling sales. The track holds about 50 races each year, with international meetings in summer and also a December season, which is run on a fibre track.

Le Pays d'Auge

Distillery visits

To see Calvados, cider and *pommeau* being made, and enjoy a taste of it too, these traditional Pays d'Auge distilleries in Calvados are open to visitors (see page 261 for more).

Calvados Boulard Moulin de la Foulonnerie

In village Coquainvilliers (6 km from Lisieux), T02 31 62 60 54, calvados-boulard.com.
Apr-Sep. 1-hr visit, €3.30.

Calvados Père Magloire

route de Trouville, Pont l'Evêque, T02 31 64 30 31, calvados-pere-magloire.com.
May-Oct. 45-min guided tour, €2.50.

Christian Drouin

Domaine Cœur de Lion, Coudray-Rabut (2 km from Pont l'Evêque), T02 31 64 30 05, coeur-de-lion.com.
All year. Free (including tasting).

Les Plages du Débarquement (Landing Beaches)

Tours

Battlebus

Bayeux, T02 31 22 28 82, battlebus.fr.
Day trips €85.

Long-standing business run by an English-French couple offering a good selection of full-day and custom-made private tours of the British, Canadian and American beaches in eight-seater minibuses accompanied by British guides. Tours start in Bayeux.

D-Day Tours

6 rue St-Jean, Bayeux, T02 31 51 70 52, normandywebguide.com.
Half-day prices from about €40 per person, reductions for students.

One of several companies offering a choice of full-day and half-day guided tours by minibus to the different beaches. Private guided tours are available. Start in either Caen or Bayeux.

Mémorial de Caen Battlefield Tours

Le Mémorial de Caen, esplanade Général Eisenhower, Caen, T02 31 06 06 45, memorial-caen.fr/fr/circuit_tour.
Day trip €109.50.

The Mémorial runs its own full-day minibus tour, which includes a visit to the Mémorial de Caen followed by a tour of the Landing Beaches. Tours start out from an assembly point at Caen railway station.

Utah Beach

Ste-Mère-Église tourist office, 6 rue Eisenhower, Ste-Mère-Eglise, T02 33 21 00 33.
A multimedia GPS video-guide for Ste-Mère-Eglise and Utah Beach is available from Ste-Mère-Église tourist office. Grandly called Musée à Ciel Ouverte (Open Skies Museum), it allows you to find, visit and explore 12 sites connected to the local D-Day landings. The guide costs €8 per day, but there is a €250 deposit.

Contents

Cotentin

Ile de Tatihou, St-Vaast-la-Hougue.

Introduction

The Cotentin Peninsula is a great wedge of northern France reaching far into the English Channel – La Manche, in French. It takes up a large part of Normandy's aptly named Manche *département*. The River Vire gives the Cotentin a boundary on the eastern side, while to the south and west the peninsula reaches down to Mont-St-Michel Bay and the River Sée. Despite the building of new road and rail links throughout Normandy in recent years, most of Cotentin remains thoroughly remote and rural. Even the largest town, the port of Cherbourg-Octeville (it changed its name from Cherbourg in the year 2000), does not feel well connected. On its coasts, especially on La Hague peninsula, the Cotentin can take on an awesome aspect, rocky and wild, with sea-battered cliffs and headlands, and protected coves where little fishing harbours shelter. The coast also opens out in places, with many long sandy beaches, such as the popular seashore at Carteret and either side of the harbour resort of Granville. In the tranquil interior, a multitude of lanes banked by mature hedges thread between tiny orchards and miniature farms where a few sheep or cows graze lush pasture. There are little towns, old abbeys and the small cathedral city of Coutances, but for the most part, inland Cotentin is simply glorious countryside.

What to see in...

... one day

From Cherbourg-Octeville, travel along the shore towards La Hague. Drive along the D901 to **Goury** fishing harbour, for a seashore walk. Head south on D37 to the resort of **Carteret**. Turn inland to visit **Coutances** and its cathedral. Cut across country via Carentan, to reach **Ste-Mère-Eglise**. End the day on the peninsula's eastern tip, in **St-Vaast-la-Hougue** and **Barfleur**.

...a weekend or more

Follow the coast from Cherbourg-Octeville to **Cap de la Hague**. Take the road to Carteret, and continue to **Granville**, an old coastal resort. Take a trip along D13 to **Abbaye de Hambye**. Compare it with the cathedral at **Coutances** and on D2, the twice-rebuilt Norman Romanesque **Abbaye de Lessay**. Cross the peninsula to the wartime sights of **Ste-Mère-Eglise**, and head towards **St-Vaast-la-Hougue** and **Barfleur**. It's a short distance through the green Val de Saire back to your starting point.

Jardin des Plantes, Coutances.

Cherbourg-Octeville

In the peaceful post-war years, Cherbourg-Octeville became a major cross-channel ferry port, and today is visited by more yachts than any other harbour in Europe There is a bustling, enjoyable atmosphere in the old town centre as well as an attractive waterfront plaza, some pedestrianized streets lined with attractive old stone buildings, pleasant cafés and good shops. The marina and centre of town lie on the west bank of the harbour, while the ferries and commercial shipping are kept on the east bank. You can still see, though, that Cherbourg-Octeville, with its mighty harbour defences, has a military heritage. Indeed, it's still one of France's largest naval ports. Cherbourg-Octeville originally sprang from an idea in the mind of the 17th-century military architect Marquis de Vauban. His vision was of a fortified trading and naval port at the very tip of the Cotentin, greatly enlarged by man-made harbours, which could be made suitable for large ocean-going vessels. The idea was far ahead of its time. A breakwater strong enough to make this possible could not be built for 150 years, the naval port finally opening in 1858, long after Vauban's death. The town's heyday came in the 1930s, when the largest and most luxurious ocean cruise ships, as well as a huge tonnage of industrial shipping, were docking at Cherbourg. During the Normandy Invasion in 1944, Cherbourg was the centre of a huge battle (13-26 June) to drive out the Germans, after which it was developed as the main port for supplies to the Liberation forces. While that period robbed the town of its historic appearance, it has allowed Cherbourg to redevelop, modernize and remain a major port town.

Essentials

❶ Getting around Daytime public transport right across the city of Cherbourg-Octeville is provided by **Zéphir Bus** (T08 10 81 00 50, zephirbus.com) between about 0620 and 1945 Monday-Saturday, about 0750-1900 Sunday, additional limited service Friday and Saturday nights. Their website details routes, timetables and discount tickets. The central point for town buses is boulevard R Schumann where most lines intersect.

❷ Bus station Avenue Jean-François Millet, T02 33 44 32 22. For details of regional bus services, see page 273.

❸ Train station Avenue Jean-François Millet, T02 33 44 36 35. For details of regional rail services, see page 271.

❹ ATM There are 10 banks with ATMs in the centre of town, including two in rue Foch.

❺ Hospital Hôpital Louis Pasteur, 46 rue du Val de Saire, T02 33 20 70 00.

❻ Pharmacy There are many pharmacies in the town centre, including: **Pharmacie Goffin**, 1 place Géneral de Gaulle, T02 33 20 41 29, and **Pharmacie Lepetit-Dupas**, 49 rue Foch, T02 33 43 13 42.

❼ Post office Place Divette, T02 33 08 87 01, Monday-Friday 0800-1900, Saturday 0900-1200.

❽ Tourist information 2 quai Alexandre III, T02 33 93 52 02, octcherbourgcotentin.fr, September-May 0900-1200 and 1400-1800, June 0900-1230 and 1400-1830, July-August 0900-1830.

It's a fact...

Cotentin's eastern flank gives way to the flatter, sandier shoreline where American forces arrived on 6 June 1944, codenamed Utah beach, north of the town of Carentan. See page 183.

Parc Emmanuel Liais

Rond Point Leclerc, between rue de l'Abbaye and la rue de la Bucaille, T02 33 53 12 31.
Open from about 0800 to evening – varies throughout year. Free.
Map: Cherbourg-Octeville, p206.

For a quiet stroll in the town centre, visit these public botanic gardens, bursting with 500 varieties of tropical plant, laid out in the 19th century.

Around the region

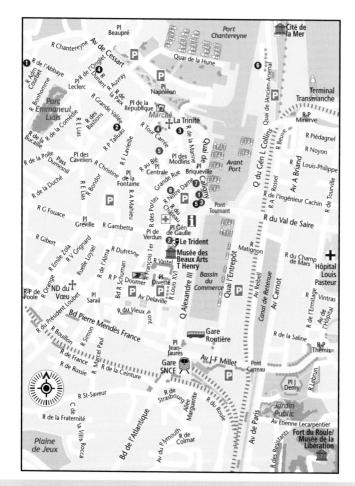

Cherbourg-Octeville listings

① Sleeping
1 Auberge de Jeunesse de Cherbourg-Octeville *55 rue de l'Abbaye*
2 Hôtel Angleterre *8 rue P Talluau*
3 Hôtel de la Renaissance *4 rue de l'Eglise*
4 Hôtel Le Louvre *2 rue Henri Dunant*
5 La Régence *42 quai Caligny*
6 Mercure Cherbourg Plaisance *allée du Président Menut*

① Eating & drinking
1 Café de Paris *40 quai Caligny*
2 Café du Théâtre *8 place Général de Gaulle*
3 La Régence *42 quai Caligny*
4 Le Faitout *25 rue Tour Carrée*
5 Le Plouc 2 *59 rue Blé*
6 Le Pommier *15 bis rue Notre Dame*
7 Le Vauban *22 quai Caligny*

Redoubtable, the nuclear submarine at Cité de la Mer.

Tip...

Cherbourg-Octeville has no proper beach, but during July and August there is a bus, Le Bus Plage, running from the city centre to the Plage de Collignon, just east of town, and Plage de Querqueville, to the west.

Cité de la Mer

Gare Maritime Transatlantique, T02 33 20 26 26, citedelamer.com.
Open 0930-1800 or 1900, with variations depending on school holidays, last tickets sold 1 hr before closing. Low season €15.50, €10.50 child (under 5s free), high season €18, €13 child (under 5s free).
Map: Cherbourg-Octeville, p206.

If you have some hours to pass in Cherbourg-Octeville, it's worth crossing to the right bank to visit this family attraction. There is a good aquarium here, said to be Europe's deepest, but the focus is on our relationship with the sea. The main attraction is an interesting self-guided tour of the nuclear submarine, *Redoubtable*. The Cité is located inside the former transatlantic station, next to the transatlantic dock, so with luck there may be a cruise liner moored alongside.

Musée des Beaux-Arts Thomas Henry (Thomas Henry Fine Arts Museum)

4 rue Vastel, T02 33 23 39 30.
May-Sep Tue-Sat 1000-1200 and 1400-1800, Sun-Mon 1400-1800, Oct-Apr daily 1400-1800. Free.
Map: Cherbourg-Octeville, p206.

Behind the town's theatre, the town's most prestigious museum displays an art collection of works spanning the 15th to the 19th centuries. Among them is a work by Fra Angelico, and several by Jean-François Millet, who grew up locally.

Fort de Roule – Musée de la Libération (Museum of the Liberation)

Fort du Roule, T02 33 20 14 12.
May-Sep 1000-1200 and 1400-1800 (Sun-Mon afternoon only), Oct-Apr Wed-Sun 1400-1800)
Map: Cherbourg-Octeville, p206.

Also on the right bank, on a high ridge behind the harbour, the 19th-century Fort de Roule has a magnificent view over the town and its huge harbour. Inside the fortress, displays graphically record not simply the events of the liberation but also those that led to the defeat of France by the Nazis, and life during the German occupation. On display is an impressive collection of uniforms and weapons, maps of the period, scale models and photographs that bring the Liberation to life.

It's a fact...

Officially, there is no town in France called Cherbourg. In the year 2000, Cherbourg joined with a suburb, and changed its name to Cherbourg-Octeville

Cap de la Hague

Tip…

The Hague Peninsula has its own
tourist information office:
Office du Tourisme de la Hague,
45 rue Jaillot, Beaumont-Hague
T02 33 52 74 94, lahague.org.

Lighthouse and port of Goury.

The most dramatic of the Cotentin's rugged coastal scenery lies west of Cherbourg-Octeville, in the area known as La Hague. Within moments, you are taken on narrow lanes from awesome sea cliffs to traditional small farms with stone farmhouses and muddy farmyards.

Take the main coast road out of **Cherbourg-Octeville**, heading west from place Napoléon along the D901 Just at the edge of town, at a roundabout where the road turns away from the sea, take D45, and follow it as it leaves Cherbourg-Octeville and its suburbs behind.

You will first approach **Querqueville**, where a hilltop chapel dating from the 10th century is one of the oldest churches in France. Skirt quiet **Urville-Nacqueville**, which has a good sandy beach and a beautiful 16th-century château (Easter to end Sep Mon, Wed and Thu 1200-1700, €6) standing in sheltered, wooded grounds noted for the rhododendrons. The road climbs to the impressive towers and walls of 16th-century **Dur-Ecu manor** and arrives at the village of **Landemer**, with good sea views. Beyond it are magnificent roadside viewpoints. Just off to the right of D45, on D237, the seashore village of **Gruchy** was the birthplace of the artist François Millet (1814-1875), leading light of the Barbizon school. Child of a poor working family, he became a pioneer and one of the greatest proponents of painting natural scenes and ordinary working people. His former home can be visited on guided tours (Apr-Sep, €4).

Stay on D45 as it swings away from the seashore, eventually returning to it at little **Omonville-la-Rogue**, dominated by its solid, low 13th-century church. The village has a charming small harbour, edged with simple cottages. In the churchyard of its neighbour **Omonville-la-Petite** the poet Jacques Prévert (1900-1977) is buried. **Port-Racine**, just beyond, is another tiny and charming quayside village, and claims – quite plausibly – to be 'the smallest port in France'. The road now approaches the windy tip of **Cap de la Hague**, the far end of the

peninsula, where several small communities cluster. The village of **Goury**, right on the cape, has an attractive harbour, and is renowned for the many lives saved by its brave lifeboat crew. The Goury lighthouse is well known to sailors in these capricious waters. At low tide, razor-edged rocks can be seen just beneath the waves. Goury's near-neighbour **Auderville** has two excellent 15th-century alabasters in an otherwise plain and simple 13th-century church.

D45 ends here. Much of the terrain on the south side of the cape feels wild and untouched. Follow steep, narrow D401 (or take the busier main road D901 across higher ground) to reach the turning on the left for **Nez de Voidries** and **Nez de Jobourg**, bird reserves and rocky headlands with high cliffs and glorious views to the Channel Islands. When you get back on to D901, turn right and hurry past a large nuclear reprocessing plant.

Steep lanes run between the main road and the sea. Take D318 from Beaumont-Hague down to **Vauville**, a delightful village of dry-stone walls and old stone houses. From here the D237 to Biville has magnificent coastal views. **Biville** is the home of a rather obscure cult, the veneration of Thomas Helye (1187-1257), known as *Le Bienheureux* (Blessed), a priest whose supposedly miracle-working remains are preserved in a modern shrine in the 13th-century church. A footpath (about 20 minutes each way) leads to a granite crucifix on a high point, known as the **Calvaire des Dunes**, from which there is a magnificent vista along the western Cotentin coast from Flamanville to Nez de Jobourg.

From Biville, climb D118 back to D901. Turn right for Cherbourg-Octeville. A turning on the right, rue du Bigard, leads up to the modern, family-oriented (but French only) **Ludiver Planétarium de la Hague** (T02 33 78 13 80, ludiver.com; site open Jul-Aug daily 1100-1830, rest of year Sun-Fri 1400-1800; planetarium shows Jul-Aug daily at 1130, 1500 and 1630, rest of year at 1500 only; €7.50, €5.50 child and concessions), which has a museum about stars and planets, children's entertainment as well as the planetarium. D901 takes you the short distance back into Cherbourg-Octeville.

Northern Cotentin

At first sight, the northern (or upper) Cotentin seems dominated by the modern industrial port town of Cherbourg-Octeville at its tip. Yet this part of the peninsula also preserves the greatest sense of unharnessed and unspoiled nature. It was here that the first Norse invaders set foot in Normandy, and here that they clung on longest to their old culture. Many village names incorporate a *bec* (stream, in Norse), *tot* (house) or *hougue* (low hill). Rocky headlands, panoramic sea views and enchanting little fishing harbours characterize the wild Cap de la Hague area, west of Cherbourg-Octeville. The temptation to get out of the car and have a good walk is irresistible! Everywhere, the sea feels close. The highlight is the lofty Nez de Jobourg cliffs facing towards the Channel Islands across the dangerous currents of the Alderney Races. East of Cherbourg-Octeville lies the more sheltered Val de Saire, where the little Saire river running through tranquil, rustic countryside. Barfleur and St-Vaast-la-Hougue are fishing ports with charming, old-fashioned quaysides and good little hotels and seafood restaurants. For a surprising contrast, head away from the coasts into the lanes and villages of the interior, a gentle, quiet landscape of streams and wildflower meadows, fields and woods of beech and oak.

There's a long history behind the delightful scene of Barfleur's bustling fishing harbour, with its cobbled quaysides and simple stone houses looking on to the working trawlers and the dockside activity. It used to make a popular weekend outing for the residents of Cherbourg, but today is relatively little visited.

It was once a much larger town and more important harbour. In 1066 William the Conqueror's ship set sail from here on his campaign against England (William himself boarded it at Dives, on the coast near Caen), and it was from Barfleur that Richard the Lionheart set sail to England in 1194 to be crowned king. In 1120 the *Blanc Nef* foundered on the rocks off Pointe de Barfleur, just north of the town, with the loss of some three members of the Anglo-Norman nobility – among them the heir to the English throne, William, son of Henry I.

Phare de Gatteville

25c la Route du Phare, Gatteville-le-Phare, T02 33 23 17 97, pharedegatteville.com.
Daily Feb-Mar and Oct 1000-1200 and 1400-1600, Apr and Sep 1000-1200 and 1400-1800, May-Aug 1000-1200 and 1400-1900, closed in bad weather, about €2, children free.

Today, a seashore path takes you 4 km to the huge Gatteville Lighthouse, which now casts its warning

Northern Cotentin essentials

ℹ Tourist information Barfleur: 2 rond Point Guillaume le Conquérant, T02-33 54 02 48, ville-barfleur. fr, July-August 1000-1230 and 1430-1900; April-June and September Monday-Saturday 0930-1230 and 1430-1830, sometimes open Sunday 1000-1230 and 1430-1900. **Barneville**: 10 rue des Ecoles, T02-33 04 90 58, Mon-Sat 0900-1200 and 1400-1800. **Carteret**: place Flandres Dunkerque, T02-33 04 94 54, daily July-August 1000-1230 and 1500-1900. **Lessay**: 11 place St-Cloud, T02-33 45 14 34, canton-lessay.com. **Northern Cotentin**: 2 quai Alexandre III, T02-33 93 52 02, otcherbourgcotentin. fr, September-May 0900-1200 and 1400-1800, June 0900-1230 and 1400-1830, July-August 0900-1830. **Ste-Mère-Eglise**: 6 rue Eisenhower, T02-33 21 00 33, sainte-mere-eglise.info. **St-Vaast-la-Hougue**: 1 place du Général de Gaulle, T02-33 23 19 32, saint-vaast-reville. com, open morning and afternoon Monday-Saturday (and Sunday April-September).

from that treacherous headland. Almost 75 m tall, with 365 steps to the top, on a clear day the lighthouse gives a view reaching 30 km out to sea.

Tourist information: 1 place du Général de Gaulle, T02 33 23 19 32, saint-vaast-reville.com.

With a name clearly revealing its Norse origins, St-Vaast is famous in France for its crabs and other shellfish and especially its high-quality oysters. Along the quayside, fishing boats are moored and lobster pots stacked high as fishermen sit fixing the snags in their nets, while scores of small yachts jostle at floating pontoons. The quayside leads round to a long jetty projecting into the waves and protecting the harbour. Such a large and deep harbour – and fortified, too – is far more than the fishermen or even the yachtsmen need. Those features date from past centuries, when St-Vaast was a bigger town, and much involved in wars between France and England. In a crucial episode, England's Catholic King James II, displaced by the Protestant William of Orange, massed a great Irish and French 'Catholic fleet' at St-Vaast in 1692. He

Tip...

Locals call their town simply 'St Va'.

Amphibious boat at St-Vaast-la-Hougue.

St-Vaast-la-Hougue harbour.

intended to launch a great attack on England and regain his crown. But the Irish and French sailors would not work together and, coming under a surprise attack by an English and Dutch 'Protestant fleet', were routed before they had even set sail, in what was known as the Battle of La Hougue.

Ile de Tatihou

tatihou.com.

Just offshore is Tatihou Island; fortified by Vauban, it is now inhabited mainly by a huge number of seabirds. Access to the island is limited to 500 visitors per day (to protect the wildlife; no dogs are allowed). At low tide, if the tidal coefficients are right, it's sometimes possible to get to it on foot on a path called the Rhun that winds through the oysterbeds. If not, you can ride in a curious amphibious three-wheeled **ferry boat** (Quai Vauban, St-Vaast-la-Hougue, T02 33 23 19 92; Apr-Sep daily and Oct-Mar Sat-Sun, approximately 1000-1730 every 30-60 mins, timings according to the tide, 10-min trip; return €7.80, €3.20 child, under 4s free, includes entry to

the Tour Vauban fort and museum on the island; return crossing only, €4.60, €1.50 child, one-way €3, €1.50 child).

It was on Tatihou that King Edward II landed in 1346 to place his feet on French soil and claim the throne of France.

On the island, there are gardens, old shipwright's workshops and a modest **maritime heritage museum** as well as Vauban's **fort** or tower (fort and museum €4.60, €2.30 child, under 4s free, all tickets should be bought from the Accueil Tatihou on quai Vauban in St-Vaast). The 21-m-tall tower, declared a World Heritage Site in 2008, contains a gunpowder store, sleeping quarters and

Tip...

Warning: always check the tidal coefficients before crossing to Tatihou on foot. Even if the path appears to be safely uncovered, the coefficient must be 70 or more to allow sufficient time to cross safely there and back. The tourist office on the quayside can assist in case of uncertainty.

Five of the best

Places to see on the Cotentin coast

❶ The shores of Mont-St-Michel Bay – take D911 south of Granville along the coast to Jullouville and Carolles for long sandy beaches, promenades, flowers and dreamily beautiful views.
❷ Granville – place de l'Isthme, the main square in the Upper Town, has an immense coastal vista.
❸ Cap de la Hague – rocky headlands, tiny harbours and dramatic views towards the Channel Islands.
❹ Barneville-Carteret – an elegant belle epoque resort, glorious beaches and majestic views.
❺ St-Vaast-la-Hougue – stroll the busy, picturesque working fishing harbour and take a trip to little Tatihou Island, just offshore.

Carteret.

canon platform, and has its own fortified farm. The high point of Tatihou's year is the folk festival held every August, with plenty of events held on the St-Vaast quayside. It is possible to stay on the island in simple lodgings (see Sleeping, page 224).

Ste-Mère-Eglise

This village lies just inland from Utah Beach (see page 183). German soldiers marched into Ste-Mère on 18 June 1940 and established Nazi rule here, as everywhere in the Cotentin. Almost four years later, in the evening of 5 June 1944, the sky over the village was filled by 811 US Air Force planes, which dropped 14,238 parachutists of the 82nd and 101st airborne divisions on to Ste-Mère. The Americans took control of the village just before midnight.

Eglise

Place de l'Eglise.
Daily, about 0800-1800.

Famously, during the night of 5 June 1944 one wretched American parachutist got caught on the **church tower** and hung there for hours – an incident shown in the film *The Longest Day*. A dummy representing him, his billowing parachute caught above, remains there to this day and is still a shocking and pitiful image. Inside the church, the oldest parts of which date from the 11th century, a vivid modern stained-glass window depicts the Virgin Mary surrounded by parachutists and planes. A second window is a gift from US parachute regiment veterans. You'll see other memorials of the Liberation around the church square.

A dummy airman hangs from the church roof at Ste-Mère-Eglise.

Coastline at Barneville-Carteret.

Tip…

For a good coastal walk, take the old Sentier des Douaniers (Customs Officers' path), which follows the cliff top around Cap de Carteret.

Musée Airborne

14 rue Eisenhower, T02 33 41 41 35, musee-airborne.com.
Apr-Sep 0900-1845, Feb-Mar and Oct-Nov and part of Christmas/New Year period 0930-1200 and 1400-1800, €7, €4 child, veterans free.

Just across the square from the church, the town's museum is in two buildings, one under a roof representing a landing parachute and the other representing the wing of a plane. Displays range from a genuine Douglas C47 plane and WACO glider to uniforms, vehicles, weapons and evocative documents and photographs.

Barneville-Carteret

Barneville and Carteret (barneville-carteret.fr) are neighbouring small towns that have joined together administratively, yet preserve quite distinct and separate characters. Between them lies a large natural harbour in the estuary of the River Gerfleur. From the harbour, you can catch a ferry to Jersey. It's close enough for a day trip. On the south side of the Gerfleur, set back from the harbour, quiet **Barneville** is mainly residential. At its heart is an 11th-century church and there's a good street market on Saturdays with masses of fresh fish and shellfish. Between the harbour and the sandy seashore, Barneville's rather sedate but very popular well-equipped modern family beach resort is called **Barneville-Plage**.

On the north side of the harbour is the livelier and more atmospheric small fishing town of **Carteret**. There's a sandy beach on this side too, smaller but well sheltered. It leads out towards a rocky cape called Cap de Carteret, last of the Cotentin headlands before the tamer coasts of Southern Cotentin. On the cliff top stand a chapel and a lighthouse.

Tip…

At low tide, miles of sand and rock pools along the Barneville-Carteret waterfronts are exposed. You can find a huge selection of shellfish, especially crabs and shrimps.

Lessay

In what was then an open and uninhabited part of the Cotentin – today it is lightly wooded farming country – 1000 years ago the quiet village of Lessay grew around a lonely abbey. The Benedictine community built a fine **abbey church** (usually open daily 0900-1800, except during services) here in 1050. It later years it was altered, and for centuries was considered one of the loveliest examples of Norman Romanesque architecture and a pioneer in its development of the style. During the bombardment of 1944, the church was very badly damaged, but was skilfully repaired by stonemasons from 1945 to 1958. Sturdy, plain and unadorned, it is quiet, restful, perfectly symmetrical and pleasingly proportioned. The masons used the same elegant pale stone as

before, although the older stone appears to have a slightly pinker tint. The church contains a modern organ, installed in 1994, and is a delightful place to enjoy classical concerts during July and August.

Tip...

Mont Castre, about 10 km northeast of Lessay, was the site of one of the greatest battles between the Gauls and the Romans. Thousands of fighting men of the Unelli and other tribes, under their leader Viridovix, died here in 56 BC in their struggle to prevent Roman rule.

Southern Cotentin

Inland, especially in its southern half, the Cotentin peninsula broadens out into the varied and attractive small-scale farming country called *bocage*. The sea feels further away and less dominant. The land becomes gentler. Sunken lanes weave between tall hedges and orchards and fields of good rich pasture. Several of the thriving little country towns have a long history – this was a centre of pre-Roman civilization, then of Roman rule and was populous in the Middle Ages too. Among those towns that reward a visit are ancient Coutances and curiously named Villedieu-les-Poêles (God's Town of Pans). Along its west coast, the Manche *département* intersperses sandy beaches and dunes, marshes where seabirds cluster, small harbour towns and rocky headlands. Here and there are remnants of German gun emplacements. There's a string of little holiday resorts, including Portbail, with its Romanesque church and Gallo-Roman baptistry, and Coutainville, with superb beach and fin-de-siècle charm. Granville is altogether bigger and busier, with plenty of interest in its Upper and Lower towns. The coast road south of town curves along the Bay of Mont-St-Michel at the foot of the Cotentin Peninsula, giving some exquisite views.

Occupying a hilltop position, this appealing and attractive small cathedral city has existed here in one form or another for at least 2000 years. Under the name Cosedia, it was the main settlement of the Unelli tribe whose resistance to Roman rule proved troublesome to Caesar. Eventually subdued by Rome in 56 BC, it had to be defended during the Roman occupation. By about AD 500, Coutances became the seat of an important bishopric whose authority included the Channel Islands, and had a cathedral. Ninth-century Viking raiders almost destroyed the town and drove away the clergy and the rest of population, but rebuilt a Norse town of their own among the ruins, complete with a new cathedral in their Norman Romanesque style. In 1218, Coutances was damaged again, by fire, which is why its present cathedral dates from that time. Bombed in 1944, the town has once more recovered and much of it has been restored, although the loss of many buildings is plain to see.

Southern Cotentin essentials

❶ Tourist information Coutances: place Georges Leclerc, T02 33 19 08 10, in summer season Monday-Friday 0930-1830, Saturday 1000-1230 and 1400-1800, Sunday 1000-1300; rest of year Monday-Friday 0930-1230 and 1400-1800, Saturday 1000-1230 and 1400-1700. **Villedieu-les-Poêles:** 43 place de la République, T02 33 61 05 69, ot-villedieu.fr, July-August daily 0900-1800, September-June Monday-Saturday 0900-1200 and 1400-1730. **Granville:** cours Jonville, T02 33 91 30 03, granville-tourisme.fr, summer Monday-Saturday 0900-1300 and 1400-1900, Sunday 1000-1300 and 1500-1800; winter Monday-Saturday 0900-1230 and 1400-1730.

Cathédrale de Notre-Dame de Coutances

Rue Tancrède, cathedralecoutances.free.fr. Daily 0900-1900 (1800 in winter). Free; extensive programme of guided tours available, ask at tourist office.

Luckily, Coutances' greatest possession survived the war. The cathedral stands on the main street at the summit of the town. Its three tall towers are visible from afar, one of them a massive octagonal lantern tower soaring to 41 m. Beautiful inside and

Tip...

Most medieval stained-glass windows tell a story, often from the Bible or the lives of saints. Look closely at the stained glass in the north transept of Coutances cathedral and you'll see that it tells the story of Thomas à Becket, who was murdered in Canterbury cathedral in 1170.

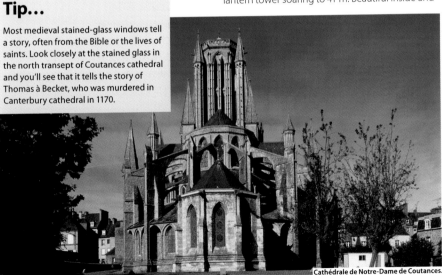

Cathédrale de Notre-Dame de Coutances.

out, Coutances cathedral is numbered among the great masterpieces of Norman Gothic architecture. Yet curiously, although built in the 13th century, it was constructed closely around the framework of its 11th-century Romanesque predecessor, parts of the building being Gothic stonework attached to the Romanesque structure.

The total effect is of elegant simplicity and masterful workmanship, bringing together solidity and finesse. Inside, arches are high and narrow, the aisles open on to a succession of side chapels, and the inside of the lantern tower is surprisingly beautiful. Some of the sculpture and the rich blue stained glass on the west front dates right back to its 13th-century reconsecration. There is plenty of later work, too, including the very striking and graceful **Notre-Dame de la Circata**, a 14th-century marble sculpture of a colourfully draped Madonna and Child depicted as essentially just an ordinary, wistful mother (albeit wearing a crown) holding her little boy on her arm. This touching image, standing in the painted Lady Chapel, attracted large numbers of pilgrims during the turmoil of the Hundred Years War.

The much-revered **Chapelle Religeuse** displays a remarkable collection of body parts and bodily fragments, supposedly being the relics of numerous important saints, bishops, abbots, priests, martyrs and other Catholic celebrities, as well as pieces of the Cross and even the crown of thorns.

Jardin des Plantes

Rue Quesnel-Morinière, T02 33 19 08 10. Daily Jul-Aug 0900-2330 with illuminations, otherwise Apr-Sep 0900-2000, Oct-Mar 0900-1700. Free.

The square in front of the cathedral is the town's marketplace, and just a few minutes' walk on the other side of it is the entrance of the extensive 19th-century Jardin des Plantes. This delightful green park has wonderfully imaginative herbaceous displays, lawns, copses and narrow, flowery paved terraces with fountains. In summer, illuminations and music make it quite magical. At the entrance to the gardens, **Musée Quesnel-Morinière** (2 rue Quesnel-Morinière, T02 33 07 07 88, Mon and Wed-Sat 1000-1200 and 1400-1700 (Jul-Aug 1800), Sun 1400-1700, €2.50, children free) displays a variety of local arts and traditional regional craftsmanship, and there are some good paintings too, with some surprises – notably, a painting by Rubens of *Lions and Dogs Fighting*.

Quel est le fou sublime qui osa lancer dans les airs un pareil monument?

(What sublime madman dared launch such a monument into the air?)

The 17th-century military engineer Vauban on seeing Coutances cathedral with magnificent architecture perfect in every aspect.

Jardin des Plantes.

It's a fact…

The Cotentin Peninsula takes its name from Coutances. The town's Roman name was Constantia, while the majority of the peninsula, ruled from here, was a *pagus* (district) called Constantinus.

Abbaye de Hambye & Villedieu-les-Poêles

Abbaye de Hambye

12 km north of Villedieu-les-Poêles on D9 and D51, T02 33 61 76 92, sitesetmusees.cg50.fr.
Apr-Jun and Sep-Oct Wed-Mon 1000-1200 and 1400-1800, Jul-Aug daily 1000-1200 and 1400-1800 (but published times sometimes not adhered to), closed winter, except by appointment. €4.20, €3.20 concession, €1.75 child, includes guided tour of the private monastic quarters.

In a calm, utterly rural setting hidden in the valley of the little River Sienne, the ruins of this exquisite abbey, founded in 1145, look as if they could be quickly repaired and brought back into use by the community that now lives at the site. Inside the majestic, austere Gothic abbey church, the open sky provides the roof. The evocative rooms around the former cloisters, the chapter house, dormitory and 13th-century kitchen with its impressive fireplace have been restored. The former refectory is decorated with fine old tapestries. The community's farm buildings, with stables and cider press, survive almost as they were in the 16th century.

Villedieu-les-Poêles

The strange name – God's Town of Pans – honours almost 1000 years of excellent workmanship making hand-crafted copper pots, flagons, milk-churns, casseroles and of course pans, as well as many other metal goods. The craft was originally brought here by the Knights of Malta, honoured by the town in the **Grand Sacré** festival every four

years (next in 2012, villedieu-grandsacre.fr). Metal-working industries continue, with factories making water tanks and central heating boilers. Despite its industrial heritage, Villedieu is a pleasing town, lying on both banks of the River Sienne. It preserves many historic streets and courtyards, where you'll find several remaining small workshops. Walk along the main street, place de la République and rue Carnot, to find many small shops selling high-quality copper kitchenware.

Fonderie Cornille-Havard (10 rue du Pont Chignon, T02 33 61 00 56, cornille-havard.com, mid-Feb to 11 Nov Tue-Sun 1000-1230 and 1400-1800, Jul-Aug daily 0900-1800, 20-min guided

Granville.

tours in English and other languages, €4.90, €4 child) is one of the last remaining traditional bell foundries still in business. Lace making has been another local craft. Several museums, all close together in the town centre, explore Villedieu's traditional manufacturing trades, among them **Musée de la Poeslerie – Maison de la Dentellière** (Museum of Pan-making – House of Lace, Cour du Foyer, 25 rue du Général Huard, T02 33 69 33 44, museesvilledieu.sitew.com, Tue 1400-1830, Wed-Sat 1000-1230 and 1400-1830, and every second week Sun 1400-1830, €4, €2 child, under 10s free), tucked away in a picturesque yard.

Granville

Larger than the other Cotentin beach resorts, Granville attracts summer crowds, and has done for more than a century. It's divided into the sombre fortified Upper Town (Ville Haute), high on a rocky ridge rising sheer from the sea, and the newer Lower Town (Ville Basse). The Upper Town came into being as an English fort in the 15th century. They rapidly lost control of it, and in 1695 it was the English themselves who almost destroyed the town when they attacked corsaires (pirates)

who were based here. Granville began to flourish again with the growth of its fishing harbour, which grew to become the Lower Town, and in the 19th century began its career as a holiday resort.

Cross the drawbridge and pass through the **Grande Porte**, a 16th-century gatehouse, into the Upper Town. Just inside the gate, the **Musée du Vieux Granville** (2 rue Lecarpentier, T02 33 50 44 10, Apr-Sep Wed-Mon 1000-1200 and 1400-1800 (1830 in Jul-Aug), Oct-Dec and Feb-Mar Wed, Sat and Sun 1400-1800, €1.70, €1 concessions and under 11s free) gives background information about the town that proves useful when you are strolling around. Turn right along quiet, narrow and atmospheric old streets of granite 18th-century houses to reach the large and airy main square, **place de l'Isthme**. The square gives spectacular sea views. From here, the **Iles Chausey**, 16 km away, seem very close. Further away, the hills of Brittany rise from the horizon. If you're tempted to visit the Chausey Islands, which are administratively part of Granville, you can catch a ferry there from the harbour in the bustling and lively Lower Town (see right), where the animated marina is the focal point.

Musée d'Art Moderne Richard Anacréon

Place de l'Isthme, T02 33 51 02 94.
May-Sep Tue-Wed 1100-1800, Oct-Apr Wed-Sun 1400-1800. €2.60, €1.40 concessions, under 10s free, fees liable to alteration, temporary exhibitions may have their own opening hours and entry fees.

The art museum in the Upper Town's main square came into being when a private collector gave Granville his whole collection of 280 works of art and 550 annotated books, forming an unrivalled assembly of modern late 19th and 20th-century art and literature. Painters in the collection include Derain, van Dongen, Vlaminck, Utrillo, Laurencin, Signac, Friesz, Cross and Luce. Among the books and manuscripts are extraordinary rare volumes and first editions, by such authors as Apollinaire, Cocteau, Colette, Genet, Loti and Valéry. The museum hosts a succession of prestigious temporary exhibitions.

Musée Christian Dior

Villa Les Rhumbs, rue Estouteville, T02 33 61 48 21, musee-dior-granville.com.
Summer only, dates variable but generally 1 May-20 Sep, daily 1000-1830, €6, €4 concessions, under 12s.

Overlooking the sea from the north side of the Lower Town, the museum occupies the childhood home of the great *couturier*. A grand 1920s private house, it exhibits a dazzling collection of Dior's work as well as personal memorabilia. Every year there's an all-summer special exhibition. The park-like garden, too, with lawns, trees and colourful flowerbeds, is very beautiful, especially the rose garden. There's also an elegant *salon de thé*, with tables on the lawn.

Iles Chausey essentials

❶ Getting there
Ferry Iles Chausey are one hour by ferry from Granville, services operated by **Vedettes Jolie France** (Gare Maritime 2ème bureau, T02 33 50 31 81, vedettejoliefrance.com). Crossings daily year round, from one to two return crossings per day to up to five, depending on the date. Return fare €21.30, €13.10 child three to 14 years, €5 under threes.

Iles Chausey (Chausey Islands)

The Chausey Islands have an exceptionally large tidal range, with 14 m difference between low and high tide. At low tide, hundreds of rocks and small islands are revealed. The largest of the 50 islands that are still visible when the tide comes back in, and the only one inhabited, Grande Ile de Chausey has a permanent population said to number fewer than 10 people, but in summer scores of visitors, fishermen and sailing enthusiasts spend time in this away-from-it-all haven. It's fascinating to walk the paths of Grande Ile and explore the simple watery world of these granite islands. The Chausey Islands are the only Channel Islands under the control of France. All the Channel Islands remained a possession of the Dukes of Normandy after the French crown abolished the Duchy in 1469 and in 1500 the Chausey Islands were abandoned by the Channel Islands government based in Jersey and were granted to France.

Though apparently just low-lying fragments of rock when seen from a distance, when one steps ashore on to Grande Ile de Chausey it is transformed into a spacious, airy, green landscape of stony hills, dunes and heathland, wild flowers and seabirds. There's a church and cottages, a hamlet called **Les Blainvillais** and cultivated fields and gardens. Two old forts stand guard, 16th-century at one end of the island, 19th-century at the other. There's also a hotel and restaurant.

Sleeping

Cherbourg-Octeville

Mercure Cherbourg Plaisance €€€-€€

Allée du Président Menut, T02 33 44 01 11.
Map: Cherbourg-Octeville, p206.
Standard rooms at this three-star right-bank hotel may be considered a little short of the usual Mercure level, but the chief attraction here is proximity to the ferry terminal, just a few minutes away. The pricier Superior rooms do provide decent comfortable accommodation, with harbour views. The hotel has a restaurant with familiar French fare, but the town centre is only about 10 minutes' walk for better value.

Hôtel Le Louvre €€

2 rue Henri Dunant, T02 33 53 02 28, hotel-le-louvre-cherbourg. com.
Map: Cherbourg-Octeville, p206.
A decently comfortable, modern and efficiently run two-star hotel about 15 minutes' walk from the port and town centre, the Louvre is in a neighbourhood that can be a little noisy, but it has good soundproofing. Catering for both family holidays and business travellers, services and facilities are of a good standard and include Wi-Fi.

La Régence €€

42 quai Caligny, T02 33 43 05 16, laregence.com.
Map: Cherbourg-Octeville, p206.
This town centre family-run hotel on the quayside, very convenient for the car ferry, is more comfortable and better equipped than its two stars would suggest, with simple, uncluttered, tastefully decorated rooms. Service is friendly and efficient, and there's free Wi-Fi.

Auberge de Jeunesse de Cherbourg-Octeville €

55 rue de l'Abbaye, T02 33 78 15 15, fuaj.org.
Reception 0800-1200 and 1800-2300, hostel open all year except Christmas and New Year.
Map: Cherbourg-Octeville, p206.
For low-budget accommodation in the city centre, the youth hostel is well placed in an attractively refurbished former French Navy building.

Hôtel Angleterre €

8 rue P Talluau, T02 33 53 70 06, hotelangleterre-fr.com.
Map: Cherbourg-Octeville, p206.
A modest, simple tourist hotel in solid corner premises in a quiet street, yet in the heart of the town, the Angleterre offers adequately equipped and inexpensive rooms.

Hôtel de La Renaissance €

4 rue de l'Eglise, T02 33 43 23 90, hotel-renaissance-cherbourg.com.
Map: Cherbourg-Octeville, p206.
Well placed in the city centre, this two-star hotel offers clean, neat, rooms with views towards the port and the sea. No restaurant, but there are several nearby.

Northern Cotentin

Marine €€€€-€€€

11 rue de Paris, Carteret, T02 33 53 83 31, hotelmarine.com.
Mar-23 Dec.
With a bright beachy atmosphere and a seafront terrace in the heart of the resort, this small 19th-century hotel (run by the same family since opening) has comfortable, light and airy bedrooms and one of the best restaurants in the *département*.

Ormes €€€-€€

Promenade Barbey-d'Aurevilly, Carteret, T02 33 52 23 50, hoteldesormes.fr.
Closed Jan.
A solid and comfortable, ivy-draped boutique hotel (12 rooms), exquisitely decorated in warm soothing pale tones contrasting with white, and furnished in the best home-from-home style (if only one's home *could* be as nice as this!). Outside there's a lovely garden terrace and harbour views. The hotel also has a good restaurant.

Conquérant €€

16-18 rue St-Thomas-à-Becket, Barfleur, T02 33 54 00 82, hotel-leconquerant.com.
Closed mid-Nov to mid-Mar.
In an appealing 17th-century stone building close to the port, this traditional two-star hotel has simple, pleasing rooms, all very varied, most with a view into the lovely garden. Breakfast is served, and in the evening dinner with savoury and sweet crêpes.

France-et-Fuchsias €€-€

20 rue Marechal, St-Vaast-la-Hougue, T02 33 54 40 41, france-fuchsias.com.
Closed some weeks during the winter, closed Mon Oct-May and Tue Nov-Mar.
This satisfyingly traditional place, set back from the street behind a cobbled courtyard and gorgeously draped in fuchsias, is a delightful little hotel of charm and character. Steep, narrow stairs climb to simple, pleasant rooms, with wicker furniture. There's a strong fuchsia theme throughout, with fuchsia-coloured carpet, wallpaper, picture frames, lampshades… It's noted too for its excellent seafood restaurant; strictly speaking, the France is the hotel, and the Fuchsias the restaurant, but both are known as France-et-Fuchsias. It's just a few paces from St-Vaast's bustling, picturesque quayside. Outstanding value.

Hotel France-et-Fuchsias, St-Vaast-la-Hougue.

Le Moderne €

1 place de Gaulle, Barfleur, T02 33 23 12 44, hotel-restaurant-moderne-barfleur.com.
Closed Jan to mid-Feb.
This interesting building just a few minutes' walk from the harbour is a classic *restaurant avec chambres* – the main business is eating, while the plain and simple bedrooms above are simply a place to lie down and sleep afterwards! If that's all you need, the inexpensive Moderne could be a good choice.

Chambres d'hôtes

Chambres d'Hôtes Les Deux Caps €

2 La Brasserie, Carneville, T02 33 54 13 81, gitedesdeuxcaps.com.
Exceptionally good value, this high-quality B&B is close to Cap Lévy, 12 km from Cherbourg, in delightful Val de Saire countryside with a spacious garden and views towards the sea (it's about 2.5 km from beaches). The house is attractively decorated and furnished with rustic touches. Rooms are comfortable and simple, with calm, pale colours. The owner is a former chef who has worked in Michelin-starred restaurants. She serves an excellent *table d'hôte* (set dinner) for an additional €20 per person, drinks included.

Tatihou Island €
Ile Tatihou, T02 33 54 33 33, tatihou.com.
Always contact in advance to check availability.
In the island's sturdy granite buildings there is simple accommodation of single, double and triple rooms with en suite facilities. Enjoy nature, peace, the sea and the stars. Prices are €76 for full-board (€38 child) or €55 half-board (€29 child). There is no room-only rate.

Southern Cotentin

Fort et Iles €€€
Grande Ile de Chausey, T02 33 50 25 02, hotel-chausey.com.
Mid-Apr to end Sep. Prices are for half-board.
Look not for creature comforts but for peace and quiet and even a touch of romance about the location when the day-trippers have departed. Chausey's simple, old-fashioned little hotel (just eight rooms, four with sea views) offers utter tranquillity. Rooms are small and service arguably lacks polish, but the white-washed maritime freshness of the decor and the garden setting have a good deal of charm.

Mercure Le Grand Large €€€-€€
5 rue Falaise, Granville, T02 33 91 19 19, mercure-granville.com.
With an appealing decor of pale woods and rugs, and a bright maritime feel on balconies and terraces, this comfortable, modern little resort hotel well deserves its three stars. It stands in a lofty position by the sea (there's a steep climb to reach it), overlooking the beach in one direction, the rooftops of the town centre in the other. It also has a good spa with seawater treatments.

Auberge de l'Abbaye €€
5 route de l'Abbaye, Hambye, T02 33 61 42 19.
Closed 2 weeks in Oct, 3 weeks in Feb.
In rustic tranquillity, with hardly a sound except hens clucking and the gentle rushing of the nearby stream, this family-run hotel is in a spacious, handsome stone house just a short stroll from the Abbaye de Hambye. It also boasts an elegant restaurant.

Cositel €€
Rue St-Malo, Coutances, T02 33 19 15 00, cositel.fr.
The twee name conceals a comfortable low-budget modern hotel, with simple neat decor and bright uncluttered interiors all adding up to something perhaps better than its two-star rating suggests. There's free broadband internet access in all bedrooms and the hotel also has its own restaurant serving modern French cooking, artfully presented.

Bains €
19 rue Clemenceau, Granville, T02 33 50 17 31, hoteldesbains-granville.com.
Closed most of Jan.
By the waterfront just below the old town, at one end of the beach, the hotel is part of the 1920s complex that includes Granville's casino. Pleasantly decorated in pale tones, rooms are modest and rather variable, but some are attractive, with sea views and jacuzzi.

Taverne du Parvis €
Place Parvis Notre Dame, Coutances, T02 33 45 13 55, hotelleparvi.free.fr.
Facing the front of Coutances cathedral, this traditional old hotel-restaurant-brasserie has a dozen simple one-star rooms with shower and TV, at very inexpensive prices. Especially good value is the overnight half-board (€48 for dinner, bed and breakfast, Mon-Thu only).

Chambres d'hôtes

Le Mascaret €€€-€€
1 rue de Bas, Blainville sur mer, T02 33 45 86 09, restaurant-lemascaret.fr.
Closed most of Jan and 10 days in Nov.
Off the beaten track, by the sea near Coutances, this is a guesthouse with a difference. Instead of the usual home-from-home feel, here is a luxurious haven, an 18th-century house, courtyard and garden, with

Eating & drinking

interesting, elegant rooms and suites, some decorated with Baroque exoticism, as well as pampering spa treatments, excellent breakfasts and a Michelin-starred restaurant.

Gites

Iles Chausey Gîtes Communaux €
Ancien Presbytère, Grande Ile de Chausey, T02 33 91 30 03.
Closed Jan and part of Feb.
The former school and rectory building close to the old fort on Grande Ile are divided into four gîtes providing adequate accommodation that captures something of the flavour of island life. The gîtes can each accommodate from four to six people. Bookings must be made through the Office de Tourisme in Granville.

Cherbourg-Octeville

Café de Paris €€
40 quai Caligny, T02 33 43 12 36.
Mon 1900-2145, Tue-Sat 1200-1400 and 1900-2145, usually closed 2 weeks early in the year and 2 weeks in Nov.
Map: Cherbourg-Octeville, p206.
This popular and legendary fish and seafood restaurant was founded as long ago as 1803, but looks and feels modern. There are three dining rooms and outdoor tables too, and it could hardly be better placed, right on the main quayside.

La Régence €€
42 quai Caligny, T02 33 43 05 16, laregence.com.
Daily 1200-1430 and 1930-2200.
Map: Cherbourg-Octeville, p206.
This is the restaurant of a two-star hotel, attractive with awnings and flowers outside and a warm, rich Edwardian-style decor inside, with velvet and polished woods and partitions. It's very conveniently placed on the busy quayside near the bridge to the right bank and the car ferry. Service is friendly and efficient, with a choice of menus of French and Norman cooking, emphasising fresh shellfish.

Le Plouc 2 €€
59 rue Blé, T02 33 01 06 46.
Mon-Sun 1900-2130, Tue-Sat 1200-1400 and 1900-2130.
Map: Cherbourg-Octeville, p206.
Atmospheric with old beams and tiles, much liked by locals for straightforward menus of French cooking skilfully and imaginatively prepared, as well as generously and attractively presented. Good wine list.

Le Vauban €€
22 quai Caligny, T02 33 43 10 11.
Tue-Fri 1200-1400 and 1900-2100, Sat 1900-2100, Sun 1200-1400, closed spring and autumn half-terms.
Map: Cherbourg-Octeville, p206.
A popular and highly regarded bright modern restaurant on the quayside, with a glass-enclosed front section overlooking the street. Excellent French cooking with the emphasis on seafood.

Le Faitout €€-€
25 rue Tour Carrée, T02 33 04 25 04, restaurant-le-faitout.com.
Mon-Sat lunch and dinner, closed 2 weeks May, 1 week beginning Nov, 2 weeks Christmas.
Map: Cherbourg-Octeville, p206.
In the main shopping area, this appealing, attractive and unpretentious bistro-style restaurant offers classic French fare, such as chicken liver terrine or salmon tart, at very reasonable prices.

Le Pommier €
15 bis rue Notre Dame, T02 33 53 54 60.
Tue-Sat 1200-1400 and 1900-2230, closed 2 weeks in Jan, 3 weeks in Nov.
Map: Cherbourg-Octeville, p206.
There's good value for money at this rather stylish bistro-style restaurant serving traditional French dishes, such as pigeon in pastry. Modern art hangs on the walls, and there are periodic temporary exhibitions.

Cafés & bars
Café du Théâtre
8 place Général de Gaulle, T02 33 43 01 49.
Mon-Sat 0800-0100.
Map: Cherbourg-Octeville, p206.
Once part of the ornate, Italianate theatre which is right in front of it, this is now a lively ground floor bar and upstairs brasserie, ideal for drinks and people-watching before or after a show. If you're hungry, there's a choice of inexpensive dishes.

Tip...
In St-Vaast-la-Hougue, take your shopping basket to Maison Gosselin, a renowned *épicerie* with top-quality cheeses, pâtés and other ready-to-eat foods.

Northern Cotentin

Restaurant de la Marine €€€€-€€€
11 rue de Paris, Carteret, T02 33 53 83 31, hotelmarine.com.
Mar-11 Nov, contact for opening hours.
Eat in the light and airy dining room with sea views, or get even closer to the view on the terrace, at this Michelin-starred restaurant noted for imaginative French and Norman cooking.

France-et-Fuchsias €€€
20 rue Marechal, St-Vaast-la-Hougue, T02 33 54 40 41, france-fuchsias.com.
Lunch and dinner, closed some weeks during the winter, Mon Oct-May and Tue Nov-Mar.
In St-Vaast's quiet 'main street' a few minutes' walk from its attractive fishing harbour, this enticing restaurant (more correctly just called Les Fuchsias, while its hotel is La France) is draped in the foliage and flowers of a huge climbing fuchsia. Inside, the decor and menus are tasteful and traditional, but high quality. Fresh seafood is very much the speciality, but there are plenty of other dishes too. Sample mackerel stuffed with leeks, and sea bream with cream of cauliflower, broad beans, peas and chorizo. Many of the ingredients come from their own farm, close by.

Le Rivage €€€-€€
Promenade Barbey-d'Aurevilly, Carteret, T02 33 52 23 50, hoteldesormes.fr.
Tue-Sat lunch and dinner, Sun lunch, closed Tue in winter, closed Jan.
In the elegant, charming Hôtel des Ormes, draped with the foliage of an climbing plant, this is a place to sample local lamb and the freshest fish and seafood, beautifully cooked and presented. At lunchtime, eat out of doors and enjoy sea views.

Hôtel du Fort et des Iles €€
Grande Ile de Chausey, T02 33 50 25 02, hotel-chausey.com.
Mid-April to Sep Tue-Sun lunch and dinner (open Mon on national holiday weekends).
Jolly and informal, with two rooms and an outdoor dining area with wonderful sea views, the restaurant offers limited set menus naturally strongly focused on fish and especially the Chausey islands' renowned lobster and other ocean-fresh shellfish.

Le Moderne €
1 place de Gaulle, Barfleur, T02 33 23 12 44, hotel-restaurant-moderne-barfleur.com.
Closed Jan to mid-Feb.
This attractive building with terrace in front is a good-quality country restaurant, with slightly fussy decor, correct service, and well-prepared menus. The speciality is local fish and

It's a fact...

The oysters of Cotentin are acclaimed in France. Those produced on the stretch of Cotentin coastline from Granville to Portbail are especially renowned. Gourmets discern a distinctive 'flavour of the ocean' in these *pleine mer* (open seas) oysters, thanks to the clear waters and strong currents.

seafood, especially oysters, but there's a wide range of other French and Norman dishes.

Southern Cotentin

La Citadelle €€€-€€
34 rue du Port, Granville, T02 33 50 34 10, restaurant-la-citadelle. com.
Thu-Tue lunch until 1400, dinner until 2130, closed Tue Oct-Mar, and school half-terms in Feb and Nov.
Enjoy attractively presented fresh fish, local lobster and other seafood, as well as other French and Norman dishes, in a restaurant whose light, fresh decor of blue and white with pale wood gives a distinctly nautical feel. There's an enclosed outdoor terrace at the front.

Le Mascaret €€€-€€
1 rue de Bas, Blainville sur Mer, T02 33 45 86 09, restaurant-lemascaret.fr.
Lunch and dinner, closed most of Jan and 10 days in Nov, and Sun and Wed evenings excluding mid Jul-end Aug.
By the sea near Coutances, in an elegant, imaginative and luxurious setting, this highly inventive Michelin-starred restaurant brings together many influences to create delicious dishes in a relaxed, spontaneous style. Local carrots, for example, could appear as anything from crisps to ice-cream, while desserts may involve liquid nitrogen. The flagship menu promises to combine the arts, technology and tradition!

Auberge de l'Abbaye €€
5 route de l'Abbaye, Hambye, T02 33 61 42 19.
Lunch and dinner, closed 2 weeks in Oct, 2 weeks in Feb.
This traditional family-run hotel-restaurant is in a spacious, handsome stone house south of the village of Hambye, within easy walking distance of the abbey. Despite the rustic setting, the cooking and the dining room are sophisticated and elegant.

Taverne du Parvis €
Place Parvis Notre Dame, Coutances, T02 33 45 13 55, hotelleparvi.free.fr.
Open all day.
Facing the front of Coutances cathedral, this hotel-restaurant-brasserie has an old-fashioned pub-like appeal, with wooden façade, tiled floors, brass fittings and beer and cider on tap. Salads and snacks are on offer, as well as good-value set menus of classic French, Norman and Alsatian brasserie fare at modest prices, such as ham braised in cider, *choucroute* and *flammeküche*.

Cafés & bars

Salon de Thé – Musée Christian Dior
Musée Christian Dior, rue Estouteville, Granville, T02 33 61 48 21.
Jul-Aug daily 1100-1830.
At this elegant villa where haute-couturier Christian Dior spent his childhood, and which is now a museum devoted to him, there's a delightful *salon de thé* with tables on the lawn and views of the sea.

Entertainment

Cherbourg-Octeville

Bars & clubs

Casino de Cherbourg
18 quai Alexandre III,
T02 33 20 53 35.
Daily 1030-0400 (0500 at
weekends), daytime bar opens
1200, nightclub Fri-Sat
2200-0500.
Reputedly the oldest casino in
France, the building itself was
destroyed during the war, and its
successor completely refurbished
in 2000. Perhaps lacking the
glamour of the original, this is still
a place to enjoy a dance, a dinner
and glitzy show and a roll of the
dice – or at least, of the slot
machine. Enjoy a dinner dance at
its nightclub, L'Amirauté, or cross
the road to the casino's diner,
themed as 1950s Americana and
appropriately named Fiftys Diner.

Le Requin Marteau
20 rue de la Paix, T02 33 53 15 74.
Thu-Sat evenings.
The most popular dance disco
with the young Cherbourgeois. It
is sometimes overcrowded and
often busy in the early hours of
Saturday night and Sunday
morning. It's right in the city
centre, close to place Napoléon.

Tip...

Pick up the latest copy of *Le Mois*
from shops or the tourist office
to find out what's on this month
in Cherbourg-Octeville.

Children

Cité de la Mer
Gare Maritime Transatlantique,
T02 33 20 26 26, citedelamer.com.
Opens 0930, closes between
1800 and 1900, with variations
depending on school holidays.
Last tickets sold 1 hr before
closing, low season €15.50,
€10.50 child (under 5s free),
high season €18, €13 child
(under 5s free).
'Sea City' near Cherbourg's ferry
dock is a child-oriented
attraction all about our
relationship with the sea. The
main attraction is a genuine
nuclear submarine, see page 207.

**Ludiver Planetarium and
Observatory**
Beaumont-Hague, T02 33 78 13 80,
ludiver.com.
Jul-Aug daily 1100-1830, rest of
year daily excluding Sat
1400-1800; planetarium shows
Jul-Aug daily at 1130, 1500 and
1630, rest of year at 1500 only;
€7.50, €5.50 child/concession.
You may need a bit of French to
get the best out this high-tech
attraction 10 km from
Cherbourg, but it's child
oriented, with dynamic
planetarium shows and
educational children's
entertainment.

Festivals & events

Charivarue
*Centre des Arts du Cirque de
Basse-Normandie, rue de la
Chasse Verte, T02 33 88 43 73,
arts-du-cirque.com.*
1 week Jun-Jul.
For a week soon after the
summer solstice, music, dance,
drama and magic and circus
entertainment burst on to the
streets of Cherbourg-Octeville.

Music

**Le Trident, Scène Nationale
de Cherbourg-Octeville
(Trident National Stage)**
*Place du Général de Gaulle,
T02 33 88 55 50,
trident-scenenationale.com.*
Cherbourg's remarkable
19th-century 600-seat theatre,
built in an Italian style of ornate
opulence (and today known as
the Théâtre à l'Italienne), is the
grandest of the three venues
used by the Trident combined
stage companies of Cherbourg-
Octeville for an interesting
programme of arts and
entertainment including modern
and classical dance and music.
The two other venues are the
400-seat Théâtre de la Butte and
240-seat Le Vox, the latter often
hosting innovative modern
dance, drama and music.

Shopping

Festivals & events

La Foire de Ste-Croix (Holy Cross Fair)
Lessay, 3-4 days every Sep on the 2nd weekend.
On these end-of-summer days, Lessay hosts one of Normandy's biggest, liveliest and oldest country fairs. The main activity is the trading of cattle, horses and other animals. Lambs are grilled throughout the fair.

Music

Les Heures Musicales de l'Abbaye de Lessay
Eglise Abbatiale de Lessay, bookings via Lessay tourist office, 11 place St Cloud, Lessay, T02 33 45 14 34, concertsheuresmusicales@canton-lessay.com. Latest details at http://lesheuresmuses.blogspot.com.
The beautiful Romanesque abbey and its convent buildings provide the setting for this annual programme of concerts of classical music and choral performances for about six weeks during July and August.

Les Traversées Tatihou
On the island of Tatihou and waterfront of St-Vaast-la-Hougue, T02 33 54 33 33, book online at evene.fr/culture/agenda/les-traversees-tatihou-5464.php.
4 days usually on the 3rd weekend in Aug.

Tatihou's festival of folk music, with the emphasis on Celtic and traditional music and seafaring culture. There is a special atmosphere thanks to the remote and enchanting setting, and the crossing to the island, which many festival-goers do in bare feet. Performance times have to be arranged according to the tide, though there are also late-night festival events at St-Vaast on the quayside and in the bars.

Southern Cotentin

Festivals & events

Festival des Coquillages et des Crustacés
Granville.
Early Oct.
A cornucopia of crustaceans are dished up at this jolly gourmet extravaganza in France's leading shellfish port. Vast quantities are sold ready-to-eat and consumed on the spot, and there are also stalls where you can learn how to cook, open and eat them.

Granville Carnival
Granville.
Weekend before Mardi Gras (Shrove Tuesday).
Ancient traditions of a seafaring community live on in these four days of parades, music and festivities under the rule of a Carnival King.

Cherbourg-Octeville

Antiques & second-hand

Flea market
Place des Moulins, place de la Révolution, rue d'Espagne and Parvis de la Basilique Ste Trinité.
1st Sat of the month, 0800-1800.
There are regular produce markets every day of the week (except Monday) in Cherbourg-Octeville and throughout the region. Once a month comes the much bigger Marché aux Puces (flea market) filling Cherbourg-Octeville's central squares with a variety of bric-à-brac, household goods and clothing ranging from fine antiques to junk.

Northern Cotentin

Food & drink

Maison Gosselin
27 rue de Verüe, St-Vaast-la-Hougue, T02 33 54 40 06, maison-gosselin.com.
Tue-Sat 0900-1230 and 1430-1900, Sun 0900-1230.
One of the highlights of a visit to St-Vaast-la-Hougue is to look in at this legendary *épicerie*. Opened in 1889 by Clovis Gosselin, it has remained in the family ever since. With a gleaming red façade, it's now run by Clovis' great-granddaughter Françoise and her husband Bertrand. Along with a vast array of ordinary products, its shelves are loaded with the finest Normandy cheeses and their

Maison Gosselin, St-Vaast-la-Hougue.

own wide range of top-quality home-made pâtés and terrines (for example, pork pâté mixed with Livarot cheese), *tripes à la mode de Caen*, conserves and confectionery. In addition to such edible treats, the shop also stocks unusual souvenirs and children's toys, such as dolls' house furniture.

Southern Cotentin

Kitchenware
Walk along the central place de la République and rue Carnot and the side streets in Villedieu-les-Poêles to find many small shops selling high-quality copper kitchenware.

Markets
Le Grand Marché
Place des Halles, place des Costils, place de la République and place du Presbytère, Villedieu-les-Poêles.

Always an important centre for trade and commerce, Villedieu still has one of the biggest markets in the Manche *département* every Tuesday morning. It's divided into sections, each in their own square, but the emphasis is firmly on local Normandy produce, with sellers of sausages, crème fraîche and butter, eggs and hens, fresh fish, home-made preserves and much more, including on-the-spot cooking of favourite snacks and takeaway fare.

Activities & tours

Cherbourg-Octeville

Guided tours

Cherbourg-Octeville guided walking tours

2 quai Alexandre III,
T02 33 93 52 02,
otcherbourgcotentin.fr.
Cherbourg-Octeville tourist office run guided walking tours visiting the sights of the town each Sunday afternoon, except in July and August when tours are almost every day. The tours are free, and leave from the tourist office at 1430. Contact the tourist office for information

Southern Cotentin

Golf

Granville Golf Club

Bréville-sur-Mer, T02 33 50 23 06,
www.golfdegranville.com.
This excellent course, 6552 yards long, combines an 18-hole course and a nine-hole which meander through natural dunes and undulating fairways close to the sea just north of Granville.

Guided tours

Granville Office de Tourisme

Cours Jonville, Granville, T02 33 91 30 03, granville-tourisme.fr.
€2.70, under 12s free, evening tour of Christian Dior gardens free.
Granville tourist office provides several themed guided tours (in French only) to enable visitors to discover the cultural heritage and maritime history of the town. All start at 1500 at the tourist office and last about 1½ hours, except the unusual and enjoyable evening visit to the gardens at the Musée Christian Dior, which is free, and starts at the entrance to the gardens.

Le Perche.

Contents

Southern Normandy

Introduction

Normandy merges easily into its neighbours to the south, Brittany and Maine, where not only landscapes overlap, but history and culture too. At the foot of the Cotentin Peninsula, the shallow Baie de St-Michel separates Normandy and Brittany. In the watery sands just offshore, the abbey church of Le Mont-St-Michel is one of the most visited sites in France. By contrast few tourists venture into the rustic, rolling farmland of orchards and green pasture of the Normandy-Maine border country, where a regional nature park preserves the cool, fresh environment of streams and wooded hills. That park almost turns into another, the regional park of Le Perche, one of the least visited corners of Normandy, and the most southerly, known for charcuterie, sturdy Percheron horses and a love of tradition. There are several provincial towns worth seeing here, among them Southern Normandy's main centre, Alençon, hilltop Domfront and the surprisingly smart rural spa resort of Bagnoles-de-l'Orne. Many other sights justify a leisurely country drive, such as the châteaux of Carrouges and strangely named O. Where Orne meets Calvados there are glorious tours to be made into the Suisse Normande and Pays d'Auge, which lie in both *départements*.

What to see in...

... one day
Choose between Le Mont-St-Michel or exploring in and around Alençon. From Alençon, the Normandie-Maine regional park is close by, as is the Château de Carrouges, the cathedral at Sées and the agreeable lakeside spa of Bagnoles-de-l'Orne.

...a weekend or more
Starting from Alençon, head to Le Mont-St-Michel on the main roads (D112, N12, D976). Reaching Le Mont-St-Michel, cross the causeway and walk up to the abbey. A visit to Le Mont is best appreciated in an unhurried way, and takes several hours. From Le Mont, return first to Domfront and then to the green, peaceful woodland spa resort of Bagnoles-de-l'Orne, where it's good to linger. Continue on D908 to little Carrouges to visit the château with its gatehouse. D908 carries on to Sées, dominated by its Norman Gothic cathedral. Leave town on D438, returning to Alençon.

Le Mont-St-Michel.

Normandie-Maine

A bustling, attractive market town and a *département* capital with a long and important history, Alençon lies right on the frontier between the Duchy and neighbouring Maine and makes an ideal base for touring Southern Normandy. Even though it's not within the limits of the park, Alençon is also the main town and information centre for the Parc Naturel Régional de Normandie-Maine. This long, narrow regional park covers 235,000 ha and varies considerably throughout its range. Within its limits there are many quiet towns and rural communities, as well as protected unspoiled environments. Enchanting sylvan valleys change to broader open landscapes like the water meadows around the little cathedral city of Sées. In contrast, the landscape turns to wilder enclaves of rocky, densely wooded uplands like the Forêt de Perseigne, thick with mixed pine, oak and beech, and the vast oak woodlands of the Forêt d'Ecouves. Around Domfront, the undulating small-farm country is famed in France for its productive pear orchards, while the sedate 'green' spa resort of Bagnoles-de-l'Orne is an away-from-it-all haven of good living almost completely enclosed by the Fôret d'Andaines.

Bluebells in Forêt d'Ecouves.

Essentials

➊ Getting around All sights of interest are in the small central area of town, and you are unlikely to need to use the urban bus network. Six lines cross town via the centre. Most operate Monday-Saturday from about 0700/0900 to 1900/2000. Tickets and information from **Boutique Bus Alto**, 20 rue Ampère, T02 33 26 03 00, altobus.com.

➌ Bus station Rue St-Blaise, near Eglise Ste-Thérèse. See page 273 for regional bus travel.

➋ Train station Gare SNCF d'Alençon, rue Denis Papin, T3635 (special number). See page 271 for regional rail travel.

➒ ATM There are four in rue St-Blaise, Alençon.

⊕ Hospital The district's main hospital, beside the river south of the town centre, is **Centre Hospitalier Intercommunal Alençon**, 25 rue Fresnay, T02 33 32 74 25.

✚ Pharmacy There are three pharmacies in Grand'Rue and one in place Halle au Blé.

➔ Post office Rue de la Halle aux Toiles, Monday-Friday 0845-1815, Saturday 0845-1200.

➊ Tourist information Maison d'Ozé, place de la Magdeleine, T02 33 80 66 33, paysdalencon tourisme. com. January-March and October-December Monday-Saturday 0930-1230 and 1400-1800; April-June Monday-Saturday 0930-1230 and 1330-1830; July-September Monday-Saturday 0930-1900, Sunday 1000-1230 and 1400-1630.

Alençon

Cobbled streets and half-timbered houses hung with bright window boxes make this small manufacturing town a delight. The old town lies on the north bank of the River Sarthe. For centuries Alençon was famed for high-quality hand-made needlepoint lace, and that remains one of its attractions. The **Musée des Beaux-Arts et de la Dentelle** (Fine Arts and Lace Museum, rue Charles Aveline, T02 33 32 40 07, museedentelle-alencon.fr, Tue-Sun 1000-1200 and 1400-1800, Jul-Aug also open Mon, €3.60, €2.65 concessions, children free) gives a comprehensive overview of traditional lace-making, and Alençon's place within it, with

Tip...

It's possible to travel easily and cheaply by bus between all the main towns in Southern Normandy, particularly Alençon, Argentan and Mortagne-au-Perche. A frequent public bus service throughout the Orne *département* is provided by the publicly owned operator Cap'Orne (information from Conseil Général de l'Orne Service Transport, T02 33 81 61 95, orne. fr/orne-reseau-caporne.asp). Buy a ticket from the driver, all journeys cost just €2 regardless of distance. If you prefer, buy a ticket for 10 journeys, for just €15.

displays of some exquisite antique Point d'Alençon lace. You can also buy examples of modern hand-made needlepoint lacework here. On the other side of place Foch are the remains of a **château** of the Dukes of Normandy, notorious as a Gestapo prison and still a prison today. Nearby is the surprising circular 19th-century **Halle au Blé** (Corn Market). Alençon's large 14th-century Flamboyant Gothic **Eglise Notre-Dame** (T02 33 80 66 33, daily 0930-1200 and 1400-1730) has a three-sided porch of magnificent Gothic sculpture, and rich stonework inside, as well as excellent 16th-century stained glass. Beside the church, the château-like **Maison d'Ozé**, a fortified 15th-century granite mansion in its own gardens, is where you will find the tourist office.

For a delightful outing from Alençon, take country roads into the pretty green **Alpes Mancelles** just outside town, continuing across the regional border into Maine. Despite the name, these 'alpes' are not particularly high hills, although they can be steep and there seem to be rather a lot of them! One of the most beautiful villages in the area (and in all of France) is arty little **St-Céneri-le-Gerei**, which also has remarkably well-preserved frescoes in its Romanesque church.

Sées

Tourist information office: Office du Tourisme de Sées, place Général de Gaulle, T02 33 28 74 79. Jun-Sep Mon-Sat 0900-1230 and 1400-1800; Oct-May Tue-Fri 0900-1230 and 1400-1800, Sat 0900-1230.

Once an important ecclesiastical centre, and with a strong tradition of Christian worship reaching back to the fourth century, this small and peaceful country town on the River Orne is dominated by

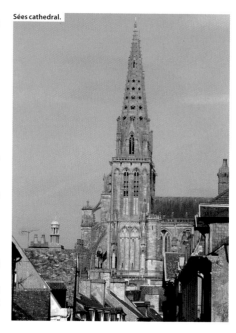
Sées cathedral.

the elegant Norman Gothic stonework of its majestic 13th- and 14th-century **Cathédrale Notre-Dame** (daily approximately 0900-1900). The present building is the fifth cathedral on this site, which was originally occupied by a Gallo-Roman temple. The cathedral's distinctive and decorative twin conical spires with their pattern of large openings are a 19th-century addition. The west façade below them lost its original grace with the addition of weighty buttresses in the 16th century. Inside, though, the building is a masterpiece of Gothic architecture, the nave in Norman style and the choir, with its expanses of the original 13th-century stained glass, a beautiful example of the more refined Ile de France Gothic. Large later stained glass rose windows light the transepts. At night, the whole cathedral is beautifully illuminated, highlighting the windows and the tracery of the spires.

It's a fact...

To make a piece of Point d'Alençon lace the size of a standard postage stamp takes a skilled worker about 25 hours. It takes eight years to learn how to do Point d'Alençon.

Château de Carrouges.

Beside the cathedral is its lovely little **Chapelle Canoniale** (canons' chapel) enclosed by a narrow wooden cloister. Having served as a covered market for a while, this is now used for art exhibitions. Behind it, in the former canons' residence, the **Musée d'Art Religieux** (T02 33 81 23 02, Wed-Mon 1000-1800, €2) displays sacred objects and treasures, religious art and liturgical vestments from the Middle Ages to the present. The town has several 18th- and 19th-century religious buildings and seminaries, most now converted to other uses, as well as an unusual circular 19th-century **Halles** (covered market) with concentric passages, which is now a public library.

Château de Carrouges

T02 33 27 20 32,
carrouges.monuments-nationaux.fr.
Daily 1000-1400 and 1400-1700 (1800 Apr-Sep, 1830 mid Jun-end Aug). €7, EU citizens aged under 26 free, €4.50 aged 18-26, under 18s free, last admission 45 mins before closing.

A long private avenue leads from the village of Carrouges to the gatehouse of the 14th to 17th-century Château de Carrouges. The **gatehouse** itself, with its patterned brick and tall, slender towers, makes a striking introduction to this grandly dignified, attractive little palace surrounded by its wide rectangular moat – almost a lake – where big fish swim and white geese glide sedately. The château, which survived the Revolution and remained in the same family for 500 years, stands in extensive calm grounds of neat lawns, terraces, fruit trees and trimmed hedges. The building is arranged around a central

Bagnoles-de-l'Orne.

Tip...

Beside the long avenue on the Carrouges estate leading from the village to the château gatehouse, notice a small Maison du Parc information desk of the Parc Naturel Régional Normandie-Maine. Stop here to pick up information on marked walking trails in the park's forests.

courtyard. Inside, the rooms are decorated and furnished in sumptuous Renaissance and classical taste, with much centuries-old original furniture. Stone and brick walls are panelled or hung with tapestries. Visit the **Chambre Louis XI**, where the king spent the night on a visit in 1473, and go below stairs to admire the enviable array of polished copperware in the **kitchens**. If you have something to celebrate, you can even hire rooms for a private reception in this prestigious setting.

Bagnoles-de-l'Orne

Tourist information office: place du Marché, T02 33 37 85 66, bagnolesdelorne.com. Apr-Oct Mon-Sat 0900-1300 and 1400-1830, Sun 1000-1230 and 1430-1830, Nov-Mar Mon-Fri 1000-1200 and 1400-1800.

A dense, pretty forest of oak, beech and pine all but surrounds this pleasant resort. At its heart, a white **casino** is reflected in a lake, and nearby the **Etablissement Thermal** (T08 11 90 22 33, free number, thermes-bagnoles.com) offers health-giving treatments using the legendary radioactive local spring water. Its curative powers are endorsed by numerous implausible legends. The **Saut du Capucin** (Capucin's Leap) is a pair of rocks between which an elderly Capucin was so reinvigorated by the waters that he was able to jump without difficulty. Apart from taking a treatment, pleasantly bustling Bagnoles has much to offer as a place for relaxation, dining, entertainment and walking beside the lake or on woodland paths.

Domfront

Tourist information office: 12 place de la Roirie, T02 33 38 53 97, domfront.com. Tue-Sat 1000-1230 and 1400-1800.

A picturesque fortified small town poised along a high, narrow ridge beside the River Varenne, quiet Domfront looks across its pear orchards, and is known for the drinks that can be made from them. Calvados Domfrontais, for example, is made with some pears in the mix rather than apples alone. At the bottom of the hill, beside D976, stands part of the lovely 11th-century Romanesque priory church **Notre-Dame-sur-l'Eau**, which was partly demolished to make way for the road. Post-war restoration work on the church uncovered a series of 12th-century frescoes in the south transept. At the top of the hill, the oldest part of Domfront, the **Cité Médiévale**, is centred on a charming little main square, place St-Julien. The concrete parish church **Eglise St-Julien**, built between the wars in neo-Byzantine style, perhaps incongruous in this historic setting, is being restored but can usually be visited. The interior is ornate, with painted walls and large expanses of modern stained glass. Walk along rue du Docteur-Barrabé to find fine medieval houses. At the western end of the little Cité, beside place de la Roirie, relics of the once-powerful 11th-century old **Norman fortress** are enclosed by public gardens with panoramic views.

Tip...

The season in Bagnoles runs from Easter to All Saints' Eve (Halloween). Between November and March you may find most things closed or very quiet.

Le Mont-St-Michel

Its setting in a vast space of sky and shore and water, and the remembrance of a time when the pious risked their lives crossing these treacherous sands and marshes on foot, and indeed the very idea of trying to build an abbey at the summit of this islet of granite, all contribute to the sense of wonder on seeing Le Mont-St-Michel. For religious and secular alike, it's an evocative, compelling sight, whether on a clear spring morning or in autumn mist, on a sunny afternoon or by moonlight, in the romantic mood of its nightly illuminations, or most especially when a high tide rushes frighteningly across the flats, now safely crossed by a causeway. The island's daunting stone ramparts rise as if part of the natural rock of the island, and from within them the lofty walls and spires of the abbey church reach up, culminating in a single immensely tall black pinnacle, on the very point of which gilded St Michael is poised triumphant. At the foot of the abbey a tiny village of narrow streets and stairs, its Grand'Rue packed with souvenir shops and cafés and distractions, caters to huge numbers of tourists crowding their way to and from the narrow Grand Degré steps that lead into the abbey precincts.

Essentials

Parking On reaching the causeway you will be directed to available parking spaces. The price of parking is €4 for a car, €8 for a campervan or similar, €1 for a motorbike. Cars with a disabled badge have to pay, but are given places reserved for them at the far end of the causeway.

Orientation From the causeway, walk through the fortified Porte de l'Avancée gateway that leads through the ramparts on to Grand'Rue, the main street of Le Mont-St-Michel.

Tourist information There's a tourist office in the **Corps de Garde des Bourgeois**, a 16th-century guard house, just inside the gateway on to the island, T02 33 60 14 30, ot-montsaintmichel.com.

Sightseeing Along Grand'Rue are refreshments, shops, a parish church and museums. The street slopes upwards slightly and ends in steps that you must climb to continue to the abbey. Reaching the abbey, pay for an entry ticket. You may visit the abbey in a group or on your own.

Avoiding the crowds Come in springtime, early in the morning, or late in the afternoon, to see Le Mont-St-Michel without tour-bus groups. Better still, stay overnight in one of the island's hotels.

Warning Never be tempted to make the crossing to Le Mont-St-Michel on the sands at low tide, or even to take a short walk from Le Mont. When the tide turns, the sea races back over the flats at about 1 m per second. Victor Hugo described it coming in at "the speed of a galloping horse".

Abbaye de St-Michel.

Tip...

Wear comfortable walking shoes and be prepared for a lot of exercise. The Grand Degré has 350 stairs, followed by several hundred more while visiting the abbey. The only part of Le Mont-St-Michel that can be accessed without climbing any stairs is Grand'Rue.

Abbaye de St-Michel

T02 33 89 80 00,
mont-saint-michel.monuments-nationaux.fr.
Daily, May-Aug 0900-1900, Sep-Apr 0930-1800, last admission 1 hr before closing. In addition to normal opening hours, Jul-Aug Mon-Sat 1900-2230 pre-booked groups can visit without a guide. €8.50, EU citizens under 26 free, €5 aged 18-25, under 18s free. There's no charge to enter the abbey if you are attending Mass. Times of services are shown on the community's website, abbaye-montsaintmichel.com.

You can tour the abbey on your own or pay an extra €4.50 for an audioguide, which will lead you on a tour of about one hour 15 minutes. Guided tours are possible only for pre-booked groups.

From the **Grand Degré** steps, wider stairs lead to the **Plate-forme du Saut Gautier** (Gautier's Leap Terrace), which gives access to the **Eglise Abbatiale** (abbey church) and the maze of other abbey buildings. The abbey came into being in AD 708 after Bishop Aubert of nearby Avranches had

visualized it standing on the rock which at that time was called Mont Tombe (another smaller outcrop to the north is still called Tombelaine). Within 150 years the abbey he founded was attracting pilgrims. In the 10th century it became a border outpost of the new Duchy of Normandy, and was heavily fortified by the Norsemen, who peopled it with a Benedictine community. The enlargement of the abbey and rebuilding in Romanesque style began.

During the wars between the Anglo-Normans and the French, the buildings had to be repaired and partly rebuilt and the ramparts enlarged. Le Mont and its abbey became not only an increasingly popular and prestigious pilgrimage centre, but also a powerful French garrison. At the same time, beautiful Gothic construction started to replace the crumbling Romanesque structures. 13th-century additions on the north side, commissioned by the French monarch, still known as **La Merveille** (The Marvel), are on three levels, with two wings (east and west), attached to the Romanesque crypt at the bottom, and the church at the upper level. More fine Gothic work was added at the end of the 15th century.

Highlights of the Eglise Abbatiale

The exterior of the Eglise Abbatiale (Abbey church) is a triumph of exuberant Gothic craftsmanship. Inside, the church is spacious and combines the sturdy, simple elegance of the older Romanesque crypts and nave with a glorious later Gothic choir. From the nave, pass into the wonderfully graceful **cloister** with elegant twin arcades and enter the monks' vast **refectory**. You are now on the upper level of **La Merveille**. Provisions were brought to the upper level using **the great wheel**, a huge pulley operated by a treadmill. On lower levels, the **knights' hall** and **guests' hall** are awesome spaces supported by rows of columns. On a guided group tour, you may visit the older crypts that support the abbey buildings, including the most ancient and affecting, **Notre-Dame-Sous-Terre** (Our Lady Below Ground).

In the 16th century, the abbey began a long decline, and by the time of the Revolution had all but ceased to function. The buildings were turned into a prison, and so remained until Victor Hugo led a campaign to rescue Le Mont-St-Michel for the nation. In 1874, having closed the prison, the French government set out to restore and enhance the abbey, in the process making many changes to its appearance, rebuilding much of Grand'Rue and creating the solid causeway. That process has continued right up to the present day. The cloister gardens were added as recently as the 1960s. A religious community took up residence in the abbey once again in 1966.

Avranches

Tourist information office: 2 rue Général de Gaulle, T02 33 58 00 22, ot-avranches.com.

For more than 1000 years the story of this attractive town on sa lope above the River Sée has been linked to that of Le Mont-St-Michel. The far end of its colourful **Jardin des Plantes** (created over 200 years ago, but re-laid after wartime damage) gives an ethereal view across the expanse of the Sée estuary and the Baie du Mont St-Michel with the

It's a fact...

Silt and land reclamation have deprived Le Mont-St-Michel of its isolation. Salt meadows, with sheep grazing on them, approach the island. The solid causeway, built in 1879, prevents the tide from washing away accumulating sands. An effort is underway to prevent further silting around Le Mont. One proposal is to replace the causeway with a raised footway that allows the tide to flow beneath.

enigmatic form of Le Mont-St-Michel rising in the distance. The fortified **old town** is at the top of the hill, where picturesque narrow streets converge on Place Daniel-Huet. There was once a cathedral behind the square, but it collapsed in 1794. Where it stood is now a garden known as **La Plate-Forme**, and from here the vista towards the bay is even wider. From this spot Bishop Aubert envisioned an abbey standing on Mont Tombe, which was to become Le Mont-St-Michel.

Avranches is the official repository for the abbey's many precious medieval manuscripts at **Le Scriptorial d'Avranches – Musée des Manuscrits du Mont-St-Michel** (place d'Estouteville, T02 33 79 57 00, scriptorial.fr, Tue-Sun Oct-Apr 1000–1230 and 1400–1700, May-Sep till 1800, Jul-Aug no midday closing, closed Jan, last entry an hour before closing, €7, €5 over-60s, €3 unemployed and students, under-10s free, audioguide additional €3). This is also a fun and interactive place where visitors can learn about writing and books in general, and the abbey's manuscripts in particular.

It's a fact...

At a junction in Avranches below the town centre, in a square now called place Général Patton, a dignified stone monument (with a Sherman tank beside it) honours and records General Patton's success in July 1944 in the action known as the Percée d'Avranches which broke the German hold on the town and opened the way for an American advance that was to continue to Belgium. The whole square has been ceded to the USA as sovereign American territory.

Pays d'Argentan

The extensive forests and open grassy plains reaching from Argentan to the Pays d'Auge, and encompassing the Pays d'Exmes, overlap with neighbouring Calvados and share its appearance and history. This is pre-eminent horse-breeding country, which is why it was chosen for Louis XIV's Le Pin Haras National (Le Pin National Stud Farm), still one of the most respected in France. So tranquil now, these woods and meadows echoed with the sound of war in 1944. This area formed part of the Falaise Pocket where some of the bloodiest confrontations of the Battle of Normandy took place and the Nazis made a last stand. The dead are remembered on the lofty Mémorial de Coudehard-Montmorel in the midst of the battlefield. The medieval lace-making town of Argentan, almost entirely destroyed in that struggle, stands on the River Orne not far from where the valley deepens to become the centre of the scenic Suisse Normande. Many other streams spring from the high, open country, including the rivers Dives and Touques, which mark the limits of the Pays d'Auge. Camembert, one of the most famous Auge villages of them all, is here, as well as another great name in Normandy cheese, Vimoutiers.

Argentan

Office de Tourisme d'Argentan, Chapelle St Nicolas, T02 33 67 12 48, argentan.fr.
Sep-Jun Mon-Fri 0930-1230 and 1400-1800, Sat 0930-1230 and 1330-1730; Jul- Aug Mon 0900-1300 and 1400-1830, Tue-Sat 0900-1830. See also papao.fr.

Although 80% of Argentan was demolished by the ferocious Allied bombardments aimed at dislodging the Nazis in August 1944, the residents returned afterwards and began to reconstruct their town. The result is functional, but pleasantly bustling, and a few attractive old buildings have survived. There are two old churches (one now housing the tourist office), and the **donjon** is a remnant of medieval ramparts. The 14th-century **château** survives as today's law courts. Argentan was for centuries renowned for intricate high-quality lace. At **Maison des Dentelles** (House of Lace, 34 rue de la Noé, T02 33 67 50 78, Apr-18 Oct Tue-Sat 0900-1130 and 1400-1730, Sun 1500-1730, €3, €2.30 students, unemployed and children over 10, under 10s free) that heritage is beautifully explored, with fine pieces of work on display, and some that you can buy in the museum shop.

Haras National du Pin

Le Pin-au-Haras, on D926 15 km east of Argentan, T02 33 36 68 68, haras-national-du-pin.com.
Apr-Sep 1000-1800, Oct-Mar except French half-term holidays 1400-1700, Oct-Mar French half-term holidays 1030-1200 and 1400-1700. Guided tours of the stables €5, €3 students and children over 10, €2 child 7-10 years, under 7s free, unaccompanied Discovery Trail walk in the estate additional €4 (€3 child 7-10 years, under 7s free), combined visit to stables and château (possible only on selected dates typically 21 and 28 Feb, 6 Mar, 10, 17 and 24 Apr, 1 and 8 May, 29 Oct, 5 Nov, 23 and 30 Dec) €8, €5 students and schoolchildren, €3 other children.

Louis XIV had scoured France for the best place to rear horses and was advised to choose this very

Haras National du Pin.

Tip...

Thursdays from around 5 June to 25 September are the best days to visit the Haras National du Pin as there's a musical show of stallions with traditional horse-drawn carriages. In July and August, if you miss the Thursday show it can be seen on some Tuesdays. The stallion shows start at 1500 and cost €5.

estate. His 'Versailles of the Horse' was created for him by Jules-Hardouin Mansart, the architect of the real Palace of Versailles. When Mansart died in 1708, the work of building the stables and château was continued by Robert de Cotte, who had also worked on Versailles. Le Pin encompasses 1100 ha with vast, majestic stables. Here fine horses are raised, all the crafts of the stables are taught and perfected, and ten pure breeds are preserved.

Château de Sassy

St-Christophe-le-Jajolet, T02 33 35 32 66.
Easter to All Saints 1500-1800, except 15 Jun-15 Sep 1030-1230 and 1400-1800. Garden free, château €5.

On the very edge of the Forêt d'Ecouves, this 18th-century mainly red-brick palace overlooks its extensive formal gardens, laid out in the 1920s, which are reached by descending three terraces. Superb 18th-century Aubusson and Gobelins tapestries hang inside the house, which belonged to Duc Pasquier, Louis XVI's defence counsel in the Revolutionary show trial. Also on display is a lock of the king's hair presented to the duke.

The secrets of Marie Harel

According to a much-loved legend, Camembert cheese was invented in the 1790s by a young farmer's wife called Marie Harel, née Fontaine, who lived at Beaumoncel Farm in the village of Camembert. She gave shelter to one of the many fugitive priests who, after the Revolution, were crossing Normandy in the hope of escaping France and making their way to England. The priest, who was from the great cheese-making region of Brie, told her some secrets that Marie used to create one of Normandy's best loved cheeses. The legend continues that, in 1863, the Emperor Napoleon III visited the area for the opening of the railway from Paris and was greeted by large crowds. Out of the crowd stepped one of Marie's grandchildren, who thrust a cheeses into his hand. He liked it so much that he asked to have one delivered every day. Camembert's success was assured.

The likely truth is that a cheese resembling Camembert had been made in the area for centuries. Camembert, after all, is just up the road from Livarot. Social historian Pierre Boisard explains in his book *Le Camembert, Mythe Français* that local parish records show Marie Harel (1761-1812) never lived in Camembert – and it was not Marie but her father's second wife who came from Beaumoncel Farm. Marie herself married a farmhand who had worked at the farm. There seems no evidence for the priestly tale, nor for the encounter with the Emperor. What is clear is that Marie Harel really did discover a way of making exceptionally good mature cheeses, because they were renowned at Vimoutiers and Argentan markets, where she sold them. She passed on the secret to her daughters, whose husbands all started successful dairies specializing in Camembert à la Marie Harel.

Château d'O

Mortrée, T02 33 39 55 79.
Usually open Jul and Aug, contact in advance confirm entry times and fees.

The home of the Lords of O, looking very much like a Loire valley château, is a beautiful early Renaissance building of delicate white stonework, highlighted with brick patterns, under steep dark roofs, and all completely surrounded by an expanse of gently flowing water. The whole scene is perfectly romantic. Originally a Norman Gothic fortress, it was reconstructed in the 15th century by the family of O, for generations political and financial advisers to the French crown. Enlarged in the 16th century, and internally renovated in the 18th, it is still a private house. The surrounding grounds are a delightful mix of rose gardens, woodland, formal gardens and a productive kitchen garden. Inside the château, admire 17th-century *trompe l'œil* murals of Apollo and a flock of eagles representing his nine muses.

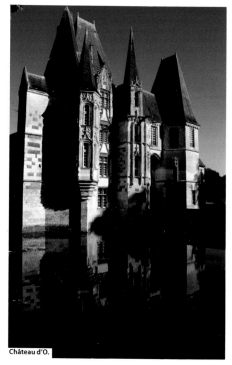

Château d'O.

Mémorial de Coudehard-Montormel

Les Hayettes, Montormel, T02 33 67 38 61, memorial-montormel.org.
Apr daily 1000-1700, May-Sep daily 0930-1800, Oct-Mar Wed, Sat and Sun 1000-1700. €5, veterans of Second World War free, €4 veterans of other wars, €3.50 students and children over 12 years, €2.50 under 12s.

High on this battleground in what was known as the Falaise Pocket, from 18-22 August 1944 the Allies finally defeated the Germans in the last encounter of the Battle of Normandy. The site has a commanding view over the area north-east of Argentan where British, American and Canadian forces had encircled the Nazi forces, whose only escape route lay within range of this hill. The memorial complex honours the success and the sacrifice of the Allied forces – in particular, a Polish division installed here – who picked off the retreating German forces and drove away Panzer divisions attempting to come to their aid, while themselves coming under sustained heavy attack. The battle's course is explained in the museum.

Pays d'Auge Ornais

Tourist information office: Office de Tourisme du Pays du Camembert, 21 place de Mackau, Vimoutiers, T02 33 67 49 42, cdc-camembert.com.
Tourist information open Jun-Aug Mon 1400-1800, Tue-Sat 0930-1230 and 1400-1800, Sun 1000-1230 and 1400-1600, Sep-May Mon 1400-1730, Tue-Sat 1000-1200 and 1400-1730, national holidays from May to June 1000-1300.

The pretty Auge country crosses the border of Calvados and continues into the Orne *département*, where **Vimoutiers** is the main centre for the attractive rural Livarot and Camembert cheese-making areas. Despite massive wartime destruction, and hasty reconstruction, the little town has plenty of charm. There's a folksy little museum all about the local cheeses, the **Musée du Camembert et Conservatoire des Traditions du Pays d'Auge** (10 av du Général de Gaulle, T02 33 39

Camembert online

paysducamembert.unblog.fr.
vimoutiers.fr.
camembert-country.com/vimoutiers/infeng01.htm.
maisonducamembert.com/acces.htm.

30 29, Mar-Oct Mon 1400-1800, Tue-Sat 0900-1200 and 1400-1800, Sun 1000-1200 and 1430-1800, €3, €2 children 7-14 years, under 7s free), as well as a statue of Marie Harel, the plaque carefully describing her as the 'possessor of the secret of making Camembert,' and even a full-size statue of a cow, *'à la gloire de la vache normande'* (to the glory of the Norman cow), in front of the town hall. Just a short distance away, **Camembert** itself is a tiny and surprisingly uncommercialized village with good views. Here another museum about the local cheese-making tradition, the **Maison du Camembert** (place du Camembert, T02 33 12 10 37, Easter to All Saints Wed-Sun 1000-1800, May-Aug open daily, free), has an eye-catching façade resembling an open Camembert cheese box. Directly opposite, **Ferme Président** (T02 33 36 06 60, fermepresident.com, Jun-Aug daily 1000-1215 and 1400-1830, call to check new entry fee) – run by large dairy manufacturers Président – puts on guided tours around a show farm that includes restored 18th-century rooms and dairy, a video, and a chance to see Camembert being made in modern conditions. **Beaumoncel** (T02 33 39 27 01), the farm where the legendary Marie Harel supposedly created the famous cheese, is also open to visitors on summer afternoons, as are some of the other local dairy farms.

La Suisse Normande

La Suisse Normande doesn't have much in common with La Suisse. No snowy peaks, glaciers or Alpine meadows. No ski resorts. No Swiss chalets. What this part of Normandy does have are delightful green hills, sparkling rivers, exquisite villages, rich pasture and tranquil countryside. Although there are no significant sights, this is one of the loveliest parts of the Duchy for a leisurely drive or a vigorous cycle ride. For walkers or canoeists, this is an area to explore.

La Suisse Normande follows the twists and turns of the Orne valley from Putanges-Pont-Ecrepin to Thury-Harcourt, so is shared between the Calvados and Orne *départements*. A good base, close to the southern end of the route, is Argentan. From here take D15 for 16 km to **Putanges-Pont-Ecrepin**, a handsome old town rising from a weir on the River Orne. It has a lively air, with a cobbled market square, hikers arriving and leaving, little hotels and busy cafés. Climb away from the town on D909 (in the direction of Falaise) and turn left (D239) for Rabodanges, where there's a 17th-century château and an access road to **Barrage de Rabodanges (Rabodanges Dam)**, which has created a lake with a popular waterside recreation area. Continue above the edge of the spectacular **Gorges de St-Aubert** to Menil-Hermei, and turn left (D21), winding downwards to cross the river. The narrow road (D301) climbs to the landmark **Roche d'Oëtre**, a striking crag of rock jutting up above the valley of the Rouvre. Even at a mere 120-m altitude it gives spectacular views, and is the nearest thing to a mountain in the Suisse Normande. Follow the road down to the picturesque village of **Rouvrou**, with its grey stone cottages rising from a big meander in

the River Rouvre, and turn (D43) to cross the Orne and take the road to the busy and delightfully pretty waterside village of **Pont d'Ouilly**. Its seven-arched stone bridge spans the Orne at a point where the river broadens after emerging from the gorge. Follow the right bank of the river, pausing at the 16th-century **La Chapelle-St-Roch**, which has modern frescoes. The church is the scene of a pilgrimage in traditional costume on 15 August. Reaching St-Christophe, take D23 which climbs away from the river and travels through very attractive countryside all the way to Acqueville, where **Château de la Motte** (T02 31 78 31 73, Easter to All Saints Tue-Sun 1400-1900, €4, under-12s free) has a 19th-century walled garden complete with an 130-year-old greenhouse. Take D6 to **Thury-Harcourt**, at the northern end of la Suisse Normande, and one of its busiest little tourist villages.

Turn back towards the south here, taking D562 to **Clécy**, which rises beside a curve in the River Orne. All the countryside round about is very beautiful, and you could follow some of the marked footpaths which lead from here into the hills. Scenic D562 climbs steeply, reaching a summit with broad views to the northwest. On the descent, pass La Fresne and turn left into the next village, **St-Denis-de-Méré**. Take D256, joining D511 and crossing the River Noireau at the old railway station of Pont Erambourg. This is the starting point for a fun and unusual excursion, the **Vélorail de la Suisse Normande** (Apr-Oct daily, T02 31 69 39 30, rails-suissenormande.fr, €15), a people-powered train of open-air carriages moved by cycling. You travel along the disused railway here to a point near Clécy, and return. D15 runs from here back to Putanges-Pont-Ecrepin and into Argentan.

Le Perche

In the past, much of the population abandoned the wild, unworkable hills of Le Perche and made their way to Quebec and the new world. Especially in the 17th century, and then in the 19th, many sought a better life in a richer land. Yet today its natural unspoiled landscapes of oak forests and lakes and grassy pasture are the greatest asset in this long-disputed border country where Normandy reaches deep into Maine. Le Perche indeed continues across the border, and locals of this divided region are more likely to identify themselves as Percherons than Normans. Percheron is also the name of the large and sturdy horse breed that originates here. While such powerful horses are little in demand nowadays, Le Perche is still dotted with stables and horse studs raising other breeds. There are dairy farms and orchards too, on a traditional small scale, and pig farms producing the region's highly esteemed butchers' products – to French gourmets Le Perche brings to mind award-winning charcuterie and *boudin* (black pudding). You'll find plenty of shops offering these meaty specialities in Mortagne-au-Perche, the former capital of Le Perche, still its main town and a good base for exploring the area.

It's a fact...

The name Perche has nothing to do with the English word perch, or with the fish of the same name, and was originally spelled Perx. It is thought to come from a Celtic origin.

Mortagne-au-Perche

Tourist information office: Office de Tourisme, Théâtre-Halle aux Grains, pl Gén de Gaulle, T02 33 85 11 18.
Tue-Sat 1000-1230 and 1500-1800.

A busy working town in a lofty position on the northern reaches of Le Perche, Mortagne is the region's principal commercial and cultural centre. However, it has remained relatively small and has plenty of charm, with several 16th to 18th-century buildings and an agreeably unpretentious atmosphere. In and around its two adjoining main squares, place du Général de Gaulle and place de la République, several little butchers' shops offer varieties of their own home-made *boudin*, for which Mortagne is well known among connoisseurs. **Porte St-Denis** is a remnant of 15th-century fortifications, now topped by a little museum of local history. **Eglise Notre-Dame**, from the same period although much altered over the centuries, has some excellent woodwork inside and a stained-glass window commemorating those who left to settle in Canada in the 17th century. A few paces south of place de la République, the flower-filled **Jardin Publique** (public garden, daily 0800-1900, free) gives sweeping views to the south-west across the wooded hills of the Perche region.

Tip...

The whole town of Mortagne-au-Perche has free Wi-Fi. Check local connections and click on Mortagne-au-Perche Wi-Fi Offert. You have to reconnect after 15 minutes online.

Manoir de Courboyer

Maison du Parc, Courboyer, Nocé, T02 33 25 70 10, parc-naturel-perche.fr.
Daily 1030-1800 (July-Aug 1830, Nov-Mar 1730).
Free, except château interior €2, under-16s free.

To learn more about Le Perche, see some Percheron horses and enjoy walking on some well-marked paths, call in at this little 15th-century fortified château in the heart of the Perche countryside. It serves as the Centre d'Acceuil et d'Information Touristique (Welcome and Tourist Information Centre) for the Parc Naturel Régional du Perche, which extends across the whole region.

Plaque of a breeder of Percheron horses.

Five of the best

Places for a walk

❶ **Forêt de Mortain** One-hour hike beside the River Cance, taking in La Grande Cascade, at Mortain.
❷ **Forêt des Andaines** 11 marked trails starting from roadside car parks near Bagnoles-de-l'Orne.
❸ **Forêt d'Ecouves** Marked 1½ to four-hour trails from the Rocher du Vignage, near Alençon.
❹ **Suisse Normande** Challenging hike on GR36 path in wild Gorges de St-Aubert, near Putanges.
❺ **Le Perche** Short country walk at Manoir de Courboyer, and marked forest trails nearby.

Sleeping

Normandie-Maine

Le Manoir du Lys €€€€-€€
La Croix Gautier, route de Juvigny, near Bagnoles-de-l'Orne, T02 33 37 80 69, manoir-du-lys.com.
Closed 3 Jan-14 Feb.
Just outside Bagnoles in a tranquil farmland setting close to the edge of the forest, this smart family-oriented four-star Relais de Silence has comfortable, colourful rooms and suites of great character and style, a heated pool and plenty of sports facilities as well as a Michelin-starred restaurant.

O Gayot €€-€
2 av de la Ferté-Macé, Bagnoles-de-l'Orne, T02 33 38 44 01, ogayot.com.
Closed 23 Dec-10 Feb, and Sun evenings Nov-Mar.
Rooms in this inexpensive, centrally located two-star hotel have bright, minimalist and uncluttered decor with clean lines and combinations of blue, grey, green and red. The accommodation is modest and functional, but rooms are comfortable and quiet, have flat-screen TVs, and there's Wi-Fi throughout.

Ibis €
13 place Poulet-Malassis, Alençon, T02 33 80 67 67.
This useful budget chain, with functional comfortable modern rooms, has a hotel in Alençon in a mainly residential area yet close to the town centre and within 200 to 300 m of the sights. It has a 24-hour bar and Wi-Fi.

La Potinière €
2 rue des Casinos, Bagnoles-de-l'Orne, T02 33 30 65 00, hoteldelapotiniere.com.
13 Feb-16 Nov.
Beautifully located in the heart of the resort, beside the lake with a view across the water to the white casino, this two-star family-run hotel is a striking landmark with its red and white chequered corner turret. Inside, rooms are pleasingly simple and traditional, with basic facilities. The hotel has a popular restaurant serving local cuisine.

Le Mont-St-Michel

La Mère Poulard €€€
Grand'Rue, Le Mont-St-Michel, T02 33 89 68 68, merepoulard.com.
You are paying for location, not service or facilities, at this adequately comfortable establishment at the entrance to Grand'Rue, associated with the famous restaurant of the same name. It can be a slog up the stairs to your room, rewarded by views of the bay.

La Croix d'Or €€
83 rue de la Constitution, Avranches, T02 33 58 04 88, hoteldelacroixdor.fr.
A spick-and-span classic family-run small hotel, amiable and helpful, this half-timbered former 17th-century inn gives excellent value for money. Accommodation is simple but attractive and well-maintained. There's a delightful garden, free Wi-Fi and a good restaurant too.

La Digue €€
At the mainland end of the causeway, Le Mont-St-Michel, T02 33 60 14 02, ladigue.eu.
Ivy clad, moderately priced and almost as close to Le Mont as you can get without actually being there, this heavily used hotel provides a well-located base. Most rooms are on the small side, adequately equipped but well worn, with tiny bathrooms. Some look towards Le Mont, as does the restaurant, where fresh local seafood is on the menu.

Au Jardin des Plantes €€-€
Place du Jardin des Plantes, Avranches, T02 33 58 03 68.
Well placed for the Jardin des Plantes, some rooms with distant views of Le Mont-St-Michel, this calm, family-run hotel is in two sections. It offers a friendly welcome and simple classic rooms, with basic comforts. The hotel's restaurant serving traditional French cuisine is popular with locals.

Hostellerie de la Renaissance €€

20 av de la 2e Division Blindée, Argentan, T02 33 36 14 20, hotel-larenaissance.com. Closed 2nd fortnight in Jul, and last week in Mar.

Often regarded as a *restaurant avec chambres*, the family-run Renaissance has comfortable modern rooms of elegant simplicity and taste, attractive in pale or muted colours. The restaurant (see page 258) is a high point.

Le Lion Verd €

Place de l'Hôtel de Ville, Putanges-Pont-Ecrepin, T02 33 35 01 86, hotel-restaurant-lion-verd.com.

This handsome, flower-decked stone mansion has long been a substantial presence in the riverside main square (and Saturday marketplace) of this little town at the southern end of the Suisse Normande. Better known as a restaurant, it is also a good little two-star hotel with traditional, adequately equipped rooms at a value-for-money price. Breakfast costs just €4.

Tribunal €€

4 place Palais, Mortagne-au-Perche, T02 33 25 04 77, hotel-tribunal.fr.

A substantial medieval stone building on a corner a few hundred metres from the town centre and main squares, this family-run hotel combines a sense of history with stylish interiors and a touch of luxury.

Villa Fol Avril €€

2 rue des Fers Chauds, Moutiers au Perche, T02 33 83 22 67, villafolavril.fr.

In a quiet village deep in the countryside of the northwestern reaches of the Parc Naturel Régional du Perche, this stylish small hotel occupies a former 19th-century coaching inn. Decorated with flair, with muted colours, natural materials, quarry tiles, rustic touches and antique furnishings, yet with plenty of light and modern comforts. There's a pool and garden.

Chambres d'hôtes

La Renardière

Bellou-le-Trichard, T02 33 25 57 96, perchedansleperche.com.

In the most southern reaches of Le Perche Normand you can get into the woodland spirit of the region and sleep up in the branches of trees. Climb the steps to this five-berth tree house built in an old chestnut tree. It has a terrace, comfortable chalet-style rooms, fully equipped kitchen corner and bathroom. It's insulated from the weather and has good heating. You can rent by the night, or for longer stays. The price for a week for two people is €795 with breakfast, €700 without.

Eating & drinking

Le Manoir du Lys €€€

La Croix Gautier, Route de Juvigny, Bagnoles-de-l'Orne, T02 33 37 80 69, manoir-du-lys.com.
Daily lunch and dinner (except Nov-Apr – closed Sun dinner, Tue lunch and all day Mon), closed 2 Jan-13 Feb.
Between the town and the forest edge, enjoy lavishly inventive cooking on a distinctly Norman theme in the acclaimed Michelin-starred restaurant of a converted manor house. Dine in the smart interior, decorated in soothing pale colours, or out on the attractive terrace, with succulent dishes like Normandy beef fillet with bacon and foie gras potato.

Au Petit Vatel €€

72 place du Commandant Desmeulles, Alençon, T02 33 26 23 78.
Thu-Tue lunch and dinner except Sun dinner and Tue dinner.
Green-tinted paint and window boxes bursting with flowers brighten up this grey-stone building near the town centre. Inside, ambitious tasty dishes, strong on seafood and Normandy flavours, are served in a lively setting decorated in pastel hues. For an unusual cheese course, choose fried Camembert with salad.

Tip...

One of the gourmet treats of Normandy is *agneau de pré-salé* (salt meadow lamb) from the flood meadows close to Le Mont-St-Michel. The sheep graze on pasture that is constantly washed with salt water, and contains plants adapted to such a salty environment. As a result, the meat is exceptionally tender and juicy, with hints of herb flavours.

La Potinière €

2 rue des Casinos, Bagnoles-de-l'Orne, T02 33 30 65 00, hoteldelapotiniere.com.
Daily 1130-1330 and 1830-2130.
This bright lakeside restaurant with a red and white turret has plenty of windows with good views across the lake towards the casino. It offers a variety of inexpensive menus with French and Norman classic dishes.

O Gayot €

2 av de la Ferté-Macé, Bagnoles-de-l'Orne, T02 33 38 44 01, ogayot.com.
Fri-Wed lunch and dinner except Sun dinner (open Thu in Aug, closed Mon lunch 15 Nov-Mar).
The brasserie of this hotel has a covered pavement terrace and is a model of good-quality informal inexpensive eating. Perhaps not surprising, since it's overseen by the chef of Michelin-starred Manoir au Lys and offers such dishes as *œuf cocotte à la crème de foie gras.*

La Croix d'Or €€

83 rue de la Constitution, Avranches, T02 33 58 04 88, hoteldelacroixdor.fr.
Daily lunch and dinner, except Sun dinner from 15 Oct-31 Mar.
Bare stone, wooden beams and polished copper pots and pans give rustic charm to this excellent restaurant in a half-timbered 17th-century coaching inn. Tables are laid with white cloths, and the food, emphasizing Normandy specialities, is exceptional. Menus include both cheese and dessert.

La Mère Poulard €€

Grand'Rue, Le Mont-St-Michel, T02 33 89 02 02, terrasses-poulard.fr.
Daily lunch and dinner.
Its name apparently a play on words meaning Mother Hen, this simple traditional diner is surely the second most famous address in Le Mont-St-Michel after the abbey itself. Acclaimed by gourmets for its omelettes, it also serves generous *fruits de mer* and a wide range of other dishes, including traditional desserts.

Au Jardin des Plantes €€-€

Place du Jardin des Plantes, Avranches, T02 33 58 03 68, hotel-restaurant-avranches.com.
With varied dining areas, including a covered terrace by the pavement, this much-liked restaurant in a hotel near the

Jardin des Plantes has an appealing blue and peach colour scheme and a good range of menus. The cuisine is traditional French, with such dishes as *tripes* or foie gras.

Pick of the picnic spots

Château de Carrouges
Picnic tables among fruit trees in the quiet grounds beside the château.
Domfront public gardens
The gardens are beside a Norman fortress, with panoramic views.
Mortagne-au-Perche public gardens
The Jardin Publique has expansive views over Le Perche.

Pays d'Argentan

Hostellerie de la Renaissance €€
20 av de la 2e Division Blindée, Argentan, T02 33 36 14 20, hotel-larenaissance.com.
Daily lunch and dinner except Sun dinner. Closed 2nd fortnight in Jul, and last week in Mar.
Cosy with wooden beams, floral fabrics and an ornate old fireplace, this is the best restaurant in the area. The windows look out on a garden. Imaginative dishes, such as breast of Challans duck in a mixed-grain crust, using local ingredients, are prepared and presented with style.

Le Lion Verd €€
Place de l'Hôtel de Ville, Putanges-Pont-Ecrepin, T02 33 35 01 86, hotel-restaurant-lion-verd.com.
The menus here are pleasingly uncomplicated, with little or no choice, offering good value and good-quality classic French and Norman cooking. The restaurant, in a flower-decked stone mansion beside the river, is a large, modern room, but with

pretty, rosy-hued decor and big picture windows. For an even better view, eat on the waterside terrace. It makes an excellent start or finish to a tour of the Suisse Normande.

La Roche d'Oëtre €
La Roche d'Oëtre, near junction of D329 and D301 near Rouvrou, T02 31 68 87 45.
Daily lunchtime and Fri-Sat dinner.
Close to the top of the highest point in the Suisse Normande, this simple spacious buffet restaurant offers drinks, snacks, inexpensive set lunches – and terrific views. The nearest village is Rouvrou, about 2 km away.

Le Montormel €
Croix Tiret, Mont Ormel, T02 33 12 58 09.
Daily lunch.
Convenient for a pause before or after visiting the Mémorial de Montormel, about 200 m away, this simple Armenian family-run bar and restaurant offers good, generous home-cooking of Armenian as well as French and

Norman dishes. The €17 *formule* includes three courses, coffee and wine or cider.

Brasseries
Au Pont de l'Orne
1 place de l'Hôtel de Ville, Putanges-Pont-Ecrepin, T02 33 36 14 84.
Mon-Sat 0800-2300.
As the name makes clear, this popular brasserie is right beside the river bridge in the heart of Putanges. Relax with a drink, or tuck in to a wide range of snacks and inexpensive home-made dishes ranging from crêpes or sauerkraut to paella or couscous.

Delabroise Mireille
2 rue du Château, Alençon, T02 33 26 14 08.
Mon-Sat 0800-2300 (phone to confirm).
This town centre brasserie is on the ground floor of a magnificent half-timbered 15th-century house that's thought to be the oldest in Alençon.

A patio café in Le Mont-St-Michel.

Entertainment

Tribunal €€€
4 place Palais, Mortagne-au-Perche, T02 33 25 04 77, hotel-tribunal.fr.
Flowers, bare stone and crimson and cream fabrics give a sense of opulence to this family-run restaurant in a medieval stone building a short distance from the town centre. The innovative cuisine is inspired by local tradition, and features *boudin* (black pudding), the speciality of Mortagne.

Auberge des Trois J €€€-€€
1 place Docteur Gireaux, Nocé, T02 33 73 41 03.
Wed-Sat lunch and dinner, Sun lunch, Jul-Aug also open Tue, closed 1st fortnight Jan, 2nd fortnight Sep.
In a handsome old stone and wood building in a pretty village at the heart of Le Perche, this friendly restaurant draws a crowd every weekend. They come to sample chef Stéphan Joly's refined and richly inventive French cooking with plenty of high-quality local ingredients. Three delectable *mise-en-bouche* are followed by dishes such as foie gras with *cèpes* sauce, lamb with pepper confit or bream with crayfish vinaigrette, all beautifully presented. Lovely desserts too.

Tip…
To buy traditional Perche specialities direct from the producers, ask at Mortagne's tourist office for the leaflet *Saveurs du Terroirs du Perche*, which gives addresses and phone numbers.

La Brasserie
1 place du Général de Gaulle, Mortagne-au-Perche, T02 33 25 14 77, labrasseriemortagne.com.
Sun, Tue, Wed 0900-1900 (Sun in winter closes 1500) and Thu-Sat 0900-2100, lunch served daily 1200-1400, dinner served Thu-Sat 1915-2100.
Make use of free Wi-Fi over a good breakfast, enjoy a drink or a light meal anytime, or at lunchtime you can have a three-course set menu for just €10.40. Chic and modern, with pale colours and a green and brown theme, this stylish café-brasserie with outdoor tables is on a corner of Mortagne's main square.

Bars & clubs
Casino du Lac
6 av Robert Cousin, Bagnoles-de-l'Orne, T02 33 37 84 00.
Mon-Thu 1100-0200, Fri and Sat 1000-0400, Sun 1000-0300. Entrance free, but deposit required for gaming tables. Separate fees for certain shows or *thés dansants* (tea dances).
The classy white lakeside casino at Bagnoles is a place to play the gaming tables, but also to enjoy a meal and take in a late show. For those who are not night-birds, there are evening and afternoon dance parties, including *thés dansants*. Smart dress required.

Music
La Luciole
171 route de Bretagne, Alençon, T02 33 32 83 33, laluciole.org.
Southern Normandy's main contemporary performance venue has large and small stages hosting the whole spectrum of music, including rock, pop, jazz, folk, and world, and shows. Tickets are typically around €25, but check the programme of free evening performances (all start at 1900) called *Soirées After Work*.

Scene Nationale 61
Théâtre d'Alençon, Alençon, T02 33 29 16 96, scenenationale61.fr.
The National Theatre of the Orne region stages a full programme of contemporary and classical

Shopping

arts of high standard, encompassing drama, dance and concerts in a wide variety of genres, as well as circus-style entertainment. The theatre is based in three towns, Alençon, Flers and Mortagne-au-Perche, the majority being staged here in the capital of the *département*.

Le Perche

Festivals & events

Festival de Danse Jazz et Comédie Musicale
Carré du Perche, 23 rue de Boyères, Mortagne-au-Perche, T02 33 85 23 00, lecarreduperche. com.
End of Oct.
This three-day festival of jazz dance, or jazz ballet, has become a regular fixture.

Music

Scene Nationale 61
Carré du Perche, 23 rue de Boyères, Mortagne-au-Perche, T02 33 85 23 00, scenenationale61.fr and lecarreduperche.com.
Mortagne-au-Perche is one of the three towns where performances of contemporary and classical arts are staged by Scene Nationale 61 (National Theatre of the Orne region). The venue is west of the central area.

Normandie-Maine

Art & antiques

Faïencerie de Sées T Foulon
25 rue Billy, Sées, T02 33 28 19 76.
For good-quality hand-made porcelain decorated in traditional local style, on sale at reasonable prices, visit this specialist a few minutes' walk from the cathedral.

Food & drink

Chais Calvados Comte Louis de Lauriston
Rue du Mont St-Michel, Domfront, T02 33 38 53 96, calvados-lauriston.com.
Mon-Fri 0900-1200 and 1400-1800, Sat 0930-1200.
Come to this old distillery at the foot of Domfront, about 100 m from Notre-Dame sur l'Eau chapel, for a tasting and a chance to buy. Among the products available are not just Calvados, but Calvados Domfrontais, made with pears as well as apples, and hard to find outside Normandy. Other Normandy specialities made here include cider, perry and *pommeau*.

Pays d'Argentan

Food & drink

La Galotière
Domaine de la Galotière, near Crouttes, T02 33 39 05 98, lagalotier.fr.
Mon-Sat 0900-1900.
Just outside the village of Crouttes, near Vimoutiers, this picturesque and traditional 17th-century organic apple farm and distillery of Calvados and *pommeau* is the place to see how these local specialities are made, then taste and buy. They make and sell their own apple juice and *Appellation Controlée* cider too.

Souvenirs

Maison des Dentelles (House of Lace)
34 rue de la Noé, Argentan, T02 33 67 50 78.
Apr-18 Oct Tue-Sat 0900-1130 and 1400-1730, Sun 1500-1730.
This leading lace museum also has a shop with a wide variety of tempting souvenir pieces of hand-made lace including household items and clothes on sale.

Activities & tours

Food & drink

Boucherie Charcuterie P Cedille

8 rue des 15 Fusillés, Mortagne-au-Perche, T02 33 25 10 34.

If you want to sample the best of Mortagne's *boudin* and other meat products, step into this red-fronted traditional butcher's shop on a corner near the main square. Silver cups on display testify to a whole string of charcuterie-making awards carried away by proprietor Monsieur Cedille.

Canoeing

Canoeing in the Orne valley

Details from Putanges tourist office, T02 33 36 93 73.

See the southern Suisse Normande from the water. Several options are available for trips on the River Orne, including the spectacular river gorges or easier fun rides on Lake Rabodanges. Most routes are timed for a full day or half a day. A shuttle bus takes you to your departure point for the descent and picks you up at the end of the trip.

Children

Archéoscope

Grand'Rue, Le Mont-St-Michel, T02 33 89 01 85, archeoscope-montsaintmichel.fr/ archeoscope/index.htm.

1st weekend in Feb-11 Nov daily 0900-1730 (Jul-Aug till 1830). €9, €4.50 child 10-18 years, under 10s free.

This multimedia show all about the history and construction of the abbey will appeal to adults and children alike.

Le Perche.

Rabodanges Parc de Jeux

Palm Beach, Barrage de Rabodanges, T02 33 36 03 56. An extensive play area and children's entertainment are part of this waterside leisure complex at Lake Rabodanges, the artificial lake at the southern end of La Suisse Normande.

Spa treatments at Bagnoles-de-l'Orne

Les Thermes de Bagnoles-de-l'Orne, rue du Professeur Louvel, Bagnoles-de-l'Orne, T08-11 90 22 33, thermes-bagnoles.com. Feb-11 Nov medical cures Mon-Sat 0630-1200, other treatments Mon-Sat 1430-1900 and Sun 0900-1200, 12 Nov-Jan Fri-Sat only 0930-1900. Whether for simple pampering, beauty treatments or a genuine medical cure, the Thermes provides a huge range of packages, most involving the resort's natural hot springs.

Contents

Practicalities

Pont l'Évêque.

Getting there

Air

From UK & Ireland

There are no international direct flights to Normandy. The principal air gateway to Normandy is Paris. There are several flights daily from London Heathrow, London Luton, Edinburgh, most UK regional airports and Dublin, to France's main international airport Charles de Gaulle (CDG), 22 km north of Paris. Less frequent flights depart from London Gatwick and several other UK and Irish local airports, including Cork. A small number of flights land at Paris Orly, 15 km south of the capital, most from London City airport. Airlines operating these routes include **Aeromexico**, **Air Europa**, **Air France**, **Air Mauritius**, **Alitalia**, **American Airlines**, **British Airways**, **Delta Airlines**, **EasyJet**, **Flybe**, and **Qantas**. From Scotland or Ireland **Ryanair** fly to 'Paris' (Beauvais airport, 88 km from Rouen on N31) from Glasgow, Shannon and Dublin.

From North America

Several flights depart daily from Chicago, Cincinnati, Detroit, Houston, Los Angeles, Miami, Montreal, New York, Philadelphia, San Francisco, Toronto and Washington DC to Paris Charles de Gaulle, with a less frequent service from Pittsburgh, Salt Lake City, Seattle and Vancouver.

Airports online

Beauvais aeroportbeauvais.com
Caen caen.aeroport.fr
Cherbourg welcome.aeroport-cherbourg.com
Le Havre havre.aeroport.fr
Paris (CDG and Orly) aeroportsdeparis.fr
Rouen rouen.aeroport.fr

Tip...

Time it right and you can bypass Paris by getting off Eurostar at Lille Europe station, walking 10 minutes to Lille Flandres station, and taking a train direct from there to Rouen (usually twice daily, 2 hrs 36 mins, €32.10).

From rest of Europe

All European capitals have direct flights to Paris, and there are frequent daily flights to Paris from dozens of other European cities. Within France, internal flights connect French regional airports to Normandy's small airports at Caen, Cherbourg, Deauville, Le Havre and Rouen.

Onward travel from Paris CDG & Orly airports

Seven major international car hire companies have desks at the two Paris airports. From Charles de Gaulle to Rouen is 140 km via D104, N104 and D14. From Orly to Alençon is 183 km via A86 and N12. Non-drivers should travel by RER train into central Paris and onward from Gare St Lazare to Rouen, Caen and other parts of Normandy.

Rail

Journey time from London St Pancras to Paris Gare du Nord on **Eurostar** (T08705-186186, eurostar.com) is two hours 15 minutes, plus a 30-minute check-in (from £59 return). Eurostar can add onward rail travel to Rouen or Caen. Change in Paris to Paris-St Lazare station (allow 1½ hours to change stations) to continue by TGV or intercity rail services to Rouen (journey time from Paris, from 1 hr 12 mins, from London 4 hrs 17 mins, total return fare from London from £79) or Caen (2 hrs 10 mins from Paris, 5 hrs 15 mins from London, total return fare from London from £79).

Rail travel to other destinations in Normandy can be pre-booked with **Rail Europe** (T08448-484064, raileurope.co.uk) in the UK or USA, or the French railway company **SNCF** (T08-92 35 35 35 from outside France, voyages-sncf.com) in France, or at any French train station. Catch a train at Paris-St Lazare for Bayeux, Bernay, Caen, Cherbourg, Deauville, Dieppe, Evreux, Fécamp, Le Havre, Lisieux or Rouen. Trains from Paris Montparnasse go to Alençon, Argentan, Bagnoles-de-l'Orne and Granville.

Going green

Drastically reduce your carbon footprint by travelling to Normandy by train. High-speed trains to Paris include Eurostar (from the UK), Thalys (from Belgium, Netherlands and Germany) and TGV (from southern France, Italy or Switzerland), with onward TGV services to Rouen and Le Havre. Within Normandy, rail services reach most of the towns. Major cities in Normandy have free bike schemes, so you can see the sights without using motorized transport at all.

Road

Bus/coach

Eurolines (T0871-7818181 premium rate, eurolines. co.uk) run a service from London to Paris, from where you can take a train to Normandy. The journey time is eight to nine hours and costs around £57 return, with occasional lower promotional fares. Most buses arrive at the station of Eurolines France (28 av Général-de-Gaulle, Bagnolet, T08-92 89 90 91, eurolines.fr), close to the Métro station Gallieni, with a 35-minute onward journey into Paris.

Car

The fastest way to travel to Normandy from southeast England is by road and Eurotunnel. Eurotunnel (T08443-353 535, eurotunnel.com) trains run from the M20 near Folkestone direct to autoroute A16 near Calais. It operates 24 hours a day with up to four departures an hour in peak times. Check-in and departure are rapid, and the crossing takes 35 minutes plus 30 minutes check-in, with little delay in unloading vehicles. Standard fares start from £53 single, £106 return, for a car and up to nine passengers. There are often promotions with lower fares on certain dates, and reductions for frequent travellers, while a five-day return costs £84. The onward driving time into Normandy via autoroutes A16, A28, A29 or A13 is about two hours to Rouen (215 km) or three hours 15 minutes to Caen (345 km).

Sea

Typical mid-week fares are given below, but look out for frequent bargain special offers. Crossings to Calais, Boulogne or Dunkerque are cheaper. For Le Mont-St-Michel and Southern Normandy, consider crossing to St-Malo in Brittany.

To Dieppe

From Newhaven LD Lines Transmanche (T0810-630304, transmancheferries.com) Monday-Saturday twice daily, Sunday once, crossing time four hours, plus minimum 45-minute check-in, return fare £116 for driver and car plus £34 per passenger (optional cabin from £28 each way).

To Le Havre

From Portsmouth LD Lines Transmanche twice daily. Crossing time ranges from three hours 15 minutes to eight hours, plus 45-minute check-in, typical return fare £211 for driver and car, plus £23 per passenger.

To Caen (Ouistreham)

From Portsmouth Brittany Ferries (T0871 244 0744, brittany-ferries.com) sail two to four crossings on most days, three hours 45 minutes or six hours 45 minutes or overnight crossings, plus 45-minute check-in, typical return fare £300 for car, driver and passenger, £40 return for additional passengers.

To Cherbourg-Octeville

From Poole Brittany Ferries sail twice daily, four hours 15 minutes or longer overnight crossing, additional faster crossing available May-Sep two hours 15 minutes, plus 45-minute check-in, typical return fare £280 for car, driver and passenger, £40 return for additional passengers.

From Portsmouth Brittany Ferries operate once daily, crossing time three hours, plus 45-minute check-in, typical fare £340 return for car, driver and passenger, £40 return for additional passengers.

From Rosslare Irish Ferries (Ireland T0818-300400, irishferries.com) sail this route. The number of crossings per month varies from seven in July to 14 in October, 19 to 20-hour crossing, plus one-hour check-in, from €198 return for driver and car, €20 return per additional passenger, plus compulsory cabin from €118 return.

To Normandy from the Channel Islands

Manche Iles Express (Jersey T01534-880756, Guernsey T01481-701316, manche-iles-express. com) operate seasonal ferry services between the Channel Islands and the Cotentin ports of Diélette, Barneville-Carteret and Granville.

Getting around

Rail

French trains are run by the state-owned **SNCF** (sncf.com). As in every other French region, Normandy's principal towns are all connected by fast modern trains several times daily. The main rail routes are Cherbourg-Octeville to Paris (3 hrs, €44.10) via Caen (1 hr 10 mins); Caen to Paris (2 hrs 10 mins, €31.20); Caen to Rouen (1 hr 35 mins, €23); Rouen to Paris (from 1 hr 11 mins, €20.50); and Rouen to Le Havre (42 mins, €13.60).

For Normandy rail information, check SNCF's dedicated website for the regions, ter-sncf.com.

Rail passes

InterRail France (interrailnet.com/interrail-one-country-pass-france) gives unlimited travel on French trains for three to eight days during one month. A three-day InterRail France pass costs €189, €125 for under-26s. It must be bought outside France.

Remember that on the site, Normandy is two regions – Basse Normandie and Haute Normandie.

Dieppe and Le Havre The national rail company **SNCF** (T0825 000 276, ter-sncf.com/haute_normandie) runs buses (in cooperation with other companies) as well as trains that together provide a good network of regional services between towns in Upper Normandy. Main rail lines from Rouen go to Le Havre (51 mins) and Dieppe (45 mins), with changes for other towns, for example Rouen-Fécamp (one change, 1 hr-1 hr 40 mins). Other bus and rail routes link towns in the north of the region, and a rail service also loops through the area south of the Seine. An SNCF bus links Rouen directly to Evreux (1 hr). There's a map of the complete SNCF network in Upper Normandy at ter-sncf.com/haute_normandie/carte_horaires/index.asp.

Côte d'Albâtre There is a service between Le Havre and Fécamp (40 mins).

Calvados There are direct trains between Paris-St Lazare and Caen (2 hrs 10 mins), and others stopping only at Lisieux, several times daily. There is more than one train an hour between Caen and Bayeux (about 15 mins), continuing to Cherbourg-Octeville (1 hr 10 mins). There are several trains from Caen to Alençon (about 1 hr 13 mins), some stopping at Argentan and Sées. There are services from Lisieux to Trouville (22 mins) and along the Côte Fleurie to Dives/Cabourg (another 30 mins).

Cherbourg-Octeville Regular rail services connect Cherbourg-Octeville to Paris-St Lazare (3 hrs), via Caen (1 hr 10 mins), and, with one change, to Rennes (3 hrs 37 mins) via Coutances (1 hour 38 mins), and, with one or two changes, Granville (about 2 hrs). A TGV service currently connects Cherbourg-Octeville to Dijon via Caen, Roissy and Marne-la-Vallée (Disneyland), but as there is no high-speed line between Roissy and Cherbourg-Octeville, the trains do not travel at TGV speeds and journey times remain unchanged.

Southern Cotentin A line connects Granville to Paris Montparnasse (3 hrs 13 mins) via Argentan (1 hr 15 mins).

Southern Normandy Alençon is on the Caen-Tours intercity line with frequent services during the day to Le Mans for onward travel to Paris (about 1½ hrs) or, in the other direction, to Caen (about 1 hr 13 mins, some trains stopping at Argentan and Sées). There are also train services from Paris to Argentan (about 2 hrs) and Briouze (about 2 hrs 10 mins), where there is onward bus travel to Bagnoles-de-l'Orne (additional 40 mins).

Road

Bicycle

Picturesque countryside, quiet country lanes and gently challenging topography make Normandy a good region for cycling. Long-distance cycle routes cut through the region, including the Voies Vertes (green ways), former railway lines.

IGN Cartes de Promenade maps, intended for walkers, are useful. IGN Serie Bleue maps cover a smaller area in more detail. Most tourist offices have information about cycle trails in their area, and can give the addresses of local bike hire firms – usually at least one in every town. Many focus on VTT (mountain bikes) but it is also possible to hire touring cycles. Shop around, as hire fees vary considerably. Expect to pay around €80 a week or €12-€15 a day for a touring bike, or €90 a week, €15-€17 day, for a mountain bike. Prices for children's bikes are likely to be almost as much.

Normandy's two main cities operate free bike schemes. Cy'clic in Rouen and V'eol in Caen both give 30 minutes' free hire, followed by increasing charges for subsequent periods. You have to register for the schemes, and use your credit card to pick up the sturdy roadsters from stands all around town.

Côte d'Albâtre There is little public transport between towns along the coast between Fécamp, Dieppe and Le Tréport. Regular bus services between Etretat, Fécamp and Le Havre are operated by Cars Périer (T02 35 46 37 77, cars-perier.com).

Calvados A frequent modern public bus service throughout the Calvados *département* is provided by Bus Verts du Calvados (T0810 21 42 14, Mon-Sat 0700-2000, busverts.fr). Tickets for single journeys are available from the driver on the bus, and all other tickets from Bus Verts sales points at bus stations. Their website gives routes, timetables and discount tickets, including the Ticket Liberté, which gives the freedom to travel on most of the network for periods of a day (€12.90), three days (€25.16) or one week (€36.12).

Cotentin A public bus service throughout the Manche *département* is provided by Manéo Services (T0800 15 00 50 Mon-Fri 0800-1900, mobi50.com). Tickets for single journeys are available from the driver on the bus. Their website details routes, timetables and discount tickets.

Bus/coach

Every *département* in Normandy has a local bus network, with timetables geared to the needs of workers and schoolchildren. Most do not cross the *départemental* boundary. Out-of-town sights like the Landing Beaches can be hard to reach by public bus. National rail operator SNCF also runs bus routes to supplement train services; these are shown on railway timetables. Fares vary from one *département* to another, but typically work out at about €2.20 for up to an hour's travel. In some cases (Manche, Orne) there is a flat rate for all journeys, while in others the price depends on the distance travelled. In Calvados, fares depend on the number of zones travelled, starting at €1.25 for any journey within a single zone.

Car

Travelling by car makes it easy and enjoyable to explore Normandy's rural areas. However, with autoroute tolls, fuel costing about €1.30 per litre and the euro riding high against sterling, driving has become a more expensive option. In addition, traffic congestion, traffic-free streets, and finding somewhere to park all make car travel difficult in main towns, especially Rouen and Caen.

Speed limits are generally 110 kph (68 mph) on dual carriageways, and 130 kph (80 mph) on motorways (sometimes lower on toll-free motorways). Otherwise, the maximum speed is generally 50 kph (31 mph) in town, 90 kph (55 mph) out of town. Insurance documents, car registration papers and a full driving licence issued by any EU

Driving times from Paris

Rouen one hour 30 minutes
Deauville two hours
Le Havre two hours
Caen two hours 20 minutes
Omaha Beach two hours 50 minutes
Cherbourg three hours 30 minutes
Le Mont-St-Michel three hours 30 minutes

Tip...

No need to use up holiday cash paying autoroute tolls. All the tollbooths accept Mastercard, Visa and other credit cards, even for the smallest amounts.

country or the US must be carried when driving. Third party insurance is compulsory. Comprehensive insurance issued by UK insurers is valid throughout the EU (a so-called Green Card is no longer required). The minimum driving age for a car or motorcycle is 18.

By law you must stop immediately after an accident, with minimum obstruction to traffic. If anyone has been injured, or is under the influence of alcohol, call the police. French motorists must complete an insurance form verifying the facts and all parties must sign to show that they agree that it is a true account. Non-French motorists should exchange details with the other parties. If you break down, put on hazard warning lights (or display a warning triangle).

Police levy hefty on-the-spot fines for speeding, worn tyres, not wearing a seat belt, not stopping at a Stop sign and overtaking where forbidden. The amount is likely to be about €135, but can be considerably more. Issuing a receipt is part of the on-the-spot procedure – always be sure to get one, and keep it carefully. Serious violations such as drink-driving could lead to your car being impounded, as well as heavy fines or imprisonment.

Service stations, especially on autoroutes, sell a range of excellent road atlases and maps, including the well-respected Michelin and IGN. Bison Futé (bison-fute.equipement.gouv.fr) publish an annual map showing less congested itineraries, free from tourist offices and gas stations.

Parking meter charges are relatively modest, but it can be difficult finding a space. Payment is required typically Monday-Friday 0900-1800, Saturday 0900-1200. A good time to find a parking space is lunchtime (1200-1400) and there's often no charge for parking then. Parking spaces painted

with blue lines are Zone Bleue, where parking is free for 90 minutes if the time of arrival is displayed in the windscreen with a 'disque horaire pour les zones bleue', known as a Disque Bleue. Blue EU Disabled Parking photocards issued in the UK are valid in France, but in a Zone Bleue must be used in conjunction with a Disque Bleue.

Car hire

Car hire is widely available from both international and local firms. At airports, stations and main roads in the cities and resorts you'll see all the familiar car rental names. Prices are generally higher than in other countries, especially for drivers under 25. Before signing the rental agreement, check that any existing damage on a vehicle you are about to rent has been noted. Make sure your rental is for unlimited mileage – some firms may place an upper limit on the free mileage. Be sure to return the car with the same amount of fuel as at the start of the rental, as fuel charges may be imposed by car rental companies.

Priorité à droite

Misunderstanding this important rule is the main cause of accidents involving foreign motorists in France. Drive on the right and always give way to anything approaching from the right, except where signs indicate to the contrary. The main priority signs are a rectangular yellow sign if you have priority, and a yellow rectangle crossed out meaning you no longer have priority. Where two major roads merge, look out for signs showing who has priority (*Vous n'avez pas la priorité* and/or *Cédez le passage*). Two important exceptions are that vehicles emerging from private property don't have priority over traffic on the public highway, and most roundabouts give priority to vehicles already in the roundabout (as in the UK).

Directory

Customs & immigration

UK and other EU citizens do not need a visa to visit France. Travellers from USA, Australia, New Zealand and Canada may stay up to 90 days without a visa. There are no restrictions on importing legal articles for personal use.

Disabled travellers

France is aware of the needs of disabled travellers but provision for them is patchy. New public buildings are obliged to provide access and facilities, but problems can be acute in areas with cobbled paving and medieval buildings. For parking, display your EU blue photocard as in the UK. French organizations for the disabled focus on residents, not tourists. Normandy Tourism produces useful booklets (in French, but using easy-to-understand symbols) detailing tourist establishments with facilities for the disabled. They are available online at normandie-tourisme. fr/normandy-tourism/more-information/ disabled-friendly-normandy-179-2.html.

Etiquette

Most French people rigorously observe conventions of politeness, always shaking hands on first introduction, moving on to kisses on the cheek (two, three or four depending on the nature of the relationship) with friends. The formal word *vous* should be used for 'you' until a fine line of intimacy has been crossed, then you should stick to *tu*. Punctuality is fairly strictly observed. Dress in public places is usually smart casual and stylish. Address strangers as *Monsieur*, *Madame* or *Mademoiselle*. Entering or leaving small shops or offices, greet those inside with a quick '*Messieurs-dames*'.

Families

Normandy, like most regions of France, is extremely family friendly. Children are welcomed in restaurants with their own menu. Hotels often have family rooms, or can wheel in an extra cot or bed for a few euros extra. Discounts are usually offered at sights and attractions.

Health

Comprehensive travel and medical insurance is recommended. EU citizens should apply for a free European Health Insurance Card or EHIC (ehic.org), which entitles you to emergency medical treatment on the same terms as French nationals. Note that you will have to pay all charges and prescriptions up front and be reimbursed once you return home. If you develop a minor ailment while on holiday a visit to any pharmacy will allow you to discuss your concerns with highly qualified staff, who can give medical advice and recommend treatment. Outside normal opening hours, the address of the nearest duty pharmacy (*pharmacie de garde*) is displayed in the pharmacy window. The out-of-hours number for a local doctor (*médecin généraliste*) may also be listed.

In a serious emergency, go to the accident and emergency department (*urgences*) at the nearest Centre Hospitalier (numbers listed in the Essentials section at the beginning of each chapter) or call an ambulance (SAMU) by dialling 15.

Insurance

Comprehensive travel and medical insurance is strongly recommended, as the European Health Insurance Card (EHIC) does not cover medical repatriation, ongoing medical treatment or treatment considered to be non-urgent. Check for exclusions if you mean to engage in risky sports. Keep all insurance documents to hand; a good

way to keep track of your policies is to email the details to yourself. Make sure you have adequate insurance when hiring a car and always ask how much excess you are liable for if the vehicle is returned with any damage. It is generally worth paying a little more for collision damage waiver. If driving your own vehicle to France, contact your insurers before you travel to ensure you are adequately covered, and keep the documents in your vehicle in case you need to prove it.

Money

The French currency is the Euro (€). Euros are available from ATMs using credit or debit cards. Credit cards are widely accepted by shops, restaurants, museums, attractions, petrol stations, etc, but may be refused in shops for purchases below about €5. Remember you need your PIN for every transaction. Cash is needed for buses, taxis, bars and markets.

Police

To call police in an emergency, dial 17. French police are divided into different forces with different roles. *Gendarmes* are armed units on call to deal with crime, especially outside urban areas. *Police Nationale* are ordinary employees under the control of the mayor, dealing with routine policing issues. *CRS* have a wide remit to prevent violent civil disturbance.

Post

The post office (PTT, or La Poste) provides communications services, generally including stamps, phone, Minitel and internet access. Offices are open (with local variations) during normal working hours Monday to Friday, and usually Saturday morning. Stamps (*timbres*) can also be bought in newsagents and little stores known as *tabacs*. A stamp for an ordinary letter (up to 20 g) or postcard within France costs €0.56; within the EU €0.70; to the US, Canada, Australia and most other countries €0.85. Letter boxes are yellow.

Safety

All towns and rural areas in Normandy are generally safe, with little crime. However, sensible precautions should be taken; for example, don't leave anything valuable on view in cars.

Telephone

French phone numbers indicate which region and which town they are in (all Normandy numbers begin with 02, for example), but there are no area codes and you must dial all 10 digits when phoning from inside France. The prefix for France is +33 and drop the initial 0 of the number you are phoning. For international operator assistance, dial 3212.

France is well covered by mobile phone (cell phone) reception. European (including UK) visitors can use their phones normally. Visitors from the US and Australia should call their provider to check their package. On arrival in France you will receive a text informing you of the charges. All public phones required a pre-paid card, available from newsagents, *tabacs*, etc.

Time difference

France uses Central European Standard Time and Central European Daylight Saving Time (ie GMT+1 and GMT+2 respectively). CET Daylight Saving Time (Summer Time) starts at 0200 on the last Sunday in March and ends at 0300 on the last Sunday in October.

Tipping

Tipping is not necessary in France. Hotel, restaurant and bar bills include service and no tip is expected, although small change is often left for service at an outdoor table. Taxi drivers do not expect tips, though many people do round the fare up. For good service anywhere, just say 'Merci!'

Tourist information

For regional information, contact the Normandy Tourism (CRT Normandie), T02 32 33 79 00, normandie-tourisme.fr. For local information: Alençon, T02 33 80 66 33, paysdalencontourisme.com; Bagnoles-de-l'Orne, T02 33 37 85 66, bagnolesdelorne.com; Bayeux, bayeux-tourism.com; Caen T02 31 27 14 14, tourisme.caen.fr; Cherbourg-Octeville T02 33 93 52 02, otcherbourgcotentin.fr; Deauville, T02 31 14 40 00, deauville.org; Dieppe, T02 32 14 40 60, dieppetourisme.com; Giverny T02 32 51 28 22, giverny-village.fr; Honfleur T02 31 89 23 30, ot-honfleur.fr; Le Havre T02 32 74 04 04, lehavretourisme.com; Le Mont-St-Michel T02 33 60 1430, ot-montsaintmichel.com; Rouen T02 32 08 32 40, rouentourisme.com.

Voltage

The power is supply in France is 220 volts. Circular two-pin plugs are used.

Language

Basics

hello *bonjour*
good evening *bonsoir*
goodbye *au revoir/salut* (polite/informal)
please *s'il vous plaît*
thank you *merci*
I'm sorry, excuse me *pardon, excusez-moi*
yes *oui*
no *non*
how are you? *comment allez-vous?/ça va?* (polite/informal)
fine, thank you *bien, merci*
one moment *un instant*
how? *comment?*
how much? *c'est combien?*
when? *quand?*
where is …? *où est…?*
why? *pourquoi?*
what? *quoi?*
what's that? *qu'est-ce que c'est?*
I don't understand *je ne comprends pas*
I don't know *je ne sais pas*
I don't speak French *je ne parle pas français*
how do you say … (in French)?
   comment on dit … (en français)?
do you speak English? *est-ce que vous parlez anglais?/*
   Parlez-vous anglais?
help! *au secours!*
wait! *attendez!*
stop! *arrêtez!*

Numbers

one *un*
two *deux*
three *trois*
four *quatre*
five *cinq*
six *six*
seven *sept*
eight *huit*
nine *neuf*
10 *dix*

11 *onze*
12 *douze*
13 *treize*
14 *quatorze*
15 *quinze*
16 *seize*
17 *dix-sept*
18 *dix-huit*
19 *dix-neuf*
20 *vingt*
21 *vingt-et-un*
22 *vingt-deux*
30 *trente*
40 *quarante*
50 *cinquante*
60 *soixante*
70 *soixante-dix*
80 *quatre-vingts*
90 *quatre-vingt-dix*
100 *cent*
200 *deux cents*
1000 *mille*

Shopping

this one/that one *celui-ci/celui-là*
less *moins*
more *plus*
expensive *cher*
cheap *pas cher/bon marché*
how much is it? *c'est combien? / combien ça coûte?*
can I have …? (literally 'I would like) …' *je voudrais…*

Travelling

one ticket for… *un billet pour…*
single *un aller-simple*
return *un aller-retour*
airport *l'aéroport*
bus stop *l'arrêt de bus*
train *le train*
car *la voiture*
taxi *le taxi*
is it far? *c'est loin?*

Local tongues

The Anglo-Norman nobility who ruled both England and Normandy after the Norman Conquest had already abandoned the Viking language of their ancestors. They spoke their own brand of Old French, perhaps sprinkled with some surviving Norse words and pronunciations. In England, after a period of dominance as the language of the governing class, Anglo-Norman lost ground to the Anglo-Saxon dialects of the common people. Anglo-Norman partly survives in the old local dialects of the Channel Islands – *les Îles Anglo-Normandes*.

Normandy itself is today entirely French speaking, yet in the Cotentin and other rural districts you might hear local words inherited from Anglo-Norman and Norse, especially in landscape features and place names; for example, *hougue* and *bec* (Norse for hill and stream). Nineteenth-century linguists noted that north of a line from about Granville to Vernon, the pronunciation of local country words seemed Norse-influenced, such as 'vaque' (*vache*) and 'queva' (*cheval*) and 'gardin' (*jardin*).

Hotels

single/double room *une chambre à une personne/deux personnes*
double bed *un lit double/un grand lit*
bathroom *la salle de bain*
shower *la douche*
is there a (good) view? *est-ce qu'il y a une (belle) vue?*
can I see the room? *est-ce que je peux voir la chambre?*
when is breakfast? *le petit dejeuner est à quelle heure?*
can I have the key? *est-ce que je peux avoir la clef?/ La clef, s'il vous plaît*

Time

morning *le matin*
afternoon *l'après-midi*
evening *le soir*
night *la nuit*
a day *un jour*
a week *une semaine*
a month *un mois*
soon *bientôt*
later *plus tard*
what time is it? *quelle heure est-il?*
today/tomorrow/yesterday *aujourd'hui/demain/hier*

Days

Monday *lundi*
Tuesday *mardi*
Wednesday *mercredi*
Thursday *jeudi*
Friday *vendredi*
Saturday *samedi*
Sunday *dimanche*

Months

January *janvier*
February *février*
March *mars*
April *avril*
May *mai*
June *juin*
July *juillet*
August *août*
September *septembre*
October *octobre*
November *novembre*
December *décembre*

Index

Index

Index

Credits

Footprint credits

Project Editor: Jo Williams
Text Editor: Ria Gane
Picture editors: Kassia Gawronski,
Rob Lunn
Layout & production: Davina Rungasamy
Maps: Gail Townsley
Proofreader: Carol Maxwell
Series design: Mytton Williams

Managing Director: Andy Riddle
Commercial Director: Patrick Dawson
Publisher: Alan Murphy
Publishing managers: Felicity Laughton,
Jo Williams
Picture research: Kassia Gawronski,
Rob Lunn
Marketing: Liz Harper,
Hannah Bonnell
Sales: Jeremy Parr
Advertising: Renu Sibal
Finance & administration:
Elizabeth Taylor

Print

Manfactured in India by Nutech
Pulp from sustainable forests

Footprint feedback

We try as hard as we can to make each
Footprint guide as up to date as possible
but, of course, things always change. If
you want to let us know about your
experiences – good, bad or ugly – then
don't delay, go to footprinttravelguides.
com and send in your comments.

Every effort has been made to ensure that
the facts in this guidebook are accurate.
However, travellers should still obtain
advice from consulates, airlines etc about
travel and visa requirements before
travelling. The authors and publishers
cannot accept responsibility for any loss,
injury or inconvenience however caused.

Publishing information

FootprintFrance Normandy
1st edition
© Footprint Handbooks Ltd
May 2010

ISBN 978-1-906098-94-0
CIP DATA: A catalogue record for this
book is available from the British Library

® Footprint Handbooks and the Footprint
mark are a registered trademark of
Footprint Handbooks Ltd

Published by Footprint

6 Riverside Court
Lower Bristol Road
Bath BA2 3DZ, UK
T +44 (0)1225 469141
F +44 (0)1225 469461
footprinttravelguides.com

Distributed in North America by

Globe Pequot Press

All rights reserved. No part of this
publication may be reproduced, stored in a
retrieval system, or transmitted, in any form
or by any means, electronic, mechanical,
photocopying, recording, or otherwise
without the prior permission of Footprint
Handbooks Ltd.

The colour maps are not intended to have
any political significance.